POLICE SOCIAL WORK

D0902364

Grounded in contemporary social work practice approaches such as trauma-informed practice, cultural competency, and systems theory, this book provides a model for developing, implementing, and evaluating police social work and social service collaboration within the context of contemporary policing strategies.

The practice of professional social work in law enforcement agencies is increasingly becoming an important area of practice. Police social work, as it is known, benefits community residents and assists law enforcement agencies with accomplishing community policing and other problem-solving initiatives. Throughout 13 chapters, this book covers:

- The practice of professional social work within law enforcement agencies
- The types of social problems addressed and characteristics of police social work collaborations
- Ethical and other practice issues that arise when collaborating with law enforcement agencies and required practice skills to address these issues
- An examination of collaborations formed between law enforcement agencies and social services agencies in which the service providers are not professional social workers
- A model for developing police social work collaborations and investigating collaboration effectiveness
- Expanded roles for police social work practice such as consultation, officer selection, training recruits and police officers, and assisting their families

Police Social Work provides a wealth of case studies and other reference material to prepare students for police social work practice, as well as serving as a resource for police officers, recruits, and students majoring in policing.

George T. Patterson is Associate Professor in the Silberman School of Social Work at Hunter College, City University of New York. A certified police instructor and police social worker, Dr. Patterson has served as a visiting professor and curriculum advisor in several law enforcement training academies, trained police officers and recruits, and teaches criminal justice courses to social work students. He has published on the topics of police social work, the stress of police work, and coping among police officers and recruits. His written testimony is included in the *May 2015 Final Report of the Task Force on 21st Century Policing* established by President Barack Obama, and his research results are included in *An Evidence-Assessment of the Recommendations of the President's Task Force on 21st Century Policing.*

POLICE SOCIAL WORK

Social Work Practice in Law Enforcement Agencies

George T. Patterson

Routledge
Taylor & Francis Group

LONDON AND NEW YORK

Cover image: © Getty Images

First published 2022
by Routledge
2 Park Square, Milton Park, Abingdon, Oxon OX14 4RN

and by Routledge
605 Third Avenue, New York, NY 10158

Routledge is an imprint of the Taylor & Francis Group, an informa business

British Library Cataloguing-in-Publication Data
A catalogue record for this book is available from the British Library

Library of Congress Cataloging-in-Publication Data
A catalog record has been requested for this book

ISBN: 978-0-367-67663-6 (hbk)
ISBN: 978-0-367-67657-5 (pbk)
ISBN: 978-1-003-13225-7 (ebk)

DOI: 10.4324/9781003132257

Typeset in Bembo
by KnowledgeWorks Global Ltd.

To My Parents

CONTENTS

FIGURES

TABLES

A NOTE ABOUT THE BOOK COVER

Observing police vehicles parked in neighborhoods is not an uncommon sight. Most have seen police officers parked in marked police vehicles speaking to one another in parking lots or other spaces. Some can even identify an unmarked police vehicle parked in a neighborhood. This book cover image was selected because throughout my police social work experience, I drove an unmarked police vehicle during my shift as I responded to calls for service. Many times as a police social worker, I would meet with officers in the unmarked police vehicle to share a case outcome, to discuss other issues, or provide technical assistance to a police officer. Social work assessment, knowledge, skills, and consultation are adaptable to a range of settings.

PREFACE

This book was inspired by my professional police social work practice experience. My primary experience involved employment in a law enforcement agency providing police social work services in an urban community responding to a wide range of social problems, crises, and emergencies that came to the attention of law enforcement. My experience is perhaps atypical because I drove an unmarked police vehicle. I was dispatched to the scene by the 911 dispatcher during my tour of duty to meet with police officers and other first responders who were already on scene to provide crisis intervention to community residents.

In addition to my primary experience, I trained recruits and police officers to provide social service-related services. I also provided stress management interventions to recruits and police officers focused on stress and traumatic stress, and coping strategies.

Situating my experience as a police social worker in a law enforcement agency which is a host setting has informed me that community residents rely on law enforcement agencies to provide emergency services, particularly those with repeat calls for police services. Unfortunately, the unit where I acquired my police social work experience no longer exists. While the unit has recently changed and no longer performs its former functions, I have learned much from my professional police social work experience:

- More training and resources are needed to prepare police social workers for practice.
- Law enforcement responds to a wide range of social problems that are social service-related and involve non-crime situations.

- Even when responding to crime situations such as mass shootings, victims and survivors are in need of law enforcement services, some of which are also social service-related.
- Social problems that are addressed by law enforcement demonstrate the need for mobile, 24 hours, 7 days a week emergency crisis services in communities.

The objectives of this book are to provide a resource for police social workers, social workers collaborating with police, and social service workers who collaborate with the police. A vast amount of published materials are available that inform police social work practice. However, these materials are inaccessible without the ability to locate and retrieve the materials from databases or other sources.

At the same time that I support professional police social work practice, I also acknowledge the concerns and scrutiny expressed by some in the social work profession regarding the suitability of social work employment and collaboration with law enforcement. Social work concerns often focus on social work employment in law enforcement agencies and collaboration with an occupation that is associated with social control and social injustices such as racial profiling and excessive use of force.

Moreover, I recognize that these are not new concerns. This book is written during a time when many are discovering for the first time how prominent the service law enforcement function is in policing. Estimates suggest that approximately 80% of law enforcement functions involve providing social service-related services to community residents. This is not a new situation and has co-existed with law enforcement since the formation of American law enforcement agencies.

Significant police reforms have been implemented in the past. More than 100 years ago the Progressive Movement was determined to eliminate corruption and politics from law enforcement. Police reforms during this period included introducing merit, improving training and the use of technology, and disciplining police officers for inappropriate behaviors.

Therefore, this book traces the historical development of police social work practice and law enforcement functions. Law enforcement statistics published by the U.S. Department of Justice, Office of Justice Programs, Bureau of Justice Statistics are invaluable for understanding the characteristics of law enforcement agencies. These publications are updated every few years, and as a result, the statistics presented in this book will be updated. Readers are encouraged to seek the most recent law enforcement publications available on the Office of Justice Programs, Bureau of Justice Statistics website.

Social workers also have an ethical obligation to evaluate police social work practice and collaboration. This book introduces the POLICE Model, developed by the author, which is first presented and described in detail in Chapter 6. The model considers the importance of using data to inform police social work practice, and police and social work collaboration. Then in subsequent chapters, a brief summary of how the model can be applied is presented.

Numerous features are included in this book:

1. Case examples. These examples are based on actual police social work practice situations and highlight specific content within the chapters containing case examples. In most instances, the case examples reflect police social work practice in which the social worker is an employee of a law enforcement agency rather than a social worker who is an employee in a social service that collaborates with a law enforcement agency. These examples illustrate the range of opportunities for police social work practice.

2. Figures and tables. Several figures display chapter content for ease with conceptualizing the content. In addition to summarizing statistical data, several tables contain text that provide ease with conceptualizing the chapter content.

3. Chapter Overview. At the beginning of each chapter, readers will find an overview that summarizes and focuses attention on the content of the chapter.

4. Chapter Summary. At the end of each chapter, readers will find a summary with closing remarks regarding the chapter material. In some instances, the relationship between the chapter content and the content found in other chapters is discussed.

5. Questions for Discussion. Each chapter contains questions recommended for discussion and consideration of personal reactions to the chapter material. These questions are found at the end of each chapter.

6. Activities for Further Learning. Each chapter contains activities for acquiring additional knowledge about the chapter material. Because legislation varies among states, such as legislation that defines domestic violence and juvenile delinquency, for example, readers are encouraged to locate and retrieve information relevant for a specific state. These activities are located at the end of each chapter.

Despite concerns among some in the social work profession about the appropriateness of social work employment in law enforcement agencies or police and social work collaboration, social workers are employed in law enforcement agencies. At the time of writing, law enforcement agencies are increasingly hiring police social workers and collaborating with social workers employed in social service agencies. The most common types of collaborations respond to child maltreatment, domestic violence, mental illness, victims of crime, and youth and their families. Implementing new collaborations involves decisions such as determining which social problems, i.e., homelessness, substance abuse, neighbor disputes, should be the focus of social work interventions.

At the same time, collaborations are being proposed and implemented for social workers and collaboration partners, such as paramedics, that excludes law enforcement to provide emergency services that come to the attention of the 911 operator. Just as social work collaborations that involve law enforcement require a framework for understanding the provision of emergency services, so do collaborations that do not partner with law enforcement. Collaboration that excludes law enforcement as partners may find that law enforcement is still needed in some situations.

Social work practice in the area of emergency services requires resources to inform practice. This book is intended to provide that resource to those social workers who collaborate with police officers and are not employees in law enforcement agencies as well as those social workers who practice professional police social work practice in law enforcement agencies. This book and its accompanying features were written to achieve these objectives.

ACKNOWLEDGMENTS

First and foremost, I want to acknowledge Catherine Jones, former Editorial Assistant, Health and Social Care at Routledge/Taylor & Francis. Thank you for your patience, support, and suggestions throughout the writing process which was filled with numerous challenges as I wrote during one of the early waves of the Covid-19 pandemic. Also, a special thank you to Claire Jarvis, Senior Editor for Health and Social Care at Routledge for your support and assistance that made my long-standing vision for this book a reality. I appreciate the assistance I received from Harshita Donderia, Associate Project Manager, KnowledgeWorks Globa Ltd. who managed the copyediting process.

Thank you Dr. Lucas-Darby and Ms. Pittinger for preparing the case example titled *What is the Expected Response to Intimate Partner Violence* included in Chapter 13. Dr. Lucas-Darby is the current chairman of the Pittsburgh Citizens Police Review Board and an adjunct professor at the University of Pittsburgh School of Social Work. She holds the Ph.D. and MSW degrees from the University of Pittsburgh School of Social Work, and the M.A. in Political Science from Purdue University. Ms. Pittinger is the executive director of the Pittsburgh Citizens Police Review Board. She is also a member of the Pennsylvania State Law Enforcement Advisory Commission. She holds the Master of Public Management from Carnegie Mellon University and B.A. in Education from Marywood University. Dr. Lucas-Darby, I am grateful for the invitation and opportunity to come to Pittsburgh and share ideas about police social work practice that also informed this book's contents.

I sincerely appreciate the assistance I received from Carol Thomas with preparing the content covering domestic violence and victim assistance services. Thank you Jacob V. Gutter for your time and willingness to prepare the figures. Many thanks to the staff at the Lloyd Sealy Library at John Jay College of Criminal Justice for granting me online access while the library was closed due to the Covid-19 pandemic. Without this assistance, preparing the manuscript would have been postponed.

I am grateful to the U.S. Department of Justice, Office of Justice Programs, Bureau of Justice Statistics for the permission to reprint the law enforcement statistics prepared by your agency. Finally, I want to acknowledge the assistance of the anonymous reviewers who suggested including the international practice of police social work, among other suggestions that improved the manuscript.

ABBREVIATIONS

AMBER	Alert Program America's Missing: Broadcast Emergency Response
AMI	Any Mental Illness
BJS	Bureau of Justice Statistics
BSW	Bachelor of Social Work
CIT	Crisis Intervention Team
CJSW	Criminal Justice Social Work
CSWE	Council on Social Work Education
DHS	Department of Homeland Security
DIR	Domestic Incident Report
DSM 5	Diagnostic and Statistical Manual of Mental Disorders 5th Edition
EAP	Employee Assistance Program
EMT	Emergency Medical Technician
FBI	The Federal Bureau of Investigation
GAO	U.S. Government Accountability Office
IACP	International Association of Chiefs of Police
ICRA	The International Crime Research Association
ITRAC	The Integrated Threat and Risk Assessment Centre
JJGPS	Juvenile Justice, Geography, Policy, Practice and Statistics
LEAD	Law Enforcement Assisted Diversion
LAPD	Los Angeles Police Department
MAT	Medication-Assisted Treatment
MSW	Master of Social Work
NYPD	New York City Police Department
NAMI	National Alliance on Mental Illness
NASW	National Association of Social Workers

NCVS	National Crime Victim Survey
NIJ	National Institute of Justice
OJP	Office of Justice Programs
OJJDP	Office of Juvenile Justice and Delinquency Prevention
PINS	Persons in Need of Supervision
SAHMSA	Substance Abuse and Mental Health Services Administration
SMI	Serious Mental Illness
SRO	School Resource Officer
VRRA	Victims' Rights and Restitution Act

1

AN OVERVIEW OF LAW
ENFORCEMENT AGENCIES

Chapter overview

In 1919 August Vollmer, a well-known American police chief and policing reformer, delivered a speech titled *The Policeman as Social Worker*. The speech was delivered to the International Association of Chiefs of Police. Explicit in Vollmer's speech was the fact that police officers were performing tasks associated with the provision of social services, and collaborating with social service and community-based agencies as a crime prevention strategy. This introductory chapter provides a brief overview of the historical development of law enforcement agencies in the United States, and examines the law enforcement functions and policing strategies that address crime prevention and social problems.

In order to better understand these law enforcement functions and policing strategies, numerous characteristics of law enforcement agencies are described. These characteristics include the significance of law enforcement as a component of the criminal justice system, and the mission and structure of law enforcement agencies. The structure of law enforcement agencies examined in this chapter include organizational factors such as the paramilitary structure, agency size, types of law enforcement agencies, law enforcement agency personnel, and a summary of police officer ranks. Each of these topics is essential to understand for the practice of professional police social work.

Introduction

Substance use and abuse, alcohol use and abuse, store and shop robbery, bank robbery, suicide, accidental and natural deaths, teen runaways, missing adult persons, missing children, homelessness, fatal traffic and school bus accidents, custody visitation issues, neighbor disputes, domestic

DOI: 10.4324/9781003132257-1

violence, mental health crises, nuisance violations, parent-child conflict, landlord-tenant disputes, child abuse, child neglect, juvenile delinquency, homicide, sexual assault, victims of violent crime, non-violent and low-level offenses, natural disasters and human made disasters, school shootings and mass violence.

Although this list of incidents is not complete, the list does illustrate the wide range of incidents and calls for service that come to the attention of law enforcement. It also provides a framework for this book, given that an effective response to these incidents often requires that law enforcement collaborates with other first responders or professionals. An important question to ask at this point is – how did it happen that law enforcement agencies evolved to address such a wide range of social problems and incidents? In particular, social problems that are typically associated with the social work profession or social service providers. The answer to this question will be explained throughout the pages of this book.

The above list is also illustrative of the type of social problems and incidents during which the author provided a police social work response. In order to assist individuals who come to the attention of law enforcement police social workers, and social workers who collaborate with law enforcement require an understanding and application of both social work knowledge and skills as well as knowledge about law enforcement. As this brief introductory listing shows, a wide variety of social problems and incidents come to the attention of law enforcement. Clearly, to suggest that police social workers respond only to domestic violence, child maltreatment, or mental health crises, given the wide range of social problems that receive a law enforcement response, is inaccurate.

The focus of this book is the practice of professional police social work in law enforcement agencies. As mentioned, it is important for social workers to have an understanding of law enforcement agency functions and structure, as well as the historical role of American policing in responding to and addressing community social problems. Therefore, this introductory chapter examines law enforcement agencies.

The present chapter summarizes the history of the development of American law enforcement agencies, including the numerous policing reforms which have been implemented to enhance the law enforcement response to social problems and incidents. While a brief history of law enforcement is provided, an emphasis is placed on the role of law enforcement in responding to social problems. An overview of law enforcement agencies begins with identifying how law enforcement is one of four components in the criminal justice system.

Overview of the criminal justice system

Law enforcement agencies comprise one component of the criminal justice system among the four components that make up the criminal justice system. The

TABLE 1.1 Four criminal justice system components and general functions

Criminal justice system component	Functions
Legislation	To propose and enact legislation that may include funding and intervention provisions, define criminal offenses, or authorize criminal justice reforms.
Law enforcement	To perform order maintenance, law enforcement, and provide services.
Courts	To determine guilt or innocence and impose sanctions, to settle disputes or provide problem-solving interventions to address social problems.
Corrections	To incapacitate or provide community-based supervision and monitoring as well as rehabilitation interventions.

criminal justice system is comprised of four components: legislation, law enforcement, courts, and corrections (Alexander, 2008; Patterson, 2020; Robinson, 2010). Each of these four components is operated independently at local, state, and federal governmental levels. For example, the corrections criminal justice component operates local corrections facilities which are jails, and state and federal prisons are operated by states and the federal government. Further, in addition to operating corrections institutional facilities, community-based supervision such as probation and parole are also a part of this component.

The following summary provides a brief overview of the functions and responsibilities of each component of the criminal justice system. These general functions are also shown in Table 1.1 and graphically displayed in Figure 1.1.

Legislation

The legislative component of the criminal justice system is responsible for, among other matters, proposing and enacting legislation that identifies criminal offenses and other law violations. Some legislation includes provisions for funding provided to agencies and identifies the types of interventions that should be provided to offenders, former offenders, victims of crime, and other individuals who are in need of services.

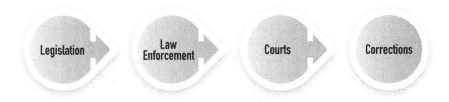

FIGURE 1.1 Components of the criminal justice system

Law enforcement

Each year, millions of individuals have contacts with law enforcement (Davis & Whyde, 2018). In general, the law enforcement component of the criminal justice system is responsible for enforcing laws, making arrests, and crime prevention. However, as we shall examine in this chapter and subsequent chapters, law enforcement provides more functions than only enforcing the law, making arrests, and crime prevention. The service law enforcement represents the function that police officers perform most often. This service function is described in greater detail in Chapter 2.

Courts

Law enforcement has a great deal of involvement with the courts. Police officers provide testimony, and crime reports and other documentation are submitted to courts as evidence. The responsibilities of criminal courts are to determine guilt or innocence and to impose sanctions. In addition to criminal courts, other types of courts exist and have district purposes. For instance, specialty courts or problem-solving courts prioritize treatment and rehabilitation instead of punitive sanctions. Examples of these courts include domestic violence courts, mental health courts, veterans courts, drug courts, and opioid courts, to illustrate a few examples. Because the primary focus of these courts is rehabilitation as opposed to punishment, law enforcement crime reports and documentation can provide valuable information to these courts.

Corrections

During pretrial or court proceedings, if bail has not been granted or posted, the corrections component has a significant role in the criminal justice system. Individuals are incapacitated or incarcerated. Incarceration is a punitive sanction. The corrections component also includes community-based supervision and monitoring.

The criminal justice system as a system

The primary responsibilities and interactions of the police social worker in the criminal justice system occur with law enforcement agencies. However, situations will arise when the police social worker may also become involved with the courts or the corrections components of the criminal justice system.

It is generally agreed that law enforcement is the primary component of the criminal justice system through which individuals enter the system. Therefore, it stands to reason that decisions and actions made by law enforcement have consequences for individuals to become involved with the courts and corrections criminal justice system components. In this way, the criminal system operates together as a system.

Each of the four components can be conceptualized as occurring in sequential order because, by and large, each of these four criminal justice system components' functions precedes the other components. Each of the four components has unique functions. For example, law enforcement is preceded by legislation defining laws and criminal violations, courts are preceded by law enforcement that determines criminal or other law violations, and corrections are preceded by courts that impose sanctions. These criminal justice system components preceding each other highlight the significant role of law enforcement as a criminal justice system component.

The criminal justice system components are also interdependent, although as individuals are processed through each component, possibilities arise for the individual to have no further criminal justice system involvement. For example, courts may dismiss charges.

A systematic relationship is also created among the four criminal justice system components. For instance, the first component, legislation, defines types of crimes and further categorizes what comprises non-violent and low-level offenses. The second component, law enforcement, not only enforces the law but also provides services. Based on legislation or law enforcement agency policies and procedures, non-violent and low-level offenders can be diverted away from the criminal justice into behavioral health services, thereby reducing further criminal justice system involvement.

In law enforcement, diversion occurs when police officers refer individuals to behavioral health and other services to address the social problem that resulted in law enforcement contact.

By diverting individuals away from arrest and utilizing other options, law enforcement precludes the further involvement of individuals in the criminal justice system. This also supports implementing police social work collaborations since one goal is to increase the use of law enforcement diversion interventions through the use of community-based services. In many instances, individuals living in the community and participating in court-ordered treatment or probation or parole supervision are likely to have additional law enforcement contacts. Depending upon the circumstances of these contacts, these individuals are often referred back to their service providers or probation or parole officers.

A brief history of American law enforcement

Law enforcement in America was formed as a component of the criminal justice system based on the law enforcement structure in England (for a more detailed historical analysis of policing from 3000 BCE in Egypt to Europe in the middle ages – see Pender 2017). A brief history of American law enforcement and its origins can be beneficial for understanding contemporary law enforcement functions and how they developed.

Policing periods

Policing in America has undergone many periods during its evolution to what now comprises contemporary policing. These periods have been described using different terms, although similarities exist among each period. Bush and Dodson (2014) articulated the following four periods: (1) the Political Entrenchment phase in which law enforcement agencies performed the service law enforcement function. This period was further characterized by law enforcement involvement in politics and corruption; (2) the Reform Efforts phase was a period during which efforts were made to end law enforcement involvement in politics and corruption. Numerous policing reforms were initiated to achieve these goals; (3) the Professional phase was characterized by more emphasis and attention given to the law enforcement function with less emphasis given to the service law enforcement function and order maintenance function; and (4) the Public and Community Relations phase is characterized by an approach that seeks to establish and maintain positive police-community relations and implement community policing strategies focused on developing collaboration with community-based agencies. This period is the current policing period.

Similarly, Cole, Smith, and DeJong (2019) described four historical periods that shaped the formation of law enforcement agencies in the United States. The authors emphasize that during each of the following historical periods, unique societal and political issues and social problems occurred that influenced policing during these periods:

1. The Colonial Era and the Early Republic – this period was characterized by the new settlers settling further westward and colonizing the land as they settled. The settlers formed an early law enforcement system with the purpose of providing community protection and safety. Not only did this system involve protecting one another from crime, they also used the system to control Native Americans.

Settlers that colonized and remained in the East formed a Watch System. The Watch System was comprised of volunteers and paid individuals who provided protection and community safety. The first Watch System was implemented in 1604 in Boston, MA. The purpose of the Watch System was for each community member to intervene to prevent crime and disorder in the community. During this period, formalized law enforcement agencies were formed.

The colonies were established from New England to the Carolinas. These colonies were not monolithic and differentiation was even found among the colonies in New England, although the New England colonies were identified as having the most structured criminal justice system. Crime rates also differed among the colonies, as well as ethnic and racial diversity, and religion and the criminal justice system were linked (Greenberg, 1982).

2. The Political Era lasted from 1840 to 1920 – during the Political Era, law enforcement became associated with politics in law enforcement agencies in which police officers were loyal to local political leaders more so than to community residents. During this period, large cities such as New York, Chicago, Philadelphia, and Boston began to reform their law enforcement agencies.
3. The Professional Model Era occurred between 1920 and 1970 – this period was shaped by the positions taken by individuals involved in the Progressive movement. In fact, the Professional Model period arose as a result of the Progressive movement. Individuals referred to as the Progressives are described as individuals who were educated and upper-middle class. They believed, among other matters, that how law enforcement agencies operate should be improved.

The Progressives' beliefs had a profound influence on law enforcement agencies and as a consequence, politics, which distinguished the Political Era, was eliminated from law enforcement operations. Improved training, discipline, technology, and merit became commonplace in law enforcement agencies. Eliminating politics and corruption from law enforcement agencies involved introducing the military model (Bittner, 1990; Toch & Grant, 2005).

4. the Community Policing Era began in 1970 and continues to the present day. The Community Policing Era is characterized by a major shift in policing functions from crime fighting to the provision of services to community residents and order maintenance. This period is primarily characterized by an emphasis on community needs such as crime and disorder.

The current Community Policing Era is maintained with an extensive infrastructure that includes research, publications, program development, and technical assistance. The U.S. Department of Justice, Community Oriented Policing Services defines community policing as "a philosophy that promotes organizational strategies that support the systematic use of partnerships and problem-solving techniques to proactively address the immediate conditions that give rise to public safety issues such as crime, social disorder, and fear of crime" (DOJ, 2014, p. 1). Collaborations and partnerships implemented to address community social problems are an essential feature of community policing and are examined throughout this book.

Each of the historical periods is distinguished by advances in policing reforms. Each period is also distinguished by advances that connect law enforcement to social work. Although the focus of this chapter is to provide an understanding of law enforcement agencies, Chapter 3 examines the development of police social work collaborations and their evolution.

TABLE 1.2 Advances in police social work during law enforcement periods

Law enforcement periods	Police social work developments
The Colonial Era and the Early Republic	Morality offenses were addressed by the faith community.
The Political Era (1840 to 1920)	1919 – August Vollmer delivered a speech titled *The Policeman* (sic) *as Social Worker* to the IACP.
The Professional Model Era (1920 to 1970)	1930 – social work is identified in the census as a profession (Stuart, 2019).
	1953 – the first description is published identifying social work employment in a law enforcement agency.
Community Policing Era (1970 to present)	1975 – Harvey Treger published the first book on the topic of police social work titled *The police-social work team*. This publication is followed by three additional books:
	1976 – *Police social work* (Colbach and Fosterling)
	1986 – *The police and social workers* (Thomas)
	1994 – *The police and social workers* (2nd ed.) (Thomas).

Applying the historical periods identified by Cole, Smith and DeJong (2019), Table 1.2 provides a summary of the connections made between law enforcement and social work that are relevant for police social work practice in law enforcement agencies. The table also shows that as American law enforcement progressed through the different periods, social work was advanced in law enforcement which did not occur solely in the community policing period. As we shall later see, the present period of community policing has evolved to include more emphasis on the community receiving social services, and the introduction of diversion, harm reduction, and a trauma-informed approach.

The earliest law enforcement agencies

The earliest law enforcement agencies were started at different times. During the latter part of the early republic period, many of the oldest law enforcement agencies were formed. Numerous law enforcement agencies identify the date the agency was formed on the agency website and also provide a brief historical overview of the agency. For example, the Rochester Police Department (RPD) was formed in 1819 (City of Rochester, Rochester Police Department, n.d.). Sixteen years later, in 1835, the Chicago Police Department was formed (Chicago Police Department, n.d.), and ten years following the formation of the Chicago Police Department, the New York City Police Department (NYPD) was formed in 1845 (NYPD, 2020).

An early system of the Texas Rangers was formed in 1823. Throughout numerous changes and until 1840, the Rangers were a defense against native Americans and later Mexicans. The "darkest period" of the Texas Rangers was between 1865 and 1873 during the Reconstruction period. On September 1, 1935, the Texas Rangers became the first state law enforcement agency (Texas Department of Public Safety, 2021).

Slave patrols

The above presentation identifying the dates that the earliest local and state law enforcement agencies were formed places these events that occurred in the United States in historical context. Other major historical events were also occurring in the United States during this time period.

Historically, examining the early formation of law enforcement agencies in the United States and in particular, the dates when they were formed reveals that slave patrols existed during the early formation of law enforcement agencies, and during the colonial period and early republic period.

The first slave patrol was formed in 1704 in the southern Colonies of the Carolinas. The formation of law enforcement agencies in the South was influenced by preserving the institution of slavery. During the Civil War, the military also provided law enforcement in the South, although during the Reconstruction period, Southern law enforcement agencies functioned comparable to the early slave patrols by denying rights to free slaves (Waxman, 2017).

The Fugitive Slave Law was passed by Congress in 1850, although an earlier Fugitive Slave Law was passed in Congress in 1793. The Fugitive Slave Law of 1793 made it legal for a slave owner or a representative for the slave owner to arrest a runaway slave even if the runaway slave was arrested in another state. The Law also made it legal to transport a runaway slave back to the slave owner. The purpose of the Fugitive Slave Law of 1850 was not to deter slaves from running away but rather to further legalize the arrest and return of runaway slaves by providing protections for slave owners or their representatives. In this way, the 1850 law strengthened the 1793 law. The number of runaway slaves that were arrested and returned to slave owners was seldom documented (Campbell, 1970). After the Fugitive Slave Law of 1793, and by 1800 each state had formed slave patrols which, after the Civil War, evolved into law enforcement agencies in the South. For that reason, while the formation of American law enforcement agencies is based on the law enforcement system in England, the formation of southern law enforcement agencies was influenced by slave patrols (Hassett-Walker, 2021).

Asserting that the aforementioned history is an important topic for students to learn, Turner, Giacopassi, and Vandiver (2006) conducted a literature review that examined 18 introductory criminal justice textbooks and 13 policing textbooks published in 2000 or later, and 14 introductory criminal justice textbooks published in the 1970s. The purpose of the review was to assess the amount of discussion given to slavery and slave patrols given the significant role of slave patrols in the formation of American law enforcement agencies. Overall, they found that these textbooks provided very modest coverage of slave patrols, if at all. They concluded more coverage of slave patrols is needed in introductory and policing textbooks to provide a better understanding of the historical context of the formation of American law enforcement agencies as well as modern-day American law enforcement.

Influential policing reformers

Several early policing reformers were influential in advocating and enacting policing reforms. Only two will be briefly mentioned. The contributions to policing reforms made by these two reformers are unparalleled. Toch and Grant (2005) describe Orlando W. Wilson (1900–1972) as "the dean of American police reformers" (p. 33). A former police chief, Wilson urged the use of social interventions as a crime prevention strategy and recognized the need for police officers to collaborate with community-based agencies. Wilson also emphasized prevention interventions such as delinquency prevention interventions.

Oliver (2017) described August Vollmer (1876–1955) as *the father of American policing* in a biographical book summarizing August Vollmer's accomplishments in policing reform. Vollmer is described as a well-known policing reformer and former chief of police in the Berkeley (California) Police Department. His significant policing reform contributions include professionalizing law enforcement agencies in the United States and internationally. He was also influential in the development of the polygraph machine, bringing about the use of radios for police vehicles for communication between officers, establishing the first crime lab in the United States, and notably establishing academic programs at the University of California, Berkeley, which evolved to become criminal justice and criminology degree programs.

This book was inspired by Vollmer's accomplishments. Vollmer urged the use of police collaboration with community-based social service agencies as a crime prevention strategy and in 1919, Vollmer was the first to coin the phrase "police social work" in a speech titled *The Policeman* (sic) *as Social Worker* (Vollmer, 1919). The collection of his writings are maintained at the Bancroft Library, University of California, Berkeley.

The civil rights movement and policing

Despite policing reforms, law enforcement relationships with the public remained tense. In the 1950s and 1960s, during the Civil Rights movement, numerous concerns about law enforcement interactions with the public, particularly interactions with the Black community were voiced. At the end of the 1960s, protests and riots occurred in large part by concerns of police officers' use of excessive force on Blacks and misconduct during police contacts with Blacks (Cunningham & Gillezeau, 2019).

Police power

The Merriam-Webster Dictionary defines police power as: "The inherent power of a government to exercise reasonable control over persons and property within its jurisdiction in the interest of the general security, health, safety, morals, and welfare except where legally prohibited" (Merriam-Webster, Inc.,

2021). The right to state police power is granted in the 10th Amendment of the U.S. Constitution (Mosk, 1981). The 10th Amendment states, "The powers not delegated to the United States by the Constitution, nor prohibited by it to the States, are reserved to the States respectively, or to the people" (U.S. Senate: Constitution of the United States, n.d.).

Galva, Atchison, and Levey (2005) elucidated the concept of police power. Police power given to each state has its origins in the colonial period and English common law. Presently, the police power to protect public health is defined in civil law, not criminal law, and provides law enforcement the authority to limit an individual's private rights when the good of the larger society is necessary. Public health and public safety in these instances are often interconnected. Examples of public health interventions upheld by police power include the authority to "enforce isolation and quarantine" (p. 20). Police power has legal support unless an individual's rights are intentionally violated.

Because police powers pertain to both public safety and public health and give law enforcement the authority to intervene in public health matters, law enforcement has been given a significant role in public health matters. DeMillo (2020) described a recent situation involving police powers that occurred during the Covid-19 pandemic when some law enforcement chiefs of police refused to implement police powers originating from state legislation mandating that masks are worn when in public to protect public health and public safety. Although some police chiefs enforced their state mandates requiring the public to wear masks, some police chiefs refused to enforce them either among the public or even within their law enforcement agency. Reasons that were given included insufficient law enforcement personnel to respond to calls involving violations of the state mandate to wear a mask or chiefs disagreeing with a state mandate. Some police chiefs also refused to allow their departments to issue tickets and fines among the public for not wearing a mask. Clearly, certain police chiefs did not perceive enforcing these public health and public safety mandates within the purview of police powers. An innovative approach to addressing state mandates was to hire members of the public including community groups to distribute masks and encourage individuals to wear them instead of using law enforcement (DeMillo 2020).

Concerning public safety during the Covid-19 pandemic, law enforcement agencies across the country reduced the number of arrests made and issued more citations. These procedures primarily applied to low-level offenses and offenders who presented a risk to public safety were arrested (Brennan Center for Justice, 2021).

Galva et al. (2005) asserted that since public health police powers are established in civil law and not criminal law among states it is important that law enforcement clarify this difference so that the public does not view public health matters as law enforcement matters. Because police social workers and professional social workers also provide assistance with public health matters it stands to reason that this distinction must also be maintained during police social work or other social work public assistance. This is particularly relevant to avoid public claims that social workers are "acting like the police."

The mission of law enforcement agencies

Numerous law enforcement agencies publish a mission statement on the agency website. In addition to identifying the agency's mission, these mission statements also provide information about the law enforcement agency and the types of services provided. In general, the mission statements primarily identify the primary tasks of serving and protecting the public.

It is necessary that police social workers understand the concepts articulated in these mission statements. As discussed in Chapters 2 and 3, these concepts play an important role in the foundation of law enforcement functions and the tasks that social workers perform as well. For purposes of illustration, four law enforcement agencies are presented. These four agencies are responsible for law enforcement in the four largest U.S. cities. Moreover, several common themes are identified among the four mission statements. These common themes include improving the quality of life and public safety within the community, reducing crime and the public's fear of crime, and developing community partnerships and collaborations. These common themes are found among the following four law enforcement agency mission statements:

> The mission of the New York City Police Department is to enhance the quality of life in New York City by working in partnership with the community to enforce the law, preserve peace, protect the people, reduce fear, and maintain order (NYPD, 2020).

> It is the mission of the Los Angeles Police Department to safeguard the lives and property of the people we serve, to reduce the incidence and fear of crime, and to enhance public safety while working with the diverse communities to improve their quality of life. Our mandate is to do so with honor and integrity, while at all times conducting ourselves with the highest ethical standards to maintain public confidence (Los Angeles Police Department, 2021).

> The Chicago Police Department, as part of, and empowered by, the community, is committed to protect the lives, property, and rights of all people, to maintain order, and to enforce the law impartially. We will provide quality police service in partnership with other members of the community. To fulfill our mission, we will strive to attain the highest degree of

ethical behavior and professional conduct at all times (City of Chicago, 2021).

The mission of the Houston Police Department is to enhance the quality of life in the City of Houston by working cooperatively with the public and within the framework of the U.S. Constitution to enforce the laws, preserve the peace, reduce fear and provide for a safe environment (City of Houston, 2021).

Law enforcement functions

Law enforcement functions refer to the general purpose of the law enforcement component of the criminal justice system. These functions are summarized in Table 1.3. Cole, Smith, and DeJong (2019) identified the following three law enforcement functions: (1) order maintenance, (2) law enforcement, and (3) the service function. A summary of the authors' descriptions are provided below:

Order maintenance function

The order maintenance function, as a crime prevention strategy, is used to maintain public safety and resolve interpersonal conflicts. The resolution of police calls for service that involves the order maintenance function is less well defined than calls that involve the law enforcement function. For example, a domestic violence police call. During an order maintenance call, police officers use their discretion to determine if a law has been violated, whether to make an arrest, divert individuals away from further criminal justice system involvement, or mediate a situation. Because law violations are less well defined during these police calls, law enforcement can be criticized for bias. This occurs because these calls are not all resolved in the same manner by all police officers and due to the differential response, racial and ethnic differences may be identified.

TABLE 1.3 Summary of law enforcement functions

Law enforcement function	*Purpose*
Order maintenance	To provide interventions focused on public safety and disorder.
Law enforcement	To investigate offenders, determine criminal charges and take offenders into custody.
Service	To provide crime prevention and other interventions to address crises, social problems, and community needs.

Law enforcement function

The law enforcement function involves a police officer determining if a law violation has occurred, and if so, the law violator is arrested. If a law violator is not arrested at the scene, an investigation to locate the offender ensues and a warrant for an arrest is issued. States have enacted different laws that define a criminal offense and police officers are trained to apply the law within their jurisdiction to determine and document which laws have been violated. Similar to the order maintenance function, law enforcement may be criticized for providing a biased police response when differential use of arrests occurs or when the law enforcement function is more focused on racial and ethnic minority and poor communities.

A social problem may be a contributing factor to a law violation. For example, an intoxicated driver who fails a sobriety test may experience an addiction to alcohol. Thus, in many instances, the social problem could be a contributing factor to the law violation. The primary goal of the law enforcement function is to address the crime and protect public safety. The officer does not examine the underlying causes or types of interventions needed. Once the court component of the criminal justice system becomes involved with the individual, these decisions can be determined.

However, this is beginning to change among law enforcement agencies as police officers address both the underlying causes and provide interventions in response to social problems associated with the law violation. For instance, Forsman, Hrelja, Henriksson, and Wiklund (2011) describe police officers collaborating with social services to initiate interventions within 24 hours following a law enforcement contact for suspected drunk driving or driving while under the influence of drugs. Such interventions are provided much earlier than court involvement and intervention decisions determined by the court. Further, it has been found that denial of drug use or a drinking problem increases shortly after police contact during which time individuals are less willing to seek services. Immediate interventions lessens these underlying issues.

The order maintenance function may involve more of an examination of these contributing factors than the law enforcement function. The service law enforcement function requires an understanding of these factors to provide appropriate crisis intervention and referrals, which is the role of the next function, the service law enforcement function.

Service function

The service law enforcement function involves responding to police calls that involve non-crime situations. This law enforcement function includes crime prevention strategies and is performed more often than the order maintenance or law enforcement functions. Examples include responding to calls to assist individuals who are ill, expressing suicidal ideation, or using substances, among others. The public contacts law enforcement or individuals come to the attention of law enforcement for numerous reasons that do not involve the law enforcement function.

Performing the service function is not a new function for law enforcement. When August Vollmer delivered his speech to the International Association of Chiefs of Police in 1919, he had already recognized that police officers were addressing a great deal of social problems and that instead of arrests individuals could receive referrals to community-based and behavioral health care providers. Bear in mind that at the time of Vollmer's speech WWI, which lasted from 1914 to 1918, had recently ended.

Mastrofski (1983) identified multiple examples of non-crime situations that comprise police calls including traffic law violations and accidents, resolving interpersonal conflicts, nuisance violations, responding to medical needs, responding to requests for information, and responding to calls for assistance. As these examples suggest performing the service law enforcement function requires that police officers provide a wide range of services and interventions such as referrals, transportation, medical assistance, crisis intervention, mediation, and emotional support, among others. The law enforcement service function is examined in greater detail in Chapter 2.

Law enforcement tasks

Law enforcement tasks refer to the duties a police officer performs. Consequently, law enforcement tasks are different from law enforcement functions with the latter referring to the general purpose of law enforcement as previously mentioned. Because this chapter provides an overview of law enforcement functions, law enforcement tasks, and the most widely implemented crime prevention strategies, it is necessary to describe the differences between these concepts.

Cole, Smith, and DeJong (2019) also identified four essential tasks that are closely aligned with the three law enforcement functions (order maintenance, law enforcement, and the service function): (1) peace-keeping tasks are used to maintain public safety and individual's rights; (2) tasks that involve arresting offenders and reducing crime; (3) crime prevention tasks that are used to prevent and reduce crime; and (4) tasks used to provide service similar to social services.

The role of law enforcement in contemporary society

The role of law enforcement in contemporary society is shaped by the law enforcement service function, which continues to comprise the majority of police officers' daily tasks. In Chapter 2, early studies that examined the amount of time police officers spend providing services that are non-crime related are summarized. As previously mentioned, this is not a new function for law enforcement. The role of law enforcement in contemporary society also includes investigating and responding to terrorism, hate crimes, cybercrimes, and other crimes that are occurring with increasing frequency.

The role of law enforcement in contemporary society is being questioned as a result of several movements such as the Defund the Police movement and the Black Lives Matter movement. In general, these questions have arisen in response to the excessive use of police force in communities of color, whether uniformed and armed officers are the most appropriate personnel to respond to community crises, concerns about militarization among law enforcement agencies and the use of military equipment when interacting with the public, and how legal proceedings should be handled when police officers are accused of brutality and misconduct. The manner in which court proceedings are conducted involving police officers and cases of police brutality have come to the attention of the Supreme Court (Fuchs, 2020; Liptak, 2020).

Contemporary concerns also suggest that many social problems such as mental health crises are perhaps best managed with a response that does not include law enforcement. Although the use of law enforcement to respond to mental health crises will be reduced apparently this involvement will not be completely eliminated (Isselbacher, 2020). As a matter of fact, police officers are performing the service law enforcement function as well as other functions while at the same time lawmakers, community leaders, and community residents are expressing concerns about the role of law enforcement in contemporary society. In response to this reality, other popular suggestions regarding contemporary law enforcement include providing more funding to law enforcement agencies to improve their ability to provide modern policing services. Additional suggestions to address concerns about policing include providing improved training on the topics of mental health and racial and ethnic diversity, hiring only police officer candidates who live within the communities that they will serve, and as mentioned eliminating the law enforcement response for certain social problems.

Law enforcement agency organizational structure

The organizational structure of law enforcement agencies is very different from a social service agency. In fact, it is also different from most other host agencies in which social workers are employed. The major differences are that law enforcement agencies are characterized by a paramilitary organizational structure, sworn police officer personnel who are armed and trained to use lethal force, and drive vehicles equipped with emergency lights and sirens.

Paramilitary structure

Law enforcement agencies are organized based on a paramilitary model. The paramilitary model became the organizational structure among law enforcement agencies in the early 1900s with the purpose of reducing crime but also removing politics and corruption from law enforcement which was prevalent during this period (Bittner, 1990; Fogelson, 1977). The Progressive movement was also influential for introducing aspects of military culture into law enforcement agencies (Uchida, 1997). Implementing elements of the military into law enforcement has continued to evolve. Kraska and Keppler (1997) found that paramilitary type policing increased 538% from 1980 to 1995. Indeed, elements of the military in law enforcement agencies are not a recent phenomenon.

Similar to the military, law enforcement agencies are characterized by a highly organized and structured chain of command. Orders or commands flow top to bottom and are expected to be followed. Orders are also written in the form of General Orders which are documents that describe specific instructions. Communication also flows upward in the chain of command for specific requests or other matters that require departmental approval. Establishing a collaboration with the law enforcement agency is an example. The law enforcement paramilitary model chain of command also includes ranks similar to the military branches.

Law enforcement officer ranks

Table 1.4 shows the typical ranks in law enforcement agencies. The numbers of officers holding these ranks, except for the commissioner and deputy commissioner, vary based on agency size and the number and type of specialty units.

TABLE 1.4 Summary of law enforcement ranks

Officer rank	General description of duties
Recruit	A recruit is a non-sworn, paid employee of a law enforcement agency participating in training at a law enforcement academy followed by a period of field training before becoming a police officer.
Police officer	This is an entry-level rank of sworn officers that includes patrol officers, and specialty police officers such as youth officers, community affairs officers, and domestic violence officers, for example.
Detective	This rank is a police officer who has been promoted to the rank of a detective with the responsibility of conducting criminal investigations.
Sergeant	This rank is above the rank of patrol officer and detective, and in general sergeants supervise patrol officers.
Lieutenant	This rank is above the rank of sergeant, and in general lieutenants supervise sergeants.
Captain	This rate is above the rank of lieutenant, and in general captains manage precincts and specialty units.
Deputy commissioner	Although different titles may be used for this position such as deputy chief, this is the second-highest or second in command position in a law enforcement agency.
Commissioner	Although different titles may be used such as chief of police, this is the highest-ranking position in a law enforcement agency and is considered as first in command.

These ranks are also based on funding to maintain such specialty units. After graduating from the recruit class in the police academy, the rank of patrol officer is the entry-level rank in law enforcement agencies. The table shows the ranks in order from lowest to highest rank and a very brief summary of the general duties of each rank.

A patrol officer is promoted through the ranks based on studying and successful completion of a civil service examination for the position of sergeant, which is an administrative position. Administrative positions involve a range of supervisory responsibilities such as scheduling assignments, providing information to officers, and completing performance evaluations. This process repeats for promotion to the next rank. The police chief is the highest-ranking member in the agency. Police chiefs in local agencies, in which police social workers are primarily employed, are typically appointed by the city mayor. Therefore, as mayoral offices change due to elections, so do police chiefs. A police chief has the authority to appoint an administrative staff. Among local law enforcement agencies, the police chief oversees the law agency and reports to the mayor.

Law enforcement agency personnel

Recruits

A recruit is a non-sworn, paid employee of a law enforcement agency participating in training at a law enforcement academy. Academy training is followed by a period of field training before the recruit becomes a sworn police officer. Field training is an essential component of recruit training and provides recruits with real-world law enforcement experience beyond classroom academy training. The supervision is provided by a field training officer. In this way, field training is similar to the experiential field-work experience of social work students who complete internships in a wide variety of settings.

Field training programs are a relatively recent development that emerged based on the programs implemented in San Jose, CA, in 1972. Because training academy classroom instruction alone is insufficient to prepare a recruit to perform law enforcement functions beyond the classroom, a field training program is an essential component of police officer training (McCampbell, 1987).

Police officers

The terms *sworn personnel* or *sworn officer* are used to designate police officers. Police officers are civil servants who have taken an oath and are authorized to carry a firearm. Sworn officers have the powers to make arrests (Hickman & Reaves, 2003).

Table 1.5 displays the number of full-time sworn police officers employed in law enforcement agencies over a six-year period from 1997 to 2016. In 2016,

TABLE 1.5 Full-time sworn police officers in general purpose state and local law enforcement agencies, 1997–2016

Agency type	1997	2000	2003	2007	2013	2016
Local police	419,996	440,770	451,737	463,147	477,317	468,170
Sheriff's office★	174,486	159,528	174,251	172,241	188,952	173,354
Primary state police	54,206	56,348	57,611	64,872	58,421	59,645
Total	648,688	656,646	683,599	700,260	724,690	701,169

★ Excludes sheriff's offices without primary law enforcement jurisdiction.

Hyland, S. (2018). *Full-time employees in law enforcement agencies, 1997–2016.* Reprinted with permission.

among the three types of law enforcement agencies, local agencies employed the most full-time police officers (468,170), followed by sheriff's offices (173,354) with the fewest police officers employed in state law enforcement agencies (59,645). In total, in 2016, 701,169 full-time police officers were employed among state and local law enforcement agencies.

Civilians

Law enforcement agencies also hire civilian personnel who are civil service employees and bound to civil service regulations. The term *civilians* refers to non-sworn personnel employed in law enforcement agencies. Civilians provide a supportive role in law enforcement agencies (Hickman & Reaves, 2003). Police social workers are an example of civilian employees.

In 2016, more civilians were employed in sheriff's offices followed by local law enforcement agencies, and finally state law enforcement agencies (Hyland, 2018). The numbers of civilian employees are shown in Table 1.6. State law enforcement agencies employed the fewest number of civilians totaling 31,452. As previously mentioned, civilian police social workers are more likely to be employed in local law enforcement agencies.

TABLE 1.6 Full-time civilian employees in general purpose state and local law enforcement agencies, 1997–2016

Agency type	1997	2000	2003	2007	2013	2016
Local police	111,317	124,874	129,013	137,880	127,642	131,332
Sheriff's office★	88,659	129,608	156,022	174,096	162,952	186,489
Primary state police	28,055	30,680	24,808	34,263	30,076	31,452
Total	228,031	285,162	309,843	346,239	320,670	349,273

★ Excludes sheriff's offices without primary law enforcement jurisdiction.

Hyland, S. (2018). *Full-time employees in law enforcement agencies, 1997–2016.* Reprinted with permission.

Volunteers

Volunteers in law enforcement agencies are also civilians. Volunteers perform supportive services in law enforcement agencies. Volunteer positions range from formalized positions to assist with law enforcement functions such as patrol and public safety to informal positions such as assisting with community organizing and police-community meetings.

Numerous volunteer opportunities are found in law enforcement agencies. For example, the Rochester Police Department operates a program known as Police and Citizens Together Against Crime Program (PAC-TAC). PAC-TAC utilizes community volunteers in a crime prevention strategy capacity together with patrol officers and crime prevention officers. These volunteers walk around their communities and establish relationships with community residents and businesses. Volunteers are trained to perform crime prevention strategies, wear a specialized uniform, and are assigned a police radio to communicate with officers (City of Rochester, n.d.).

In some communities, residents can voluntarily participate in a 12 week, 36-hour citizen police academy with the goal of acquiring a better understanding of law enforcement and improving police-community relationships (Breen & Johnson, 2007)

Student interns

The types of students completing internships in law enforcement agencies range from undergraduate students with a major in criminal justice or police science to graduate social work students. Law enforcement agency clearance is necessary to assume these positions, which also requires that intern supervisors have the appropriate training and academic background to supervise the students. In social work, it is necessary that the field instructor have a social work degree in addition to a qualification to perform field instruction.

Types of law enforcement agencies

Similar to the different types of law enforcement functions and tasks that exist different types of law enforcement agencies exist with the responsibility of providing unique law enforcement services. Thus, different types of law enforcement agencies having different goals and objectives exist. These agencies are found at local, county, state, and federal levels of government. Tribal law enforcement agencies also exist.

In general, police social workers are more likely to be employed in local law enforcement agencies. Moreover, the policing strategies of community policing, problem-oriented policing, hot spot policing, police-led diversion, soft policing, plural policing, and intelligence-led policing strategies and tasks are also more likely to be implemented in local law enforcement agencies, although other types of law enforcement agencies may also implement these strategies.

Federal agencies

Federal law enforcement officers have the authority to make arrests and carry firearms. The largest federal law enforcement agencies are the Department of Homeland Security (DHS) and the Department of Justice. In 2016, four of every five federal law enforcement officers were employed in these two agencies alone. Each of these departments includes numerous agencies. For instance, as of 2016, the DHS included: the Customs and Border Protection; Immigration and Customs Enforcement; Federal Emergency Management Agency, Mount Weather Police; Federal Protective Service; Office of the Chief Security Officer, and Secret Service. The Department of Justice agencies included: the Bureau of Alcohol, Tobacco, Firearms, and Explosives; Drug Enforcement Administration; Federal Bureau of Investigation (FBI); Federal Bureau of Prisons; and the U.S. Marshals Service (Brooks, 2019).

Perhaps the most well-known federal law enforcement agency is the FBI. In 2021, the FBI's budget was $9.7 billion with offices located both nationally and internationally. Among the agencies, priorities are protecting individuals' civil rights, addressing violent crime and white-collar crime, and protecting the United States from terrorism and cyber-attacks, among numerous other law enforcement issues (FBI, n.d.)

Tribal law enforcement agencies

As of June 2000, there were 171 American Indian tribally operated law enforcement agencies. The Bureau of Indian affairs operated 37 law enforcement agencies in tribal communities. Among these law enforcement agencies, a total of 2303 full-time sworn law enforcement officers were employed, with 94% of these agencies responding to police calls for service and 80% of the agencies performing crime prevention interventions (Hickman, 2003).

State law enforcement agencies

State operated law enforcement agencies exist in all of the 50 states. Depending on the state designation, these agencies are referred to as a state police agency, highway patrol agency, or department of public safety (Reaves, 2011).

As Table 1.7 highlights the number of general purpose local and state law enforcement agencies that operated during the 19 year period from 1997 to 2016 remained relatively stable, although a decrease of 1378 agencies existed when comparing the years 1997 and 2016 (Hyland, 2018).

TABLE 1.7 Number of general purpose state and local law enforcement agencies from 1997 to 2016

Year	1997	2000	2003	2007	2013	2016
Number of agencies	16,700	15,798	15,766	15,636	15,388	15,322

Hyland, S. (2018). *Full-time employees in law enforcement agencies, 1997–2016*. Reprinted with permission.

County law enforcement agencies

Sheriffs' offices operate in almost all counties and also operate in independent cities. The majority of sheriffs' offices (96%) perform law enforcement tasks such as patrol, responding to calls for service, and traffic enforcement. Likewise, 98% of sheriffs' offices also perform court functions such as serving notices (98%) and providing security for courts (96%). The majority of sheriffs' offices (75%) also operate one or more jails (Reaves, 2011). As these statistics indicate, sheriff's offices are involved in the law enforcement, courts, and corrections components of the criminal justice system.

Local law enforcement agencies

Local law enforcement agencies are municipal agencies. Police social workers are most often employed in local law enforcement agencies, and police and social work or social service collaborations are established among local law enforcement agencies. Community policing was identified as a policing strategy in which community partnerships are developed. In 2000, 68% of local law enforcement agencies, which also employed 90% of all local police officers, had implemented community policing as a policing strategy. Two-thirds of local law enforcement agencies, which also employed 86% of all local police officers, employed full-time community policing officers (Hickman & Reaves, 2003).

The substantial adoption of community policing strategies and employment of community policing officers among local law enforcement agencies creates possibilities for significant partnerships involving the social work profession. Recall that community policing also focuses on problem-solving, as well as partnerships, which are the components of community policing most relevant for the social work profession.

Law enforcement agency size

The size of a law enforcement agency is directly associated with its capacity to provide various types of law enforcement services. Larger agencies provide more law enforcement services, contain more specialized units, and employ more specialty-trained police officers. Smaller agencies provide fewer specialty services and have fewer specialty units, if any. Smaller law enforcement agencies are also located in communities with smaller populations, whereas larger law enforcement agencies are located in communities with larger populations.

Large law enforcement agencies

Large law enforcement agencies provide many more services than smaller agencies and also have more specialty units than smaller departments. Given the law enforcement's emphasis on crime reduction and crime prevention, larger law enforcement agencies are most likely to maintain a crime prevention unit. Smaller agencies are less likely to maintain such units. For example, the NYPD, the largest law enforcement agency in the United States, maintains a Crime Prevention Division. The tasks associated with this division include providing public safety seminars, assisting the public with registering bicycles, preventing automobile theft, and providing crime prevention information (NYPD, 2020).

Among law enforcement agencies responsible for policing large cities, Reaves and Hickman (2002) counted the full-time or part-time specialty units that performed the service law enforcement function in communities with populations of 250,000 residents or more between 1990 and 2000. In 2000, large enforcement agencies had specialty units that addressed child abuse (77%), domestic violence (84%), drug education in schools (73%), juvenile crime (68%), and missing children (66%). Some large agencies also had specialty units that provided victim assistance (47%) particularly in response to hate crimes (26%). Larger law enforcement agencies also had scuba units, mounted horse patrol units, SWAT teams, community affairs units, and canine (K-9) units.

The number of full-time police officers employed in large law enforcement ranges from more than 900 officers to more than 1000 officers. Fifty large law enforcement agencies have been identified with policing responsibilities for cities such as San Francisco, Dallas, Ft Worth, Detroit, Phoenix, and Memphis, among other large cities (Reaves, 2011). Larger law enforcement agencies also have a larger organizational structure because more specialized units exist which employ more police officers. Smaller agencies employ fewer officers, have fewer specialized units and a smaller organizational structure. Larger agencies are also characterized by more diversity among personnel. Police officers employed in large agencies are diverse in terms of race and ethnicity, level of education, sexual identification, and language than officers in smaller agencies. They also serve diverse communities.

Mid-sized law enforcement agencies

Estimating based on Reaves' (2011) figures, mid-sized law enforcement agencies employ hundreds of full-time police officers. The Rochester Police Department is an example of a mid-sized law enforcement agency. Mid-sized law enforcement agencies operate fewer specialty units than large law enforcement agencies, although more than small law enforcement agencies.

Small law enforcement agencies

Again estimating based on Reaves' (2011) figures, the majority of small local law enforcement agencies employed less than ten full-time police officers. Some small agencies employ less than 100 police officers. As mentioned having fewer police officers means having fewer resources to maintain specialty units.

Policing strategies

Policing strategies refer to approaches that are used in law enforcement to perform law enforcement functions. Recall that three law enforcement functions have been previously identified: order maintenance, law enforcement, and the service function (Cole et al., 2019).

Because the focus of this book is the law enforcement service function, several policing strategies that support the service function are presented. These strategies include community policing, problem-oriented policing, hot spot policing, police-led diversion, and soft policing. Plural policing and intelligence-led policing strategies are very briefly discussed for comparison purposes.

Multiple policing strategies exist that are used to perform law enforcement functions and tasks. In general, these strategies focus on crime reduction and prevention. A law enforcement agency may implement multiple policing strategies simultaneously. For example, an agency may implement both community policing and police-led diversion strategies. Each strategy can be implemented independently or in combination with other strategies. Policing strategies vary in their stated goals and objectives, although numerous characteristics are shared among them.

The National Institute of Justice (n.d.) reports that multiple policing strategies were developed through law enforcement practices or extensive research. Further, the common characteristics found among them occur because the strategies were created by different developers to address the same social problem or goals of crime prevention or using best practice approaches for utilizing law enforcement resources. Research is recommended as an essential endeavor for evaluating the effectiveness of these multiple policing strategies.

Community policing

Community policing is perhaps the most widely known policing strategy developed to address community social problems. Community policing consists of three components: partnerships, problem-solving techniques, and organizational transformation (Community Oriented Policing Services Office, U.S. Department of Justice, 2014). In the United States, community policing emerged as a policing strategy in Flint, Michigan. Patrol officers conducted foot patrols to better understand and address community social problems such as drug use and homelessness, and to improve police-community relations among police and people of color, gang members, youth, and undocumented immigrants (Trojanowicz & Bucqueroux, 1990).

The majority of law enforcement academies provide training covering the history of community policing, approaches for identifying social problems, utilizing problem-solving strategies, and understanding the environmental causes of crime. Further, among an average of 43 hours of community policing training provided to recruits, the majority of academies provided training focused on establishing community partnerships and collaboration with an average of 12 training hours on the topic of problem-solving skills (Reaves, 2016).

Once social workers acquire a thorough understanding of the service law enforcement function and community policing, the profession can be better equipped to develop collaborations with law enforcement agencies. Community policing initiatives and principles provide opportunities for police social workers and other professional social workers to develop collaborations with law enforcement agencies (Patterson, 2016).

Problem-oriented policing

Problem-oriented policing does not concentrate on aspects of the law enforcement organization such as its structure or personnel. This strategy instead emphasizes utilizing effective approaches for addressing community social problems. In this way, this strategy involves much more than only the identification and analysis of community problems and includes the capacity to utilize effective interventions (Goldstein, 1990). Although community policing and problem-oriented policing appear to have much in common due to their focus on resolving community social problems, Greene (2000) asserted that, in reality, these are two very different policing strategies.

Hot spot policing

As a strategy to improve public safety and reduce crime and victimization, hot spot policing refers to addressing criminal activity that occurs in concentrated locations within a community referred to as "hot spots" (Sherman, Gartin, & Buerger, 1989). In a systematic review that included only studies of randomized controlled trials, Braga (2005) found that hot spot policing was an effective crime prevention strategy in hot spots. In a pilot study, White and Weisburd (2018) found the use of a co-responder model comprised of police and mental health practitioners responding to mental health crises in hot spot areas was an effective intervention.

Police-led diversion

Law Enforcement Assisted Diversion (LEAD) is a policing strategy with the goals of diverting individuals away from arrest and thereby reducing their subsequent criminal justice system involvement. Certain types of offenses are eligible for diversion; typically, these offenses are low-level and non-violent offenses. Numerous police-led diversion programs operate and perhaps the most well-known program is the Seattle model. This model has been implemented in numerous cities (LEAD National Support Bureau, n.d.).

Soft policing

McCarthy (2013) described "soft policing" as a policing strategy in which police officers provide services to at-risk youth and also seek to improve police-community relations. Suggesting that law enforcement affords less status to police officers performing soft policing strategies, McCarthy examined the provision of soft policing services by female police officers in England and Wales. These female officers provided soft policing by collaborating with social workers and community-based agencies, which created new roles for female police officers.

Ariel, Weinborn, and Sherman (2016) conducted a randomized controlled trial comparing hotspot policing with soft policing. The soft policing strategy involved civilian law enforcement employees who conducted patrols. These civilian employees wore uniforms, although they were unarmed and had limited arrest authority. The purpose was to determine if these policing strategies were effective for reducing crime. The authors found the use of unarmed civilian law enforcement employees conducting patrol duties in hot spots was an effective policing strategy for reducing crime and police calls for services in these locations.

Additional policing strategies implemented as crime prevention strategies include plural policing, which refers to a policing strategy in which policing services are provided by non-law enforcement personnel (Eikenaar, 2019). Intelligence-led policing involves the use of intelligence officers who collect intelligence that will be used in crime prevention efforts (Telep, Ready, & Bottema, 2018).

Chapter summary

This chapter provided a brief overview of the historical development of law enforcement agencies in the United States. This brief historical summary has shown that American law enforcement agencies were developed based on the model established in England. This chapter further traced the historical development of the U.S. law enforcement agencies beginning with policing during the colonial period and the early republic, followed by the political period and the professional model period, and culminating with the community policing period, which represents the present period of American law enforcement. Significant historical events that occurred in law enforcement, such as the influence of slave patrols on the development of Southern law enforcement agencies and the Progressive movement were also reviewed.

In Chapter 2, the focus of attention turns to the service law enforcement function. This function had a prominent role in law enforcement functions historically and continues to have a prominent role in contemporary law enforcement. Contemporary American law enforcement is characterized by the use of community policing, and in fact, the current policing period was referred to as the community policing period. The community policing period is distinguished by its emphasis on law enforcement order maintenance and service functions. Before examining the service law enforcement function, it is important to understand the topics presented in this chapter such as the position of law enforcement agencies in the criminal justice system as a component that precedes courts and corrections, and the mission, structure, and organization of law enforcement agencies including agency size, personnel, and police officer ranks.

Questions for discussion

1. Among the major policing strategies presented in this chapter which strategies do you believe are the most effective for assisting community residents who experience social problems, and why?
2. Were you surprised to learn that the majority of law enforcement tasks and calls for service involve the service function?
3. Are law enforcement services in your community provided by the local police, sheriff, state police or another law enforcement agency? What is the difference among the various types of law enforcement agencies?

Activities for further learning

1. Search the LEAD website to determine if your community is exploring, developing, launching, or operating a police diversion program.
2. Search for a newspaper article or a report that describes the service law enforcement function in which an individual received assistance similar to social service assistance.
3. Search the internet to locate information about the size of the law enforcement agency in your community? Describe the agency size. What type of services are provided and what type of specialty units exist?

References

Alexander, R., Jr. (2008). Criminal justice: Overview. In T. Mizrahi & L. Davis (Eds.), *Encyclopedia of social work* (20th ed.) (Vol. 3, pp. 470–476). Washington, DC: NASW Press and New York: Oxford University Press.

Ariel, B., Weinborn, C., & Sherman, L. W. (2016). "Soft" policing at hot spots – do police community support officers work? A randomized controlled trial. *Journal of Experimental Criminology, 12*(3), 277–317.

Bittner, E. (1990). *Aspects of police work*. Boston: Northeastern University Press.

Braga, A. A. (2005). Hot spots policing and crime prevention: A systematic review of randomized controlled trials. *Journal of Experimental Criminology, 1*(3), 317–342.

Breen, M. E., & Johnson, B. R. (2007). Citizen police academies: An analysis of enhanced police community relations among citizen attendees. *Police Journal, 80*(3), 246–266.

Brennan Center for Justice at NYU Law (2021). *Police responses to Covid-19*. Retrieved from https://www.brennancenter.org/our-work/research-reports/police-responses-covid-19

Brooks, C. (2019). *Federal law enforcement officers, 2016 – Statistical tables*. NCJ 251922. Washington, DC: U.S. Department of Justice, Office of Justice Programs, Bureau of Justice Statistics.

Bush, M. D., & Dodson, K. D. (2014). Police officers as peace officers: A philosophical and theoretical examination of policing from a peacemaking approach. *Journal of Theoretical & Philosophical Criminology, 6*(3), 194–205.

Campbell, S. (1970). *Slave catchers: Enforcement of the fugitive slave law, 1850–1860.* Chapel Hill: University of North Carolina Press.

Chicago Police Department (n.d.). *History.* Retrieved from https://home.chicagopolice.org/about/history/

City of Chicago (2021). *Police – mission.* Retrieved from https://www.chicago.gov/city/en/depts/cpd/auto_generated/cpd_mission.html

City of Houston (2021). *HPD mission statement.* Retrieved from https://www.houstontx.gov/police/mission.htm

City of Rochester (n.d.). *Police and citizens together against crime program (PAC-TAC).* Retrieved from https://www.cityofrochester.gov/pactac/

Colbach, E. M., & Fosterling, C. D. (1976). *Police social work.* Springfield, IL: Charles C. Thomas.

Cole, G. F., Smith, C. E., & DeJong, C. (2019). *The American system of criminal justice (16th ed.).* Boston, MA: Cengage Learning, Inc.

Cunningham, J. P., & Gillezeau, R. (2019). Don't shoot! The impact of historical African American protest on police killings of civilians. *Journal of Quantitative Criminology, 37,* 1–34.

Davis, E., & Whyde, A. (2018). *Contacts between police and the public, 2015.* NCJ 251145. Washington, DC: U.S. Department of Justice, Office of Justice Programs, Bureau of Justice Statistics.

DeMillo, A. (2020). *Some US police refuse to enforce virus mask mandates.* Retrieved from https://www.courthousenews.com/some-us-police-refuse-to-enforce-virus-mask-mandates/

Department of Justice, Office of Community Oriented Policing Services (2014). *Community policing defined.* (2014). Retrieved from https://cops.usdoj.gov/RIC/Publications/cops-p157-pub.pdf

Eikenaar, T. (2019). Plural policing as professional strife. Municipal officers and police officers in the Netherlands. *International Journal of Police Science & Management, 21*(3), 146–155.

FBI (n.d.). *Mission & priorities.* Retrieved from https://www.fbi.gov/about/mission

Fogelson, R. M. (1977). *Big-city police.* 3rd ed. Cambridge, MA: Harvard University Press.

Forsman, Å., Hrelja, R., Henriksson, P., & Wiklund, M. (2011). Cooperation between police and social treatment services offering treatment to drink and drug drivers - experience in Sweden. *Traffic injury prevention, 12*(1), 9–17.

Fuchs, H. (2020). *Qualified immunity protection for police emerges as flash point amid protests.* Retrieved from https://www.nytimes.com/2020/06/23/us/politics/qualified-immunity.html

Galva, J. E., Atchison, C., & Levey, S. (2005). Public health strategy and the police powers of the state. *Public Health Reports, 120*(suppl 1), 20–27.

Goldstein, H. (1990). *Problem-oriented policing.* New York: McGraw-Hill, Inc.

Greenberg, D. (1982). Crime, law enforcement, and social control in colonial America. *The American Journal of Legal History, 26*(4), 293–325.

Greene, J. R. (2000). Community policing in America: Changing the nature, structure, and function of the police. In J. Horney (Ed.). *Policies, processes, and decisions of the criminal justice system, criminal justice 2000* (Vol. 3, pp. 299–370). Washington, DC: National Institute of Justice, Office of Justice Programs.

Hassett-Walker, C. (2021). How you start is how you finish? The slave patrol and Jim Crow origins of U.S. policing. *Human Rights*, *46*(2), 6–8.

Hickman, M. J. (2003). *Tribal law enforcement, 2000*. NCJ 197936. Washington, DC: US Department of Justice, Office of Justice Programs, Bureau of Justice Statistics.

Hickman, M. J., & Reaves, B. A. (2003). *Local police departments 2000*. NCJ 196002. Washington, DC: US Department of Justice, Office of Justice Programs, Bureau of Justice Statistics.

Hyland, S. (2018). *Full-time employees in law enforcement agencies, 1997–2016*. NCJ 251762. Washington, DC: U.S. Department of Justice, Office of Justice Programs, Bureau of Justice Statistics.

Isselbacher, J. (2020). *Mobile mental health teams warn their models rely on police partnerships*. Retrieved from https://www.statnews.com/2020/07/29/mobile-crisis-mental-health-police/

Kraska, P. B., & Keppler, V. E. (1997). Militarizing American police: The rise and normalization of paramilitary units. *Social Problems*, *44*(1), 1–17.

LEAD National Support Bureau (n.d.). Retrieved from https://www.leadbureau.org/

Liptak, A. (2020). *A timely case on police violence at the Supreme Court*. Retrieved from https://www.nytimes.com/2020/07/20/us/politics/supreme-court-police-brutality.html

Los Angeles Police Department (2021). *The mission statement of the LAPD*. Retrieved from https://www.lapdonline.org/inside_the_lapd/content_basic_view/844

Mastrofski, S. (1983). The police and noncrime services. In G. P. Whitaker & C. D. Phillip (Eds.), *Evaluating performance of criminal justice agencies* (pp. 33–61). Beverly Hills, CA: Sage.

McCampbell, M. S. (1987). *Field training for police officers: The state of the art*. Washington, DC: U.S. Department of Justice, National Institute of Justice.

McCarthy, D. J. (2013). Gendering "soft" policing: Multi-agency working, female cops, and the fluidities of police culture/s. *Policing and Society*, *23*(2), 261–278.

Merriam-Webster, Inc. (2021). *Police power*. Retrieved from https://www.merriam-webster.com/dictionary/police%20power

Mosk, S. (1981). Rediscovering the 10th Amendment. *Judges Journal*, *20*, 16.

National Institute of Justice (n.d.). *Policing strategies*. Retrieved from https://nij.ojp.gov/topics/policing/policing-strategies

NYPD (2020). *About NYPD*. Retrieved from https://www1.nyc.gov/site/nypd/about/about-nypd/about-nypd-landing.page

NYPD (2020). *Crime prevention*. Retrieved from https://www1.nyc.gov/site/nypd/bureaus/administrative/crime-prevention.page

NYPD (2020). *Mission*. Retrieved from https://www1.nyc.gov/site/nypd/about/about-nypd/mission.page

Oliver, W. M. (2017). *August Vollmer: The father of American policing*. Durham, NC: Carolina Academic Press.

Patterson, G. T. (2020). *Social work practice in the criminal justice system (2nd ed)*. New York: Routledge.

Patterson, G. T. (2016). *Community policing*. Oxford Bibliographies in Social Work. New York: Oxford University Press. Retrieved from http://www.oxfordbibliographies.com/view/document/obo-9780195389678/obo-9780195389678-0239.xml?rskey=zsiQqx&result=34

Pender, L. (ed). (2017). *To serve and protect: the history of policing*. New York: Britannica Educational Publishing in association with The Rosen Group, Inc.

Reaves, B. A. (2011). *Census of state and local law enforcement agencies, 2008.* NCJ 233982. Washington, DC: U.S. Department of Justice, Office of Justice Programs, Bureau of Justice Statistics.

Reaves, B. A. (2016). *State and local law enforcement training academies, 2013.* NCJ 249784. Washington, DC: U.S. Department of Justice, Office of Justice Programs, Bureau of Justice Statistics.

Reaves, B. A., & Hickman, M. L. (2002). *Police department in large cities, 1990–2000.* NCJ 175703. Washington, DC: U.S. Department of Justice, Office of Justice Programs, Bureau of Justice Statistics.

Telep, C. W., Ready, J., & Bottema, A. J. (2018). Working towards intelligence-led policing: The Phoenix Police Department intelligence officer program. *Policing: A Journal of Policy and Practice, 12*(3), 332–343.

Trojanowicz, R. C., & Bucqueroux, B. (1990). *Community policing: A contemporary perspective.* Cincinnati, OH: Anderson Publishing Co.

Robinson, M. (2010). Assessing criminal justice practice using social justice theory. *Social Justice Research, 23*(1), 77–97.

Sherman, L., Gartin, P., & Buerger, M. (1989). Hot spots of predatory crime: Routine activities and the criminology of place. *Criminology, 27,* 27–56.

Stuart, P. (2019). Social work profession: History. In *Encyclopedia of Social Work.* Retrieved From: https://oxfordre-com.proxy.wexler.hunter.cuny.edu/socialwork/view/10.1093/acrefore/9780199975839.001.0001/acrefore-9780199975839-e-623.

Texas Department of Public Safety (2021). *History of the Texas rangers.* Retrieved from https://www.dps.texas.gov/section/texas-rangers/history-texas-rangers

Thomas, T. (1986). *The police and social workers.* Aldershot, Hants, UK: Gower Publishing Company.

Thomas, T. (1994). *The police and social workers.* 2nd ed. Aldershot, UK: Arena.

Toch, H., & Grant, J. D. (2005). *Police as problem solvers: How frontline workers can promote organizational and community change.* 2nd ed. Washington, DC: American Psychological Association.

Treger, H. (1975). *The police-social work team.* Springfield, IL: Charles C. Thomas.

Turner, K. B., Giacopassi, D., & Vandiver, M. (2006). Ignoring the past: Coverage of slavery and slave patrols in criminal justice texts. *Journal of Criminal Justice Education, 17*(1), 181–195.

Uchida, C. D. (1997). Development of the American police: A historical overview. In Roger G. Dunham & Geoffrey P. Alpert (Eds.), *Critical issues in policing: Contemporary readings* (3rd ed.) (pp. 19–35). Prospect Heights, IL: Waveland Press.

U.S. Senate. *Constitution of the United States* (n.d.). Retrieved from https://www.senate.gov/civics/constitution_item/constitution.htm#amdt_10_(1791)

Vollmer, A. (April, 1919). *Writings, the policeman as social worker.* BANC MSS C-B 403, The Bancroft Library, University of California, Berkeley.

Waxman, O. B. (2017). *The history of police in America and the first force.* Retrieved from https://time.com/4779112/police-history-origins/

White, C., & Weisburd, D. (2018). A co-responder model for policing mental health problems at crime hot spots: Findings from a pilot project. *Policing: A Journal of Policy & Practice, 12*(2), 194–209.

2

THE SERVICE LAW ENFORCEMENT FUNCTION

Chapter overview

This chapter describes the service law enforcement function in sufficient detail to identify how this function supports professional police social work practice. In this regard, the chapter provides an introduction to Chapter 3 as well as providing a foundation for this book.

This chapter reviews statistics that show police officers spend more time performing the service function rather than law enforcement functions. The service law enforcement function involves responding to medical emergencies, mental health crises, victims of crime, homelessness, and substance use among other social problems that require social service assistance and interventions. Recall that law enforcement functions involve investigating offenders, determining criminal charges, and arresting offenders.

The most well-known policing strategy that exemplifies the service law enforcement function is community policing. As discussed in Chapter 1, community policing is exemplified by the principles of community partnerships, problem-solving interventions, and organizational transformation. In this chapter, we examine law enforcement preparation to perform community policing. This involves an examination of the social problem subject areas that are the most frequent focus of police and social work collaboration such as domestic violence and child maltreatment. The percentage of basic training law enforcement academies provide in these subject areas and the average number of hours of training per recruit are discussed. The same approach is used to discuss the community policing skills taught in basic training law enforcement academies. An additional policing strategy associated with the service law enforcement function discussed in this chapter includes police-led diversion.

DOI: 10.4324/9781003132257-2

Introduction

Law enforcement agencies operate 24 hours a day, 7 days a week. As mobile-first responders, police officers respond to a wide range of both crime and non-crime situations. The focus of this chapter is non-crime situations. As a result of responding to these situations, police officers can access many types of community resources. These community resources are essential for performing the service law enforcement function.

Chapter 1 introduced law enforcement as one of the four components of the criminal justice system. Chapter 1 also discussed the service law enforcement function, which involves providing a wide variety of non-crime social service-related assistance to individuals. Law enforcement is the first contact that individuals have with the criminal justice system. Consequently, when police officers utilize discretion, diversion, and provide services, individuals avoid further criminal justice system involvement and receive needed services and interventions.

Individuals and families experience emergencies that require the service law enforcement function for numerous reasons. Some of these reasons include mental health crises, medical emergencies, lack of transportation, interpersonal conflicts, and the need for information. Contributing to these reasons is the lack of health care or behavioral health care provider. Even among those who have such providers, the lack of after-hours or emergency services can result in a 911 call. These calls are certain when threatening behaviors are observed.

Other types of 911 calls can include a request to check the welfare of an individual or family member or calls are made due to a lack of understanding about what police officers can do or not do in response to the call.

In some instances, individuals are upset and feel violated by another individual and want the police to only speak with the individual. Individuals might also feel that calling the police on another individual gives them a sense of retribution.

Because of the types of calls for service received by law enforcement, police officers are likely to use the order maintenance, law enforcement, and service law enforcement functions simultaneously. Even when responding to crime situations, the service law enforcement function may be required. In other words, it is possible that each of the three functions is performed by multiple police officers responding to a single call for service. For instance, the officers consult with one another or a supervisor to make a decision about whether or not an arrest should be made. These actions involve the order maintenance function. It may be determined that an arrest should be made and when an individual is arrested, this would involve the law enforcement function. Further, there may be individuals who are in need of services such as transportation, information, or referrals. In this way, the service law enforcement function is being performed.

Performing the three law enforcement functions simultaneously also illustrates the unpredictable nature of responding to police calls for service. What may initially appear to be an order maintenance function based on information received from the 911 dispatcher may evolve into a situation that necessitates performing the three law enforcement functions. In addition to utilizing the three law enforcement functions, police officers also require knowledge about social problems, which may be the basis of the call for service. Therefore police officers should possess the knowledge and skills to perform each of the three functions.

Evidence supporting the service law enforcement function

The law enforcement function (i.e., making arrests, conducting investigations) has not comprised more than 20% of a police officer's daily tasks throughout the history of American policing. Moreover, the service law enforcement function had existed since the Colonial period when law enforcement agencies were formed, although the types of community social problems have changed over time (Strecher, 1971). Overall, the types of law enforcement functions a police officer performs depend on whether an officer is employed in a specialty unit, the type of specialty unit, and community crime rates.

Early studies have shown that the majority of law enforcement tasks involve responding to non-crime situations that are social service-related. Asserting that these tasks involve approximately 50% of a police officer's daily tasks, Peterson (1974) further asserted that a police officer is performing "as an amateur social worker" (p. 173). Treger (1987) reported a higher percentage suggesting that 50% to 90% of an officer's daily tasks are social service-related, whereas Webster (1970) found patrol officers responded to social service-related calls at a rate of 17.27% during a 54 week period.

Mastrofski (1983) provided numerous examples of crime and non-crime situations. Crime-related situations include violent crimes such as child abuse and robbery, non-violent crimes such as fraud, moral offenses such as gambling, and reporting a suspicious individual to law enforcement. Examples of non-crime situations include traffic enforcement, medical emergencies, disputes, providing information such as referrals, and providing assistance such as transportation. While finding that non-crime police calls for service comprise approximately 80% of all police calls, Scott (1981) (as cited in Mastrofski, 1983) recognized the difficulty associated with identifying the types of police calls that comprise crime and non-crime situations for measurement. This difficulty arises due to how the police call is categorized by the caller, police dispatcher, and responding police officer. Despite these difficulties, it should be noted that numerous authors have found patterns of high rates of non-crime police calls for service.

Bard (1969) suggested that as much as 90% of law enforcement tasks involve the service law enforcement function, although 99% of law enforcement training is focused on the law enforcement function. Trojanowicz and Carter (1988) described a situation in which a police officer suggested that teaching community policing was not teaching "real police work" (p. 21) but rather teaching social work. The tensions between the law enforcement and service law enforcement functions in terms of career opportunities and promotional opportunities for police officers have long been recognized.

Vollmer (1919) suggested more than 100 years ago that the number of arrests a police officer makes should not be used as the basis for evaluating the officer. Instead, he argued that crime reduction and a reduction in community social problems should be used as the basis for evaluating an officer's performance. Indeed, promotional advancement and other law enforcement rewards are given based on a police officer's ability to perform the law enforcement function.

Cole, Smith, and DeJong (2019) also identified the tensions associated with prioritizing the law enforcement function. Such prioritization results in police officer assignments to specialized units focused on crime situations being more esteemed. Police officers assigned to these specialized units, such as a homicide unit, receive more esteem within law enforcement agencies than officers assigned to patrol units or units that emphasize the service law enforcement function.

Case Example

The Law Enforcement Service Function and Police Social Work

A Neighbor Dispute

Mr. Johnson called 911 and requested that a police officer come to his home because the neighbor's children were playing in his yard. He was concerned they would destroy his landscaping. Mr. Johnson told the 911 operator this was not the first time the Smith family allowed their children to play on his landscaping. The 911 operator noticed that Mr. Johnson appeared angry. He stated he would no longer tolerate the children playing on his landscaping, and out of concern about the potential for a verbal argument to escalate into violence, he is requesting a police officer come to his home. Further, Mr. Johnson stated that he did not use the 311 non-emergency telephone number because he felt that the situation would escalate quickly and become an emergency.

A police officer was dispatched by the 911 operator and upon arriving at Mr. Johnson's home, the officer started by speaking with him first. The officer noticed that Mr. Johnson was very angry. Mr. Johnson repeated the information he told the 911 operator about the children playing on his landscaping. He added that he was concerned about the costs associated with replacing the landscaping and doubted that his neighbors could or would pay for any damages that might occur. He also added that he has previously spoken with the children's parents and asked them not to allow their children to play on his landscaping, although his request has been ignored because this is a weekly occurrence.

In response to the police officer's questions, Mr. Johnson described that a previous request he made to the parents became argumentative with shouting and threats being made. Mr. Johnson did disclose to the officer that he lost his temper and told the Smith parents that if their children returned to play on his landscaping, he would physically remove them himself. The Smith parents informed Mr. Johnson that if he touched their children, both of them would beat him up. So far, only a verbal altercation with no physical violence has occurred.

After speaking with Mr. Johnson, the police officer went next door to speak with the Smith parents. They repeated the information stated by Mr. Johnson and added they felt their children were not hurting his landscaping and that children like to play. They became angry that Mr. Johnson called the police and they felt calling the police was unnecessary.

The police officer informed both neighbors that while they have concerns about this situation because no crime had occurred at this time, the most feasible option is to resolve the situation using mediation. The officer provided some suggestions for mediation such as how the two neighbors can live side by side and respect each other's property, adding that a more formal agreement will be required. After both neighbors agreed to speak to a police social worker, the officer requested that the 911 operator dispatch a police social worker to Mr. Johnson's home. The police social worker spoke with both neighbors at the same time in an outdoor space that was as neutral as possible. Both neighbors were given a referral to contact a mediation center where they could develop an agreement to resolve this conflict.

A follow-up telephone call with Mr. Johnson and the Smith parents was conducted two weeks later by the police social worker. Mr. Johnson and the Smith parents stated they did not want this situation to escalate and have further police involvement. Therefore they have reached an agreement among themselves. The Smith parents informed their children that privileges would be taken away if they play on Mr. Johnson's landscaping and so far the children are obeying.

This case example shows how a frustrated and concerned neighbor relies on law enforcement to resolve a neighbor's dispute. In this instance, no crime has occurred, so the responding officer did not apply the law enforcement function. In many situations when no crime has occurred and individuals are in need of other services, police officers are required to perform the service law enforcement function and provide various services to individuals. This example illustrates how police officers need to be knowledgeable about resources both within the law enforcement agency and the community, and have immediate access to information so that neighbors can resolve the dispute. The police officer made an immediate referral to a police social worker and the police social worker assisted the officer with the service law enforcement function. As Stuart (2019) noted, the social work profession has a long standing history of employment in law enforcement agencies.

Police contacts with the community

In 2015, approximately 53.5 million individuals aged 16 and older had contact with law enforcement within the previous 12 month period. In 2011, more law enforcement contacts were reported (62.9 million). These law enforcement contacts are categorized as either police-initiated contacts or resident-initiated contacts. Police-initiated contacts refer to a law enforcement contact during which a police officer initiated the contact. Examples include traffic stops, being stopped and questioned by law enforcement for any reason, and being arrested. Resident-initiated contacts refer to a law enforcement contact during which an individual initiated contact with a police officer. Examples of these types of contacts include reporting a crime, requesting emergency medical assistance, and requesting assistance with a non-crime situation or other types of law enforcement assistance (Davis & Whyde, 2018). When considered together with non-crime police calls, these law enforcement contacts enhance our understanding of the service law enforcement function.

The Police-Public Contact Survey (PPCS) is a separate survey included in the National Crime Victimization Survey (NCVS). The PPCS is a nationally administered survey intended for individuals aged 16 years old and older and is found at the end of the NCVS. The questions inquire about respondents' contact with law enforcement in the 12 months prior to completing the PPCS. Overall, the results show that among individuals who called police officers for assistance the majority of these individuals, across all demographic groups, reported that police officers arrived quickly, demonstrated professional behavior, and resolved the situation. They also reported that they were either likely or more likely to contact law enforcement again in the future for assistance (Davis & Whyde, 2018).

Whereas this chapter has highlighted that the majority of law enforcement tasks involve responding to non-crime situations that are social service-related results obtained from the PPCS suggest that the majority of individuals aged 16 and older, across all demographic groups, reported a possible crime situation to law enforcement rather than a non-crime situation such as a medical emergency or a traffic accident they witnessed. The PPCS also revealed the following findings:

- Females were more likely to initiate contact with law enforcement than males.
- Individuals aged 18 to 24 were most likely to have police-initiated contact.
- Individuals aged 16 to 17 and those 65 years old or older had the fewest law enforcement contacts.
- Individuals with incomes of $75,000 or more per year were more likely to have resident-initiated contacts with law enforcement than individuals whose income was less than $25,000 per year.
- A greater percentage of blacks than whites experienced police-initiated contact during their most recent law enforcement contact (Davis & Whyde, 2018).

Specific populations and the service function

Numerous populations have law enforcement contact that results from public nuisances, offending behaviors, or public health situations such as substance use. These populations can benefit from law enforcement collaborations and the application of the service law enforcement function. For example, La Vigne et al. (2006) stated that the problem-solving techniques associated with community policing could be applied to assist prisoners during reentry. Travis, Davis, and Lawrence (2012) described numerous law enforcement prisoner reentry collaborations established between police, community-based agencies, and stakeholders. The goals of these collaborations are to enhance public safety and provide services to the reentry population.

Community policing and the service law enforcement function

Given the prominent role of community policing as a policing strategy and its emphasis on establishing partnerships and problem-solving techniques to solve community problems, it is important that police officers are trained to perform community policing. Gill et al. (2014) found that the use of community policing did not reduce crime or community members' fear of crime. On the other hand, community policing strategies increased community members' satisfaction with law enforcement and police legitimacy. The authors suggest that law enforcement implement more problem-solving techniques associated with community policing to reduce crime and fear of crime in communities.

Table 2.1 shows the special topics relevant for law enforcement partnerships to address community problems, the percentage of law enforcement academy training programs that offer the training to police recruits, and the average number of hours that each recruit receives training in the subject area. As the table also

TABLE 2.1 Special topics included in basic training programs in state and local law enforcement training academies, 2013

Subject area	Percent of academies with training	Average number of hours of instruction per recruit*
Domestic violence	98	13
Mental illness	95	10
Sexual assault	92	6
Crimes against children	90	6
Domestic preparedness/terrorism	85	9
Gangs	82	4
Victim response	80	5
Hate crimes/bias crimes	78	3
Sexual harassment	75	3
Elder abuse	73	3
Clandestine drug labs	67	4
Human trafficking	64	3
Cyber/internet crimes	57	3

* Excludes academies that did not provide this type of instruction.

Source: Reaves, B.A. (2016). *State and local law enforcement training academies, 2013.* Reprinted with permission.

TABLE 2.2 Community policing subject areas in basic training programs in state and local law enforcement training academies, 2013

Subject area	Percent of academies with training	Average number of hours of instruction per recruit*
Cultural diversity/human relations	95	12
Mediation/conflict management	82	9
Community partnership building/ collaboration	82	10
Problem-solving approaches	80	12
Total	97	43

* Excludes academies that did not provide this type of instruction.

Source: Reaves, B.A. (2016). *State and local law enforcement training academies, 2013*. Reprinted with permission.

shows, the four most frequently taught subject areas are also the areas in which law enforcement most often collaborates with the social work profession. These subject areas are domestic violence, mental illness, sexual assault, and crimes against children. The subject areas and partnerships are discussed in greater detail in subsequent chapters.

Ninety percent or more of law enforcement academy training programs provide recruit training in the aforementioned subject areas. However, as the table also shows, few hours of instruction are given to these subject areas that comprise the most common police and social work collaborations. Since the average training academy provides 840 hours or 21 weeks of training (Reaves, 2016) these subject areas are given little training time for what will involve the majority of a police officer's duties.

Table 2.2 shows the specific skills associated with community policing that were also taught in law enforcement training academies. The table shows the skills, percentage of academies that provided the training, and the average number of hours of instruction given to each recruit. Although problem-solving approaches were the subject area taught in the fewest academies, this subject was equal to cultural diversity in terms of the average number of hours of instruction provided to each recruit. It stands to reason given that community policing involves a great deal of problem-solving required for collaboration.

Organizations supporting the service law enforcement function

Law Enforcement Assisted Diversion (LEAD) was developed in 2011 in Seattle, Washington as a harm reduction approach for individuals involved in low-level offenses such as substance use. This approach was developed to reduce racial disparities in policing, and instead of arresting and formally processing offenders in the criminal justice system, police officers use their discretion to divert these individuals from further criminal justice system involvement. Law enforcement diversion occurs when police officers refer low-level offenders to trauma-informed services such as substance use treatment. LEAD was developed as a collaboration between law enforcement, community-based service providers, businesses, community stakeholders, and prosecutors (LEAD National Support Bureau, n.d.). LEAD programs are consistent with the service law enforcement function and have been implemented across the country. Numerous additional programs are under consideration as well as in planning phases.

Among LEAD core principles is the provision of intensive case management services. Another core principle requires that police officers utilize a harm reduction and housing first approach. This principle emphasizes harm reduction instead of sobriety. Because hot spots vary in their characteristics, law enforcement diversion interventions provided in hot spots should be culturally relevant. In fact, cultural competency should be applied throughout the diversion process including harm reduction, housing first, and case management interventions (LEAD National Support Bureau, 2017).

Kammersgaard (2019) described the benefits of utilizing a harm reduction approach by law enforcement that enhanced the decriminalization of substance use and public health in Copenhagen. Instead of arresting individuals using substances in public spaces, these individuals were diverted by law enforcement to legally sanctioned drug consumption rooms. This model illustrates how police officers, in order to effectively implement harm reduction in practice, need to change their attitudes about the criminalization of substance use in general and substance use in public spaces in particular.

Treatment Alternatives for Safe Communities (TASC) is a national agency, with the largest agency located in Chicago, IL, comprised of treatment professionals, case managers, and policy analysts among others. TASC provides a wide range of services meant to provide behavioral health interventions, reduce recidivism, and enhance public health and public safety among individuals experiencing substance use and co-occurring disorders. Some of these services are provided by law enforcement through law enforcement diversion interventions (TASC, 2018)

Police, Treatment and Community Collaborative (PTACC) is a collaboration established in 2017 between law enforcement, community stakeholders, behavioral healthcare providers, advocates, researchers, and policymakers. PTACC also utilizes a law enforcement diversion approach because as first responders, law enforcement has a major role in identifying and diverting low-level offenders experiencing substance use and mental health crises from further criminal justice involvement. Instead of being arrested, which results in further criminal justice involvement, individuals are referred to behavioral health and social service providers. PTACC also supports law enforcement diversion as an intervention for reducing racial disparities in the criminal justice system, and maintains that diversion should be provided without regard to racial, ethnic, abilities, and gender identities. As such, it is viewed as a strategy to decrease crime, incarceration rates, and recidivism (PTACC, 2021).

PTACC (2021) identified five Pathways to Community in which individuals are diverted from further criminal justice system involvement upon contact with law enforcement:

1. *Self-Referral* occurs when individuals self-refer to law enforcement with the knowledge that they will be referred to substance use treatment and not arrested.
2. *Active Outreach* occurs when police officers have initial contact with individuals then collaboration partners provide interventions.
3. *Naloxone Plus* refers to individuals who have experienced a drug overdose and have subsequent law enforcement contact. Treatment is provided instead of arrest and incarceration.
4. *Officer Prevention Referral* occurs when police officers provide interventions and an individual is not charged with a criminal offense.
5. *Officer Intervention Referral* occurs when police officers provide interventions. However, the individual is also given a citation although not arrested (Police Treatment and Community Collaborative, 2021).

These Pathways to Community exemplify how law enforcement can assume multiple roles and approaches that connect individuals to community-based services. A key feature of these efforts is diversion, and the majority of these efforts require that law enforcement collaborates with community-based service providers. The most severe legal sanctions given by police officers are citations.

Murphy and Russell (2020) found that police officers who responded to more drug overdose calls for service during which they provided Naloxone reported more negative attitudes toward Naloxone and substance use treatment. The authors suggested that police officers who respond to these calls for service should receive training on the topic of substance use and addiction. Similar to the need to change their attitudes about the criminalization of substance use in public spaces, police officers require more information about substance use and treatment in order to effectively utilize a harm reduction approach.

Specialized police officers and the service law enforcement function

To provide an effective response to social problems and collaborate with partners such as social workers or social service agencies requires that police officers receive specialized training. These police officers primarily perform the service law enforcement function, although as sworn police officers, they are also capable of performing other law enforcement functions as well.

As discussed in Chapter 1, larger law enforcement agencies employ police officers with specialized training who are assigned to specialized units because these agencies have more resources than smaller agencies. The following examples illustrate the types of specialized police officers who perform service law enforcement functions:

Domestic violence officers

As an example illustrating how larger law enforcement agencies are more likely to employ police officers with specialized training the NYPD, the largest law enforcement agency in the country, employs more than 400 domestic violence prevention officers. These specialty-trained officers provide support services to victims of domestic violence focused on safety planning, counseling, emergency shelters, referrals, and other types of assistance such as seeking orders of protection (New York City Police Department, 2021).

Youth officers

Youth officers have specialized training in youth issues and legal matters, and apply the service law enforcement function during their contacts with youth. As an example, the Houston Police Department operates numerous youth programs such as Gang Resistance Education Awareness Training (G.R.E.A.T), in which officers teach anti-gang and gang prevention strategies to youth in schools, and the Youth Police Advisory Council created in 1977. It is the first advisory council of its kind focused on improving relations between law enforcement and youth (Houston Police Department, 2021).

School resource officers

School resource officers (SROs) are police officers assigned to schools. SROs perform safety functions. They receive specialized training to provide these functions. Although school safety methods also include the use of metal detectors and security cameras, students felt less safe with these methods (Gonzalez, Jetelina, & Jennings, 2016).

Community affairs officers

Community affairs officers provide outreach to community members applying the service law enforcement function. They provide community presentations focused on public safety and public health, and establish collaborations with community groups, among other community activities.

Police officers with specialized mental health training

Police officers with specialized mental health training either respond independently or in collaboration with mental health practitioners to mental health crises. The most well-known specialized mental health training and collaborations include Mental Health First Aid, Crisis Intervention Team (CIT), and co-responder programs. These programs are the focus of Chapter 10.

Chapter summary

This chapter examined the service law enforcement function as a foundation for professional police social work practice and this book. It was determined that the service function comprises the majority of law enforcement tasks, and community policing is the most well-known and widely implemented policing strategy utilized to perform the service function in law enforcement agencies. Police officers respond to calls involving medical issues, mental health crises, victims of crime, juveniles, and domestic violence, among other social problems that come to the attention of law enforcement.

The amount and type of community policing preparation police recruits receive was discussed in this chapter. Training and employment of police officers who possess specialized knowledge and skills in specific areas were also discussed. Examples of these types of police officers include domestic violence officers, youth officers, community affairs officers, and police officers with specialized mental health training.

Given that one of the central principles of community policing is community partnerships, we next turn our attention to the employment of police social workers who are non-sworn civilians employed in law enforcement agencies with the purpose of collaborating with police officers when responding to calls that involve the service function. The employment of police social workers in law enforcement agencies can also be considered a policing strategy meant to address the service law enforcement function.

Questions for discussion

1. Were you surprised to learn about the wide variety of social problems that are addressed by the service law enforcement function?
2. What were your reactions to the fact that the majority of law enforcement tasks involve the service law enforcement function?
3. Can you identify the factors that explain why individuals who experience social problems seek services from law enforcement?

Activities for further learning

1. Identify the types of specialized police officers employed in your local law enforcement agency.
2. Prepare a list of additional social problems not identified in the chapter that are addressed by the service law enforcement function.
3. Identify social service agencies in your community that could assist law enforcement with responding to a community social problem that involves the service law enforcement function.

References

Bard, M. (1969). Family intervention police teams as a community mental health resource. *The Journal of Criminal Law, Criminology and Police Science*, *60*(2), 247–250.

Cole, G. F., Smith, C. E., & DeJong, C. (2019). *The American system of criminal justice* (16th ed.). Boston, MA: Cengage Learning, Inc.

Davis, E., & Whyde, A. (2018). *Contacts between police and the public, 2015*. Washington, DC: U.S. Department of Justice, Office of Justice Programs, Bureau of Justice Statistics.

Gill, C., Weisburd, D., Telep, C. W., Vitter, Z., & Bennett, T. (2014). Community-oriented policing to reduce crime, disorder and fear and increase satisfaction and legitimacy among citizens: A systematic review. *Journal of Experimental Criminology*, *10*(4), 399–428.

Gonzalez, J. M. R., Jetelina, K. K., & Jennings, W. G. (2016). Structural school safety measures, SROs, and school-related delinquent behavior and perceptions of safety: A state-of-the-art review. *Policing: An International Journal of Police Strategies & Management*, *39*(3), 438–454.

Houston Police Department (2021). *Youth programs*. Retrieved from https://www.houstontx.gov/police/youth-programs.htm

Kammersgaard, T. (2019). Harm reduction policing: From drug law enforcement to protection. *Contemporary Drug Problems*, *46*(4), 345–362.

La Vigne, N. G., Solomon, A. L., Beckman, K. A., & Johnson, K. D. (2006). *Prisoner reentry & community policing: Strategies for enhancing public safety*. Washington, DC: Urban Institute.

Law Enforcement Assisted Diversion National Support Bureau (2017). *LEAD core principles for policing role*. Retrieved from https://56ec6537-6189-4c37-a275-02c6ee23efe0.filesusr.com/ugd/6f124f_05aef9c2db0b4c1db815cac96e54368b.pdf

Law Enforcement Assisted Diversion National Support Bureau (n.d.). *About LEAD*. Retrieved from https://www.leadbureau.org/about-lead

Mastrofski, S. (1983). The police and noncrime services. In G. Whitaker & C. D. Phillip (Eds.), *Evaluating performance of criminal justice agencies* (pp. 33–61). Beverly Hills, CA: Sage.

Murphy, J., & Russell, B. (2020). Police officers' views of naloxone and drug treatment: Does greater overdose response lead to more negativity? *Journal of Drug Issues*, *50*(4), 455–471.

New York City Police Department (2021). *Domestic violence*. Retrieved from https://www1.nyc.gov/site/nypd/services/law-enforcement/domestic-violence.page

Peterson, D. M. (1974). The police officer's conception of proper police work. *The Police Journal*, *47*(2), 173–177.

Police Treatment and Community Collaborative (2021). *About PTACC*. Retrieved from https://ptaccollaborative.org/about

Reaves, B. A. (2016). *State and local law enforcement training academies, 2013*. NCJ 251145. Washington, DC: U.S. Department of Justice, Office of Justice Programs, Bureau of Justice Statistics.

Strecher, V. G. (1971). *The environment of law enforcement: A community relations guide*. Englewood Cliffs, NJ: Prentice-Hall, Inc.

Stuart, P. (2019). Social work profession: History. *Encyclopedia of social work*. Retrieved from https://oxfordre-com.proxy.wexler.hunter.cuny.edu/socialwork/view/10.1093/acrefore/9780199975839.001.0001/acrefore-9780199975839-e-623

Travis, J., Davis, R., & Lawrence, S. (2012). Exploring the role of the police in prisoner reentry. *Journal of Current Issues in Crime, Law, and Law Enforcement*, 7(3–4), 495–513.

Treatment Alternatives for Safe Communities (2018). *About*. Retrieved from https://www.tasc.org/tascweb/about.aspx

Treger, H. (1987). Police social work. In A. Minahan (Ed.), *The encyclopedia of social work* (18th ed.) (Vol. 2, pp. 263–268). Washington, DC: NASW Press.

Trojanowicz, R. C., & Carter, D. (1988). *The philosophy and role of community policing*. East Lansing, MI: National Neighborhood Foot Patrol Center, School of Criminal Justice, Michigan State University.

Vollmer, A. (April, 1919). *Writings, the policeman as social worker*. BANC MSS C-B 403, The Bancroft Library, University of California, Berkeley.

Webster, J. A. (1970). Police task and time study. *Journal of Criminal Law, Criminology and Police Science*, 61, 94–100.

3

POLICE SOCIAL WORK

Chapter overview

The preceding chapter established the service law enforcement function as the foundation for this book, professional police social work practice, and the employment of police social workers in law enforcement agencies. This chapter traces the more-than-100-year historical development of police social work practice in American law enforcement agencies as a specialty area of practice in the social work profession.

A significant event occurred when Vollmer's (1919) speech called for police officers to utilize social work knowledge and skills. This was followed by the Women's Bureaus that emerged in the 1920s in which female police officers were identified as social workers and the first documented report of a civilian social worker who was described as a liaison worker employed in a law enforcement agency to perform the tasks of referring individuals who come to the attention of law enforcement to social service agencies. The chapter also defines police social work, identifies the tasks police social workers perform, how frequently these tasks are performed, and summarizes the skills needed to practice police social work.

Introduction

POLICE SOCIAL WORKER: *Hello my name is Ms. Janet and I am a police social worker with the police department. I am like other social workers; however, the major difference is that I am employed by the police department. This means that accepting my services is voluntary. My services are voluntary for the whole family, and no family member is mandated to work with me. In other words, your family is not required to participate in my services or work with me concerning the reasons you called the police. Do you all understand?*

THE ROMA FAMILY: *Yes, we understand.*

DOI: 10.4324/9781003132257-3

POLICE SOCIAL WORKER: *Does anyone have any questions?*

MRS. ROMA: *No, I do not have any questions, but I did not know the police department had social workers.*

POLICE SOCIAL WORKER: *Yes, we assist families such as yours who have called the police for help. After we talk about your family situation and why the police were called we can consider different options you all can use resolve the situation. But as I mentioned, your family needs to agree to receive services from me. Do you all understand and agree to work with me?*

THE ROMA FAMILY: *Yes, we understand and we agree.*

MR. ROMA: *I do have a question. How long will this take?*

POLICE SOCIAL WORKER: *Usually it takes about one hour, more or less, to help families such as yours that have called the police for this type of help. Our goal for today may be to refer you all to an agency where you can all spend more time, maybe over a period of weeks, to continue to work on what we discuss today.*

MR. ROMA: *Okay, but helping our family might take 3 hours!*

Everyone laughs.

POLICE SOCIAL WORKER: *Okay let's begin with who called 911, and please tell me why you called 911 requesting the police.*

This dialogue between a police social worker and a family who called 911 illustrates an example of an introduction a police social worker might use in a law enforcement agency. It shows how during a crisis consent for services is obtained verbally and social work services are voluntary.

It is important to keep in mind that the term police social work and the job title *police social worker* refers to a social worker who is employed in a law enforcement agency and assists police officers with performing the service law enforcement function. Some law enforcement agencies may employ professional social workers to perform these service functions and assign a job title different than that of police social worker. Still, some law enforcement agencies may only use the job title of social worker, whereas other agencies may use a job title other than social worker such as counseling specialist.

Moreover, social workers who are employed in community-based social service agencies or other agencies and partner in collaborations with law enforcement agencies will not professionally identify as a police social worker. Therefore, this chapter also introduces several significant features about the practice of police social work. These features can be summarized in the following manner: (1) police social work refers to social workers who are employed in law enforcement agencies; (2) when a social worker is not employed in a law enforcement agency yet collaborates with law enforcement, the social worker will not professionally identify as a police social worker; and (3) social service workers, mental health professionals, and other partners in addition to social work also collaborate with law enforcement.

Media images that depict graphic video of police shootings and other excessive use of force on unarmed individuals, mostly men of color, may have many social workers questioning the role of law enforcement in contemporary society. Social workers may also question the adequacy and type of training that police officers receive to respond to social problems such as mental illness and domestic violence. Additional concerns include the accountability and liability of police officers and law enforcement agencies for officers' behaviors and the possibilities for diversion and collaboration with social service agencies. Indeed, all of these situations raise concerns about social justice.

Most social workers may perhaps be surprised to learn that the social work profession has a 100-year history of collaboration with law enforcement. In 1919, August Vollmer, a well-known police reformer, introduced the concept of "police social work" and "social police work" in a speech titled *The Policeman* (sic) *as Social Worker* (Vollmer, 1919) delivered to the International Association of Chiefs of Police (IACP). He stated that "police social work" and "social police work" should become standard practice in law enforcement agencies as a crime prevention strategy. The intent of the speech was to urge police officers to collaborate with social service agencies, schools, hospitals, churches, recreational facilities, clinics, public welfare, and employment agencies to address social problems such as poverty, alcohol use, unemployment, prostitution, sickness, inadequate home conditions, and poor peer relationships. In other words, because so many types of social problems were coming to the attention of police officers, Vollmer urged them to perform social work functions. Vollmer's concept of "police work social" has become a specialty area of practice within the social work profession.

Current police reform initiatives provide opportunities for expanded roles for police social work practice in response to social problems and non-violent calls that come to the attention of the emergency and non-emergency operator. Among the many examples, the Los Angeles city council made a motion to dispatch social workers instead of the Los Angeles Police Department (LAPD) to non-violent police calls. Eugene, Oregon, presently dispatches crisis intervention workers instead of armed police officers. The mayor of Sacramento, California, proposed having non-police officers dispatched to social problems. In San Francisco, California, police officers no longer respond to social problems, and similar initiatives have been proposed in Albuquerque, New Mexico (Montoya, 2020). Clinical social workers are also hired to assist law enforcement with responding to individuals experiencing mental health crises (Calzolaio, 2018). Even among law enforcement agencies that do not hire social workers police officers collaborate with social workers (Lamin & Teboh, 2016).

A brief history of police social work

Professional police social work practice has a more than 100-year history. Several major historical events summarize its development:

1. August Vollmer's (1919) speech delivered at the meeting of the IACP during which he introduced the concept of "police social work."

2. The establishment of the Women's Bureau in law enforcement agencies in 1924, although law enforcement agencies began to hire female officers much earlier (Duffin, 2010). These specialized units were comprised of female police officers who primarily performed social service functions and were previously known as the Bureau of Policewomen (Duffin), and have been recognized as social workers (Odem & Schlossman, 1991; Roberts, 2007a, 2007b; Walker, 2006). Stuart (2019) identified many social work practice settings that existed during the 1920s including law enforcement agencies.

3. The first media report of a social worker employed in a law enforcement agency to provide liaison services (Coordinating Police and Social Work, 1952).

4. The Englewood Project was a three-year experimental collaboration established between a social service agency and a law enforcement agency from August 1954 to August 1957 in Chicago. The purpose of the collaboration was juvenile delinquency prevention (Penner, 1959).

5. A project implemented in 1970 to address domestic violence was expanded to assist law enforcement with non-crime situations. In 1971, a graduate school of social work collaborated with a sheriff's department, and three social work interns partnered with sheriff's to perform the service law enforcement function. In 1972, a police social worker was hired in the sheriff's department (Colbach & Fosterling, 1976).

6. The culmination of Treger's (1987) research and program development in which he identified police social work as an emerging specialty area of social work practice. Treger's efforts to place social workers in law enforcement agencies began in 1971 (Michaels & Treger, 1973).

August Vollmer was the first to coin the phrase *police social work*. He also coined the phrase *social police work*. His intention while using these two concepts was to encourage police officers to utilize social work skills and knowledge as a crime prevention strategy to address the community social problems that came to their attention. While using these two concepts August Vollmer was not advocating for law enforcement agencies to hire police social workers, rather his intention was that police officers utilize social work knowledge and skills. To achieve these goals for police officers to utilize these skills, Vollmer argued that police officers should make referrals to community-based social service agencies and collaborate with these agencies.

In his speech, August Vollmer also recognized that police officers had little interest or time in addressing the underlying issues that contribute to social problems, providing referrals, or collaborating with community-based agencies. He purported that because police officers were beginning to perform these tasks "as a social worker" (Vollmer, 1919, p. 2) they were observing the benefits of this approach as a crime prevention strategy. Moreover, the community should be made aware of these policing services through newspaper reports, word of mouth, and short movies to learn that police officers provide referrals and assistance to individuals in need.

Thirty-three years after Vollmer delivered the speech, what appears to be the first detailed description of a social worker employed in a law enforcement agency is published, although the social worker is not identified as a police social worker. This description identified some of the types of social problems that came to the attention of law enforcement. The social worker's role was to coordinate between the law enforcement agency and social service agencies. During an eight week period in excess of 200 families having law enforcement contacts were referred to social service agencies. The presenting problems included marital and family conflict, juvenile problems, and situations involving missing persons. It was suggested that this approach would benefit the law enforcement agency by reducing crime in the community (Coordinating Police and Social Work, 1952). The publication is consistent with the speech made 33 years earlier by Vollmer, given that he suggested collaboration as a crime prevention strategy could reduce crime. The significant difference between the two events is that the latter involved collaboration tasks performed by a social worker.

Whereas Vollmer spoke the words "police social work" at IACP, intended for police officers to utilize social work skills and knowledge, Colbach and Fosterling (1976) published a book titled *Police Social Work* in which the employment and functions performed by a police social worker and social work interns placed in a sheriff's department are described. This publication was preceded by Harvey Treger's (1975) book describing the planning and development of the Police-Social Service Project (SSP). Treger's (1987) prior research and program development activities culminated in the use of the term police social work published in *The Encyclopedia of Social Work* to define it as a specialty area of social work practice. Around this time in the historical timeline of the development of police social work, other books were published on the topic (Thomas, 1986, 1994).

Case Example

An Adaptation of Crime Prevention Intervention from Vollmer's (1919) Speech

Mrs. H, a grocery store owner, telephoned 911 stating that her store security staff were detaining a mother and her young child for stealing food until a police officer arrives. Upon arrival the police officer was shown several food items the mother admitted to stealing. The value of the food items was approximately $50.00. The child was briefly separated from his mother during the police interview, assured that his mother would be fine and that she will not be arrested.

The officer inquired about the mother's living situation, employment, and income. The mother told the officer that she stole the items so she could feed her eight-year-old son. She was recently laid off from her job and not receiving unemployment or other benefits. Upon reflection and hearing more about the mother's situation the store owner told the police officer that she did not want to file charges, but she also did not want the mother to come back to her store again. The police officer documented the incident but did not complete a crime report, then referred the mother to a community-based agency that the officer and other police officers in the law enforcement agency use for these types of situations. Finally, the police officer transported the mother and her child to an emergency food distribution center where the mother was provided with one week of food for her and her child, then the mom and the child were transported home.

Unmistakably, Vollmer recognized that police officers were responding to calls that were social service related and involved the service law enforcement function. This case example is inferred from Vollmer's speech and illustrates some of the themes articulated during his speech.

He provided an example of a parent who has stolen food to feed their family. In the above example the police officer performed crime prevention consistent with Vollmer's vision for law enforcement. Further, in the speech Vollmer recognized that interventions focused on employment and social services provided by social service agencies are more effective in the long term than simply donating food. The above example shows that although the mother did receive a food donation she was also provided with a referral to a social service agency for assistance with other needs.

Police social work defined

Police social workers provide services as social problems come to the attention of law enforcement, and police officers refer or accompany the police social worker when responding to these social problems. The SSP, an early police social work program, responded to runaways, truant and unsupervised youth, mental health crises, alcohol use and abuse, substance use and abuse, individuals presenting disorderly conduct, family and marital problems, and low-level offenders involved in theft and vandalism (Treger, 1975).

Treger (1975) then categorized five social problems for which individuals were referred to the SSP and received police social work services. These services were provided to youth, their families, and adults. The social problems included: (1) criminal offenses such as drug and sex offenses; (2) problems such as running away and neighbor disputes; (3) family problems; (4) mental health crises; and (5) problems such as housing, legal, and financial needs. The majority of presenting problems that were referred to SSP were for criminal offenses, whereas individuals experiencing housing, legal, and financial needs were the least referred to SSP. Thomas (1994) identified five areas of police social work practice in law enforcement agencies that involve assisting police with responding to mental health crises, child abuse and neglect, domestic violence, juvenile offenders, and community policing initiatives.

Police Social Work **51**

Police social work is a unique area of social work practice that has been defined in various ways. One definition broadens the type of settings where police social work is practiced. However, the definitions are more similar than they are different. Because numerous types of collaborations exist that include police social workers, and because current efforts are underway to explore social workers responding to emergency and crisis situations without the presence of law enforcement, it is important to understand the varied definitions of police social work and the types of social problems that are addressed.

Treger (1987) initially defined police social work as a new area of social work practice in which social workers utilizing a social work perspective assist law enforcement with addressing community social problems. Conducting assessment and providing crisis intervention were described as key components of the social work perspective. Treger (1995) continued to enhance the definition of police social work to include the provision of services to community residents that have been referred to the police social worker by police officers. The provision of these services is provided also by social workers employed in law enforcement agencies, community-based social service agencies, and mental health agencies, as well as social workers in private practice. Treger also summarized several problematic issues that arise in police social work practice such as the lack of training opportunities.

Police social workers are professional social workers employed in a law enforcement agency. They assist individuals and families referred by police officers. In some jurisdictions police social work job vacancies do not require that applicants hold a social work degree because civil service regulations may specify that a social work-related academic degree also meets the qualifications for the position. Further, for some positions either an MSW or a BSW social work degree in addition to relevant experience is acceptable (Patterson, 2008). Knox and Roberts (2009) also defined police social work as social work employment in law enforcement agencies in which social workers are first responders to a wide variety of social problems assisting community residents.

Barker (2014) included court and jail settings in the definition of police social work, in addition to acknowledging that police social work practice occurs in law enforcement agencies. Barker also recognized that police social workers may be civilian employees in a law enforcement agency as well as sworn police officers who also hold a social worker degree. Police social workers assist victims and offenders, as well as police officers and their families. Additionally public relations and advocacy roles in law enforcement agencies were defined as components of police social work.

Patterson (2012) defined police social work as a small area of professional social work practice recognizing that more than 13,000 law enforcement agencies are found in the United States, and few law enforcement agencies employ police social workers. Several models of police social work collaboration exist that include models in which the social worker is directly employed in a law enforcement agency to collaboration models in which social workers are employed in social service agencies and collaborate with law enforcement agencies. Police social work practice is also international in scope, having been established in numerous countries.

Differences between police social work, police and social work collaboration, and police and social service collaboration

When used in this book, distinct differences exist between the terms (1) police social work, (2) police and social work collaboration, and (3) police and social service collaboration. Chapters in this book provide practice examples that illustrate these differences. Sinha (2017) also recognized these differences when differentiating between the terms police social work and social work with the police. The latter refers to non-law enforcement agencies and organizations establishing collaborations with law enforcement. Sinha also identified two models of police social work practice. One model has police social workers as employees in a law enforcement agency, and the second model involves police social workers who are not employees of a law enforcement agency but are housed in a law enforcement agency.

Police social work

Police social work is a term used to refer to a professional social worker, typically holding a graduate social work degree, employed in a law enforcement agency. This term is similar to a school social worker or a military social worker job title in which the professional social worker is employed in a school setting or a military branch. Thus, the employment of professional social workers in settings that connect the setting identity to the social work job title is not limited to only police social work.

Due to the crisis nature of their work and being embedded in a law enforcement agency in which police officers are first responders police social workers are likely to collaborate with a wide variety of partners. Examples include child protective workers, emergency medical technicians, paramedics, firefighters, and the American Red Cross. Social workers also collaborate with fire departments and provide crisis intervention (Cacciatore et al., 2011).

Collaboration requires interdisciplinary skills to communicate with these varied partners and understanding their functions. Some of these issues for collaboration are identified in Chapter 4. Assuming the role of a police social worker includes being comfortable collaborating with armed and uniformed personnel and being comfortable as a civilian working in an agency where the employees are sworn police officers. Police social workers assist police officers in performing the service law enforcement function as well as diversion interventions.

In 1975, the Association of Police Social Work (APSW) was established to meet the professional needs of police social workers near Chicago. The APSW is now referred to as the Association of Police Social Services (APSS). APSS is a not-for-profit membership organization located in Illinois that provides resources to its members such as professional development to enhance professional police social work practice and the delivery of social services in law enforcement agencies. According to its website police social work is a social work specialty area of practice in mental health (Association of Police Social Services, 2021).

Police and social work collaboration

Police and social work collaboration refers to a collaboration established between a law enforcement agency and professional social work professionals who are not employees of the law enforcement agency. These social workers are employed by social services and other types of agencies and organizations. These non-law enforcement settings include agencies such as homeless and domestic violence shelters, domestic violence service agencies, victim services agencies, outpatient mental health clinics, hospital emergency departments, and child welfare agencies. These settings are characterized by frequent law enforcement contact in which collaboration between law enforcement and social work occurs.

Similar to police social workers they also assist police officers in performing the service law enforcement function as well as diversion interventions. In addition, social workers who are not employed in law enforcement agencies can utilize police social work knowledge and skills to enhance collaboration between the social work profession and law enforcement. Dean et al. (2000) used the term social work and police partnerships to describe collaborations between law enforcement and social work. Some of these collaborations were established between social workers who were not employees of a law enforcement agency but were housed in the agency.

Collaboration between police officers and social workers who are not employees of the law enforcement agency involve performing similar tasks together. For instance, Barton (2000) recognized collaboration between police officers and social workers in response to child maltreatment cases. When collaborating on these cases police officers and social workers train together, conduct investigative interviews together, and perform shared child protection functions.

A point made throughout this book maintains this is an important distinction because clinical social workers or other social workers who partner with law enforcement may not professionally identify as a police social worker. For instance, a clinical social worker may perform interdisciplinary collaboration with psychiatrists, psychologists, and psychiatric nurses in their employment setting. At the same time this setting has established a collaboration with law enforcement to respond to mental health crisis that comes to the attention of law enforcement.

Police and social service collaboration

Comparable to police and social work collaboration, police and social service collaboration refers to law enforcement collaborations established with partners who are not employees of the law enforcement agency. These partners are social service workers who are not professional social workers but hold a related academic degree. Also comparable to police and social work collaboration are the types of settings that employ social service workers such as shelters, victim services agencies, and child welfare agencies. Social service workers are knowledgeable about confidentiality and other practice-related issues.

Patterson and Swan (2019) conducted a systematic review and found that regardless of the type of collaboration (police social work, police and social work collaboration, police and social service collaboration) similarities exist among the types of social problems that were addressed among these collaborations. The following list displays Patterson and Swan's findings that identify the types of social problems addressed among these collaborations and the frequency of these collaborations to address these social problems. Some of these social problems are also the focus of several subsequent book chapters.

- Domestic violence (20.2%)
- Mental illness (13.1%)
- Crime (10.7%)
- Juvenile delinquency (8.3%)
- Alcohol and substance abuse (7.1%)
- Child maltreatment (7.1%)
- Sexual assault (6.0%)
- Child sexual abuse (6.0%)
- Various problems affecting children (2.4%)
- Victims of crime (2.4%)
- Human trafficking (1.2%)

Goals of police social work

Given that the majority of law enforcement tasks involve the service law enforcement function, the primary goal of police social work is to provide services to individuals with law enforcement contact. These contacts primarily involve non-crime and low-level offenses but also involve crime situations involving victimization. Additional goals include providing diversion, crisis intervention, and referrals to individuals and families having law enforcement contact.

Police social work functions and tasks

Patterson (2008) identified police social work functions such as (1) training police officers in topics such as domestic violence, child abuse and neglect, and stress management; (2) providing case consultation and information to police officers about community resources and social problems; (3) counseling police officers and their family members; and (4) providing services to community residents.

Few randomized controlled trials have been conducted to demonstrate whether police social work practice is an effective approach for assisting individuals and families with law enforcement contact. More descriptive studies have been conducted. These studies identify the tasks performed by police social workers employed in law enforcement agencies. The most often performed tasks involve the provision of brief counseling, crisis intervention, and referrals to individuals and families having law enforcement contact (Patterson, 2004; Zimmerman, 1988).

These tasks are shown in Table 3.1, which summarizes the results of three studies (Patterson, 2004; Treger, 1975; Zimmerman, 1988). The table shows the number of police social work units included in each study, the types of presenting problems or populations receiving services, and when multiple police social work units were examined, the number of units providing a specific service are shown. The table shows the wide variety of presenting problems and populations that received police social work services. Importantly, the number of units that provide these services varies. Some police social work units responded to a single social problem, whereas others responded to more than one social problem.

Table 3.2 also summarizes the result of three studies (Patterson, 2004; Treger, 1975; Zimmerman, 1998). This table also shows the number of police social work units included in each study, the types of interventions provided, the percentage that these interventions were provided, and the number of interventions provided to primary clients where applicable. As the table shows, crisis intervention, counseling or therapy, and providing referrals were the three interventions provided most often. Counseling was further identified as support and psychological services and family life education.

Crisis intervention

Crisis intervention is a brief or short-term intervention. Hepworth et al. (2006) defined crisis intervention as an intervention intended "... to reduce stress, relieve symptoms, restore functioning, and prevent further deterioration within a limited time frame" (p. 384). In police social work practice the time frame can range from less than one hour to several hours. Typically crisis intervention is provided in a single session, although telephone or in-person follow-up contacts may also be provided. This suggests that police social work practice tasks such as relationship building, conducting a risk assessment or other assessment, providing intervention, and providing referrals all occur within a limited amount of time.

Indeed, in a brief amount of time the police social worker must increase the likelihood and support for follow-through when referrals are provided. These brief interventions also allow the police social worker to respond to other calls for service. While some shifts may not have many calls for service, other shifts may be very busy, and the police social worker needs to be free to respond to these other crises. Indeed, one of the concerns among police officers is the response time of the police social worker. This also applies to other collaboration partners such as child protective workers and even wait times in emergency rooms.

TABLE 3.1 Presenting problems and populations receiving police social work interventions

Study author	Number of police social work units included in study	Presenting problem	Percent provided	Presenting problem or population	Number of police social work units providing a specific service
Patterson (2004)	1	Family Problems	65	—	—
		Domestic violence	7	—	—
		Alcohol and substance use	5	—	—
		Mental health	9	—	—
		Lack of transportation	8	—	—
		Neighbor or landlord dispute	5	—	—
		Child maltreatment involving child protective services	3	—	—
		Medical needs	1	—	—
		Other needs in response to criminal offenses	9	—	—
Treger (1975)	2	Criminal offenses	44.7	—	—
		Nuisance violations	21.2	—	—
		Family and marital problems	19.9	—	—
		Mental health	11.2	—	—
		Social welfare needs	3.1	—	—
Zimmerman (1998)	21	—	—	Juveniles	9
		—	—	Families of juveniles	7
		—	—	Victims and witnesses of crime	3
		—	—	Adults	1
		—	—	Domestic violence	1
		—	—	Elderly	1
		—	—	Victims of sexual assault	1
		—	—	Sexual abuse and neglect	1
		—	—	Male youth living at home	1
		—	—	Any problem referred to the unit	9

TABLE 3.2 Interventions provided in a typical police social work unit

Study author	Number of police social work units	Interventions	Percent provided	Number of police social work units providing the intervention	Number of interventions provided to primary clients
Patterson (2004)	1	Crisis intervention	31	—	—
		Referrals	25	—	—
		Short-term counseling	19	—	—
		Follow-up with clients and social services agencies	8	—	—
		Mediation	5	—	—
		Case status information	4	—	—
		Provide information regarding law enforcement agency services	8	—	—
Zimmerman (1998)	21	Counseling or therapy	—	21	—
		Crisis intervention	—	13	—
		Referrals	—	8	—
		Assessment and consultation	—	7	—
		Community education and public speaking	—	4	—
		Advocacy	—	2	—
		Follow-up and outreach	—	2	—
		Training student interns	—	1	—
		Transportation	—	1	—
		Victims and witnesses of crime services	—	1	—
Treger (1975)	2	Support services	89.9	—	505
		Psychological services	63.2	—	355
		Family life education	53.9	—	303
		Employment and education services	24.4	—	137
		Community-based agency services	23.3	—	131
		Court services	14.9	—	84
		Food and housing services	9.1	—	51
		Marital counseling	8.5	—	48
		Health care services	8.4	—	47

According to Hepworth et al. (2006) crisis intervention is associated with a task-centered approach and is defined by six features:

1. It is provided in a limited amount of time
2. The goal is to address social problems
3. It is focused on the present social problem
4. The social worker requires skills to address the social problem and crisis
5. Tasks are assigned to resolve the crisis
6. It is adaptable to various theoretical frameworks and practice interventions.

As discussed, crisis intervention is the primary intervention approach provided by police social workers. In fact, crisis intervention is the primary approach used by police officers and law enforcement agencies when responding to police calls for service. These calls involve crisis and emergency situations. In addition to police officers, Hendricks and Byers (2002) identified other criminal justice practitioners such as corrections officers and probation officers who provide crisis intervention. They also identified firefighters, social workers, counselors, and caseworkers.

Goldstein, Monti, Sardino, and Green (1977) recognized the role of police officers providing crisis intervention while performing the service law enforcement function in response to family problems, mental health crises, alcohol and substance use, sexual assault, and suicide, for example. Goldstein et al. (1977) emphasize the importance of police officer safety among four essential tasks when providing crisis intervention: (1) monitor personal safety and the crisis intervention environment; (2) resolve the crisis using de-escalation techniques; (3) obtain information needed to resolve the crisis; and (4) provide additional interventions such as mediation, counseling, and referrals to resolve the crisis. Police social work safety is also an important issue and is discussed in the next chapter.

Case Example

A Police Social Worker Provides Crisis Intervention

A police social worker was requested by a police officer to respond to a parent-child conflict situation. Mrs. Rogers is a single parent who lives with her 11-year-old son. The police officer who responded to the 911 call assessed the situation as appropriate for intervention provided by a police social worker with the goals of visiting the family and assessing their options for resolving the conflict. No threatening behaviors, physical violence, or crime had occurred.

Upon arrival the police social worker interviewed Mrs. Rogers and her son together, focusing on the reason for the 911 call. While conducting the interview the police social worker was mindful of the crisis nature of the situation and provided emotional support to the family while also remaining focused on the current situation. Helping them to discuss their concerns then subsequently agree to a resolution became the focus of the intervention. Both Mrs. Rogers and her son discussed what their concerns were. Mom was worried because her son was not doing his chores or following the rules that she established. He has several friends whom she referred to as the wrong crowd. She told the police social worker that she became angry stating that he could no longer live in her home, and that is when she called police. She was hoping that a police officer could speak with her son and help him to realize that his friends are a bad influence on him and will get him into legal trouble.

Applying the principles of crisis intervention which includes, among others, providing an intervention in a limited amount of time, focusing on the current crisis, and resolving the crisis, the police social worker remained focused on the present conflict between the parent and child. The police social worker also focused on providing support to both the mother and son with the intended goal of not providing long-term services to their family. Both were informed about the crisis nature of the intervention that was being provided as well as the need to schedule ongoing appointments with a community-based agency specializing in parent-child conflicts. Before the crisis intervention session ended, a referral was given to Mrs. Rogers and discussed. The police social worker provided information about the agency during the intervention based on previous experience with the agency and other families who called the police.

While providing crisis intervention to the family, the police social worker was also mindful of the need to respond to other police officers' requests for interventions. Although follow-up contacts will be conducted, an ongoing series of counseling appointments will not be scheduled. These appointments would interfere with responding to other crises in the future. After ending the crisis intervention session with this family, the police social worker was informed that another family was waiting to be seen.

The following case example illustrates the procedures used to contact a police social worker for assistance. While the example does not illustrate the most common approach used to contact a police social worker, it does illustrate a specific type of police social work practice. Perhaps most approaches involve the police social worker paired with a police officer, and the pair respond together to select calls for police service. They ride together in the same police vehicle and begin and end the call for service together.

Case Example

A Police Officer Requests a Police Social Worker at the Scene of a Police Call

Figure 3.1 illustrates the process used by police officers in one law enforcement agency to request a police social worker at the scene of a police call. The figure shows this process in steps. The model can provide suggestions for other law enforcement agencies considering employing police social workers and is based on the author's police social

FIGURE 3.1 A Police social work response model

work practice experience. As the figure shows, the process begins with the first step when an individual or someone aware of the individual's situation places a call to the 911 operator. It is important to note that the individual in need of law enforcement services is not the person who makes the call in all situations. Many times an individual in crisis or with other needs comes to the attention of someone else who subsequently calls 911 after hearing about or observing behaviors that in their view warrants a law enforcement or other emergency response.

In the second step, the 911 operator dispatches a police officer to the scene. Before the officer is dispatched, relevant information is collected during the 911 call, and this information is shared with the police officer before arriving at the scene. Upon arriving at the scene the police officer performs the third step by conducting an assessment to determine if the situation is safe and an appropriate social problem for referral to a police social worker to provide intervention. If so, the officer requests a police social worker either through the 911 dispatcher or by contacting the police social worker directly using the police radio.

In this example, the police social worker has been assigned a call number, and this number is used by the officer to call the police social worker, who is also provided with a brief amount of information about the situation during the call. Police social workers, as well as police officers, also use police radio codes to communicate with each other and the dispatcher.

The fourth step occurs when the police social worker arrives at the scene in an unmarked police vehicle, often within minutes after receiving the referral. Upon arriving at the scene the police social worker informs the 911 dispatcher. This is an important and necessary step because the 911 dispatcher should be aware of the police social worker's location at all times when on the scene of a call. This is a necessary safety protocol so that police officer assistance can be dispatched immediately to the scene if needed. While at the scene the police social worker provides any number of tasks discussed in this chapter and the book. These tasks include crisis intervention, brief counseling, referral to a behavioral health care provider or community-based agency, and transportation, among others.

As mentioned, because of the safety protocol and the need for the dispatcher to know the police social worker's location when at the scene of a police call, the police social worker informs the dispatcher when the intervention has been completed and the police social worker has left the scene.

As the next case example shows, police social workers are also likely to collaborate with first responders in addition to law enforcement when providing crisis intervention. These first responders, such as firefighters, emergency medical technicians, and paramedics, can provide relevant information that police officers can use to assist individuals and families.

Case Example

Police Social Work Collaboration with Law Enforcement and Other First Responders following a Suicide

A police officer requested a police social worker to assist in response to a family crisis situation after a family member committed suicide. Upon arrival at the home, the police social worker was not required to inform the family members of the suicide given that police officers with their specialized skills and experience regarding death notifications had already notified the family about the suicide. The fire department and paramedics were also at the family's home when the police social worker arrived.

The police social worker first met with a police officer prior to assisting the family to obtain information about the situation. This information included the circumstances of the suicide and the family members' reactions to the suicide. A firefighter and paramedic provided additional information about their roles and conclusions. The father of the family committed suicide in the basement, although he appeared to be breathing when his daughter found him hanging by a rope. He was later pronounced dead at the scene.

After receiving information from all of the first responders about the circumstances of the suicide the police social worker next met with the immediate family and provided emotional support and crisis intervention services as well as discussed any probable resources the family needed. Before the police social worker arrived, the family had contacted at least a dozen other close friends, neighbors, and family members who were also present in the home, providing comfort to the immediate family. The focus of the police social work intervention was the immediate family. Therefore, these family friends, neighbors, and additional relatives were not included in the crisis intervention session. They were understanding about the need to assist the immediate family without their presence.

Prior to ending the intervention, the police social worker provided assistance with contacting and notifying additional family members at the family's request. The family was given the police social worker's contact information should the need arise in the future for additional services. A police officer also provided contact information to the family for law enforcement follow-up.

Police social work education and training

Few, if any, BSW or MSW social work educational programs offer courses or field training internships on the topic of police social work practice. Some programs offer criminal justice or forensic social work courses. Because there is a lack of educational and training opportunities to prepare social workers for police social work practice, a considerable amount of training is required on the job training. However, social work employment in other practice settings may provide relevant experience for a police social work position. These other settings include inpatient or outpatient mental health settings, child welfare settings, domestic violence, victim service, corrections, probation, and parole settings. In many of the settings, the social workers may have had prior experience collaborating with police officers while providing services to individuals. This prior collaboration experience may have provided a social worker with some understanding of the issues involved in collaborating with law enforcement.

Since so few opportunities for orientation and training police social workers exist, a ride-along can provide a useful orientation experience. A ride-along is a term used to refer to a civilian, who is not an employee of the law enforcement agency and volunteers to participate in a ride-along, pairs with a police officer for part or all of the officer's shift. This pairing includes riding in the same police vehicle together with a police officer. Participating in a ride-along can allow social workers to observe the types of calls that police officers respond to as well as the types of interventions that are provided in response to these calls. Social workers can participate in a ride-along either as a social work student or a professional social worker. In general, several requirements need to be met prior to participating in the ride-along, and typically a signed consent to participate in a ride-along is required.

Cromwell and Birzer (2012) described how a ride-along was used as an extra credit assignment in a criminal justice course. The length of time required for the ride-along was 12 hours. Upon completing the ride-along students submitted a written assignment summarizing what they learned and how the ride-along enhanced the course material. The ride-along experience improved students understanding of law enforcement functions and tasks.

The following list of activities can also prepare social workers for professional police social work practice:

- Read police reports to identify and understand the types of social problems that comprise the service law enforcement function
- Attend roll calls
- Participate in academy training
- Listen to 911 calls being dispatched to police officers
- Read law enforcement and police social work literature
- Participate in crisis intervention training
- Participate in brief counseling training
- Participate in mediation and de-escalation training
- Participate in safety training

Chapter summary

This chapter traced the historical development of police social work practice identifying when the term *police social work* was first articulated and how police social work evolved as a specialty area of practice within the social work profession.

Police social work can be viewed as comparable to other specialty areas of social work practice such as school social work, military social work, forensic social work, and medical social work in which social workers are employed in host settings and engage in interdisciplinary collaboration.

This chapter also described the goals of police social work, unique functions and tasks performed by police social workers, and the use of crisis intervention and brief intervention as the primary intervention approaches. The practice of police social work in law enforcement agencies also presents numerous ethical challenges involving privacy and confidentiality. Additional concerns associated with this type of social work practice include demographic differences between law enforcement and social work, different occupational perspectives and goals, and different attitudes toward social problems among police officers and social workers. The next chapter examines some of these critical issues.

Questions for discussion

1. What are the benefits and challenges of police social work collaboration? Do the benefits outweigh the challenges? Why or why not?
2. How do you believe that Vollmer's (1919) speech was received by police officers and state the reasons for your beliefs.
3. What were your reactions to August Vollmer's (1919) speech discussed in Chapter 2 and Chapter 3?

Activities for further learning

1. Determine whether your local law enforcement agency employs police social workers. If so, what are their primary tasks? If not, do you believe that police social workers should be employed in the law enforcement agency?
2. Find additional information about crisis intervention. Your additional information should include the theoretical framework and origins of crisis intervention.
3. Develop a list of additional police social work functions and tasks that you believe are important for police social work practice.

References

Association of Police Social Services (2021). *About APSS*. Retrieved from https://policesocialservices.org/
Barker, R.L. (2014). *Police social work. The social work dictionary* (6th ed.). Washington, DC: NASW Press.
Barton, R. (2000). Police officers and the interface with social work. In M. Davies (Ed.), *The Blackwell encyclopedia of social work* (p. 257). Malden, MA: Blackwell Publishers Ltd.

Cacciatore, J., Carlson, B., Michaelis, E., Klimek, B., & Steffan, S. (2011). Crisis intervention by social workers in fire departments: An innovative role for social workers. *Social Work, 56*(1), 81–88.

Calzolaio, S. (2018). *Franklin, Medway police will share clinician to aid in mental health-related calls.* Retrieved from https://www.milforddailynews.com/news/20181014/franklin-medway-police-will-share-clinician-to-aid-in-mental-health-related-calls

Colbach, E. M., & Fosterling, C. D. (1976). *Police social work.* Springfield, Ill: Charles C. Thomas.

Coordinating police and social work (1952). *The American City, 67,* 163.

Cromwell, P., & Birzer, M. (2012). Integrating the police ride-along as an experiential learning strategy in criminal justice courses. *Academy of Criminal Justice Science Today, 37*(5), 1–12.

Dean, C. W., Lumb, R., Proctor, K., Klopovic, J., Hyatt, A., & Hamby, R. (2000). *Social work and police partnership: A summons to the village strategies and effective practices.* Charlotte, NC: The Governor's Crime Commission, North Carolina Department of Crime Control and Public Safety.

Duffin, A. T. (2010). *History in blue: 160 years of women police, sheriffs, detectives, and state troopers.* New York: Kaplan Publishing.

Goldstein, A. P., Monti, P. J., Sardino, T. J., & Green, D. J. (1977). *Police crisis intervention.* Kalamazoo, MI: Behaviordelia, Inc.

Hendricks, J. E., & Byers, B. D. (Eds.). (2002). *Crisis intervention in criminal justice/social service.* Springfield, IL: Charles C Thomas Publisher.

Hepworth, D. H., Rooney, R. H., Dewberry Rooney, G., Strom-Gottfried, K., & Larsen J. (2006). *Direct social practice: Theory and skills* (7th ed.). Belmont, CA: Thompson Higher Education.

Knox, K., & Roberts, A.R. (2009). The social worker in a police department. In A. R. Roberts (Ed.), *Social worker's desk reference* (2nd ed.) (pp. 85–94). New York: Oxford University Press.

Lamin, S. A., & Teboh, C. (2016). Police social work and community policing. *Cogent Social Sciences, 2*(1), 1212636.

Michaels, R. A., & Treger, H. (1973). Social work in police departments. *Social Work, 18*(5), 67–75.

Montoya, K. (2020). *L.A. council wants social workers, not LAPD officers, to respond to non-violent police calls – KTLA.* Retrieved from https://ktla.com/news/local-news/l-a-council-wants-social-workers-not-lapd-officers-to-respond-to-non-violent-police-calls/

Odem, M. E., & Schlossman, S. (1991). Guardians of virtue: The juvenile court and female delinquency in early 20th-Century Los Angeles. *Crime & Delinquency, 37*(2), 186–203.

Patterson, G. T. (2004). Police social work crisis teams: Practice and research implications. *Stress, Trauma and Crisis, 7,* 93–104.

Patterson, G. T. (2008). Police social work. In T. Mizrahi & L. Davis (Eds.), *Encyclopedia of social work* (20th ed.) (Vol. 20, pp. 357–362). New York: Oxford.

Patterson, G. T. (2012). *Police social work.* Oxford Bibliographies in Social Work. New York: Oxford University Press, http://www.oxfordbibliographies.com/view/document/obo-9780195389678/obo-9780195389678-0016.xml?rskey=rvl6uQ&result=64&q=

Patterson, G. T., & Swan, P. G. (2019). Police social work and social service collaboration strategies one hundred years after Vollmer: A systematic review. *Policing: An International Journal, 42*(5), 863–886.

Penner, G. L. (1959). An experiment in police and social agency co-operation. *Annals of the American Academy of Political and Social Science, 322*(1), 79–88.

Roberts, A. R. (2007a). Police social work: Bridging the past to the present. In A. R. Roberts & D. W. Springer (Eds.), *Social work in juvenile and criminal justice settings* (3rd ed.) (pp. 126–129). Springfield, IL: Charles C. Thomas.

Roberts, A. R. (2007b). The history and role of social work in law enforcement. In A. R. Roberts & D. W. Springer (Eds.), *Social work in juvenile and criminal justice settings* (pp. 106–112). Springfield, IL: Charles C. Thomas.

Sinha, R. (2017). Police social work: Active engagement with law enforcement. In M. D. Chong & A. P. Francis (Eds.), *Demystifying criminal justice social work in India* (pp. 85–98). Thousand Oaks, CA: SAGE Publications.

Stuart, P. (2019). Social work profession: History. *Encyclopedia of Social Work*. Retrieved from https://oxfordre-com.proxy.wexler.hunter.cuny.edu/socialwork/view/10.1093/acrefore/9780199975839.001.0001/acrefore-9780199975839-e-623

Thomas, T. (1986). *The police and social workers*. Aldershot: Gower.

Thomas, T. (1994). *The police and social workers* (2nd ed.). Aldershot: Arena.

Treger, H. (1975). *The police-social work team: A new model for interprofessional cooperation: A university demonstration project in manpower training and development: Jane Addams School of Social Work, University of Illinois at Chicago Circle*. Springfield, IL: Charles C. Thomas Publisher.

Treger, H. (1987). Police social work. In A. Minahan (Ed.), *The encyclopedia of social work* (18th ed.) (Vol. 2, pp. 263–268). Washington, DC: NASW Press.

Treger, H. (1995). Police social work. In R. L. Edwards & J. G. Hopps (Eds.), *The encyclopedia of social work* (19th ed.) (pp. 1843–1848). Washington, DC: NASW Press.

Vollmer, A. (April, 1919). *Writings, the policeman as social worker*. BANC MSS C-B 403, The Bancroft Library, University of California, Berkeley.

Walker, D. (2006). Lost and forgotten: early police social workers. *The new social worker, 13*(2), 8–9.

Zimmerman, S. I. (1988). *Police social work in twenty-three programs: Program description and analysis of interdisciplinary relations*. Ph.D. diss., University of Illinois at Chicago.

4

CRITICAL ISSUES IN POLICE SOCIAL WORK

Chapter overview

Chapter 3 described the practice of police social work in law enforcement agencies, and police and social work collaboration. In this chapter, numerous critical issues that arise in these types of social work practice are examined. Indeed, the employment of police social workers in law enforcement agencies presents unique challenges for both police officers and police social workers. These challenges include practicing social work in a host setting associated with social control and authority, police social worker safety, possessing the skills and abilities to successfully provide social work services while utilizing a social work perspective amid the different occupational functions between law enforcement and social work, and negotiating challenges that arise as a result of the demographic differences between police officers and police social workers.

Additional challenges for police social workers include the lack of police social work field education opportunities and coursework preparation in social work educational programs, and the reliance on on-the-job training after a social worker has accepted a police social work position. The latter issue involves training the police social worker after employment. Ethical dilemmas are almost certain to arise when police social workers are employed in law enforcement agencies. These ethical issues must be resolved consistently with the core values of the social work profession as outlined in the NASW Code of Ethics. While the emphasis is placed on police social work, these challenges are also relevant for police and social work collaboration and police and social service collaboration.

DOI: 10.4324/9781003132257-4

Introduction

Apprehension about the appropriateness of police social work practice or social work collaboration with law enforcement is not a recent development. These apprehensions result not only because of concerns about police officers' excessive use of force and inappropriate conduct, but also because of the functional differences between law enforcement and social work, and the differences between the characteristics of law enforcement agencies and social service agencies, among other issues examined in this chapter.

Harvey Treger, whose research broke new ground for police social work practice, acknowledged these apprehensions following the conflict between demonstrators and police officers during the Democratic National Convention in 1968 and the Kent State students who were killed by the Ohio National Guard in 1970. Treger stated, "The attitude of social service agencies was such that they didn't want anybody being referred under coercion by the police... A mutual distrust had developed between the groups" (Moore, 1998).

Citing a publication that analyzed data collected from 1920 to 1932, which found that over 50% of Blacks killed during this 12 years period were killed by police officers. Ellis (1981) presented these killings as a concern for the social work profession, and police and social work collaboration.

Situating these data in the historical context of Vollmer's (1919) speech, and social work practice in law enforcement agencies during the 1920s (Stuart, 2019) reveals that the killings of Blacks by police officers have co-existed with the development of police social work. Despite concerns about the appropriateness of police social work practice or police and social collaboration, this unique field of practice appears to be growing. Numerous communities depend on police social workers or are increasing the numbers of social workers collaborating with law enforcement (Crosby, 2019; Krishnamurthy, 2016; WGME, 2021).

Police social work as interdisciplinary collaboration

No single discipline can solve many of the social problems that come to the attention of law enforcement. While recognizing that social workers are employed in many criminal justice settings such as juvenile courts, prisons, and law enforcement agencies, Bronstein (2003) argued that in order to effectively address social problems, a variety of services and interventions are necessary that require interdisciplinary collaboration. Bronstein further argued that both the benefits and barriers found among interdisciplinary collaborations should be recognized and addressed.

Indeed, the types of emergency situations that come to the attention of law enforcement often cannot be solved or resolved by law enforcement alone. Even when interdisciplinary collaboration occurs between law enforcement and police social workers, other collaboration partners are also often needed. Collaboration necessitates the development of innovative goals and tasks among the collaboration partners to meet the needs of clients (Hepworth et al., 2006).

Interdisciplinary team practice is characterized by the social worker working as a team member alongside other disciplines, typically psychiatry, psychology, and nursing. The role of the social worker is to contribute a social work perspective and expertise to the interdisciplinary team when providing services. In this way, police social work practice and police and social work collaboration can be conceptualized as interdisciplinary collaboration. While the majority of police officers do not hold licensure in a discipline, as sworn police officers, they hold academic degrees in varied disciplines such as sociology, psychology, police studies, criminal justice, and social work, among others. This further supports the use of the term interdisciplinary collaboration when conceptualizing police social work practice and police and social work collaboration.

Conceptualizing this type of social work practice as interdisciplinary collaboration has implications for social work conduct, given that the NASW Code of Ethics (2021) outlines professional conduct when social workers are partners in interdisciplinary teams. According to the NASW Code of Ethics, social workers should ensure that tasks and ethical practice guidelines for collaboration have been established, and that social workers should ensure that a social work perceptive is utilized when providing services and interacting with collaboration partners. In other words, police social workers employed in law enforcement agencies as well as social workers collaborating with law enforcement agencies should maintain a social work perspective and adhere to ethical standards for practice.

Social workers have an ethical responsibility to provide social services during public emergencies if feasible (NASW Code of Ethics, 2021). During these public emergencies, social workers are likely to be involved with police officers and other first responders depending on the nature of their involvement in an emergency situation (Patterson, 2003).

As noted throughout this book, police social work is the term used to refer to a social worker who is employed in a law enforcement agency. Social workers and social service workers who collaborate with law enforcement while employed in a community-based agency are likely to experience these critical issues as well. Consequently, these critical issues may also be relevant for any social work practitioner collaborating with a law enforcement agency to perform the service law enforcement function.

Case Example

Police Social Work Collaboration with Community-Based Agencies and Other First Responders

In the early morning hours, the fire department and a law enforcement agency responded to a large apartment fire with fatalities and injuries. Paramedics and the American Red Cross also responded to the scene. While the seriously injured had been transported to the hospital emergency department, less severely injured individuals were being treated at the scene and individuals who died in the fire were still in the apartment building when the police social worker arrived at the scene.

It was a chaotic scene when the police social worker arrived with all of the first responders already at the location, and the media that had also arrived were filming. Residents of the apartment building were walking around clothed in blankets and appeared shocked. One of the buildings in the large apartment complex was still burning and firefighters were battling the blaze. The police social worker had to determine whom to report to at the scene and who would provide information about expectations for the police social work emergency response.

The police social worker's first task was to meet with the police officers who requested a police social worker. This consultation provided the police social worker with information about the emergency response provided by all of the first responders thus far, a general estimate of the number of apartment residents who were home at the time of the fire including those who were injured and presumed to have died, the law enforcement agency tasks that were being performed, and the expectations regarding the type of assistance requested from the police social worker.

Applying knowledge of law enforcement procedures at the scene of fatal fires as well as a social work perspective, the police social worker provided a liaison role that involved information sharing between the law enforcement agency, fire department, the American Red Cross, and paramedics. Using crisis intervention skills and a trauma-informed approach, the police social worker also assisted survivors.

Crisis services at the scene focused on temporary emergency housing, transportation, food and water, emergency medical services, gathering belongings where possible, and acknowledging questions about possible causes of the apartment building fire and whether people were still inside. The police social worker also assisted with ongoing referrals and services needed following the fire. All of these services were provided at the scene as opposed to providing transportation or leaving the scene for other purposes.

Providing these interventions required that the police social worker was aware of the roles and services provided by other emergency service agencies and was able to quickly establish collaborative relationships with these providers.

As this case example has illustrated, in addition to collaborating with police officers and understanding the law enforcement agency, police social workers also collaborate with other emergency services such as emergency medical services, the American Red Cross, and the local fire department. Social workers are members of crisis response teams in fire departments (Cacciatore et al., 2011) and partner with emergency medical technicians to respond to crises (Re, 2021). Consequently, the use of police social workers in collaboration with other emergency services, in addition to law enforcement, is not surprising.

In summary, these types of emergency services interventions require that police social workers understand the roles and services provided by other first responders, emergency service agencies, and establish ongoing collaborative relationships with these responders to provide effective emergency services.

Factors affecting law enforcement and social work collaboration

In an early study, Lardner (1992) conducted a literature review to identify the characteristics that are relevant for police and social work collaboration. Lardner categorized these characteristics as individual characteristics (differences in attitudes among police officers and social workers, different levels of education, having an honest personality and sense of humor, professional experience, having the ability to manage stressful events, holding sex-role stereotypes); collaboration characteristics (the ability to develop mutual trust, understanding and lack of understanding of police officers' and social workers' roles and tasks, and the ability to engage in decision-making); and organizational characteristics (training opportunities and organizational supports, scheduling police officers and social workers to work the same shift to collaborate, effective communication across organizations, organizational feedback regarding the collaboration, different and shared organizational goals, and occupational culture).

The above categorizations summarize individual and organizational factors that can be addressed through implementing policies and procedures, and providing training and supervision. The collaboration characteristics can also be tapered by providing training, particularly joint training. During joint training, police officers and social workers can develop an understanding of each other's roles and tasks and establish trusting relationships.

Bar-On (1995) assumes a different view asserting that because the differences between law enforcement and social work are situated in the structure of law enforcement agencies and social service agencies, implementing collaboration protocols will be ineffective for overcoming these differences. When referring to these structural characteristics, Bar-On identified them as law enforcement and social work work-related functions, demographic and cultural differences, and the structural characteristics that are embedded in society. Bar-On did propose three approaches to address these issues all of which were deemed as unachievable: the first proposal is to remove the service function from the jurisdiction of law enforcement, second, to reform law enforcement agencies to become social service agencies, and third, to enhance and expand police social work and police and social work collaboration.

Bar-On (1995) suggested that each of these proposals is unattainable. Some of the reasoning was discussed in previous chapters. Due to the large percentage of police calls for service that are social service-related, it is unlikely that law enforcement agencies will cease performing the service law enforcement function. Further, police officers will resist reforming law enforcement agencies to become social service agencies and performing social service-related functions, given that performing these functions is not rewarded in the same manner as performing law enforcement functions. Finally, Bar-On argued that expanding police social work is not feasible because structural differences between law enforcement and social work persist despite these collaborations.

Law enforcement and social work functions

The order maintenance law enforcement function was previously discussed in which police officers rely on their discretion as a major factor for determining if a law has been violated, whether to make an arrest or divert individuals away from further criminal justice system involvement. While performing the order maintenance law enforcement function, a biased police response can occur because these police calls are not all resolved in the same manner. A differential response could show racial and ethnic bias among police officers resulting from varied use of discretion (Cole et al., 2019). The law enforcement function was also previously described in which police officers make arrests and investigate crimes.

Although the service law enforcement function emphasizes providing a variety of services to community residents such as referrals, crisis intervention, mediation, and emotional support to victims of violent crime, for example, and is more similar to the types of services that social workers provide in their work, there are significant differences between providing social services as a police officer and as a social worker. Many of these differences are based on the professional differences between law enforcement and social work.

The core values of the social work profession are articulated in the NASW Code of Ethics. These core values form the basis of social work practice and include the provision of services to individuals, families, groups, agencies, and communities; and the values of social justice, the dignity and worth of each individual, meaningful relationships with others, and performing social work practice with integrity and competence (NASW Code of Ethics, 2021). Whereas the service law enforcement function and the social work function of providing services are similar perspectives concerning how these functions should be achieved differ among police officers and social workers. However, these differences are narrowing.

Maintaining a social work perspective in a law enforcement agency

The law enforcement agency environment can be the source of numerous challenges to maintaining a social work perspective. The paramilitary law enforcement structure, order maintenance and law enforcement functions, and police officer's attitudes toward social problems and treatment contribute to these challenges.

Maintaining a social work perspective further implies that when police officers determine that an arrest is necessary, a police social worker should view the arrest as the law enforcement function and not make professional judgments about the appropriateness of the arrest. Police officers have a law enforcement supervisor with whom they can discuss the appropriateness of the arrest. Indeed, maintaining a social work perspective in a law enforcement agency can be challenging.

While describing his experiences with the Sacramento Domestic Violence Prevention Collaboration, Cropp (2012) observed that some police officers have "maladaptive egos and personality conflicts" (p. 213) which can be exacerbated when officers are required to collaborate with social workers, engage in community policing tasks such as problem-solving or collaborate with community-based agencies. Clearly, this does not apply to all police officers, but it is an issue that social workers should be aware of when collaborating with law enforcement. Some police officers may welcome the assistance of police social workers or police and social work collaboration with addressing community problems, whereas other may not.

Case Example

Maintaining a Social Work Perspective While Employed in a Law Enforcement Agency

A police social worker was called to the scene of a family problem because Mr. and Mrs. Henderson called 911 concerned about their 34-year-old son's alcohol abuse. The parents told the 911 operator that they are becoming increasingly concerned about Harry's drinking and feel that one day soon, he will drink himself to death. They further stated that today Harry has been acting erratic pacing around the apartment, cursing, and taking his clothes off.

The police officer remained at the scene while the police social worker interviewed the family. There were periods of silence as Mr. and Mrs. Henderson and Harry became calm during the interview and also expressed some embarrassment for calling 911 requesting assistance with their family situation. Harry explained that he knows he should stop drinking because his doctor informed him that his health is being affected by his drinking. He has an upcoming doctor's appointment during the week.

The calmness the family began to show as they spoke about their situation and the information they provided was evidence of progress toward resolving this crisis. Harry also began to share his plan for asking his doctor for a referral to a detoxification program. Suddenly, the police officer who had not spoken during the time the police social worker was interviewing the family tells the family that because she has responded to their home multiple times for the same situation, if she returns again in the future, Harry will be arrested and taken to jail. Upon hearing these comments, the family became agitated and the progress made to this point was upended as Mr. and Mrs.

Henderson, and Harry all stated that a night in jail would be best for Harry and that he should be taken to jail now.

This comment implied that an arrest would be a solution to reducing future police calls and perhaps compel Harry to stop drinking. The police officer appeared to be frustrated and impatient with Harry and his situation. She further vented that she does not understand how people can live like this and tells the police social worker that something has to be done with Harry because the apartment is disorganized and needs cleaning.

Maintaining a social work perspective in this situation is essential. First, the police social worker informed the family and police officer that a plan has been developed by the family, and the police social worker will follow up to ask how the plan has been realized. Second, the police social worker provided brief information about alcohol abuse suggesting that incarceration perhaps will not help Harry reduce or stop drinking, and may actually further exacerbate his current situation. While speaking with the family and police officer, the police social worker highlighted the need for treatment.

Social workers are required to maintain a social work respective even when employed in host settings and as members of interdisciplinary collaboration. This involves the ethical application of social work values. In this case example, the police social worker did respectfully disagree with the police officer regarding the need for an arrest. The plan developed by the family was supported given that it was appropriate and included a plan to reduce drinking or achieve sobriety, depending on Harry's goals. When the police officer provided brief information that would not resolve this situation, the police social worker did not challenge the police officer or family. Upon reflection, the police social worker realized the police officer may have expressed these ideas stemming from frustration at being unable to assist the family after multiple police calls for service from this family.

Different attitudes among law enforcement, social workers, and social service providers

Attitudes held by professionals including police officers and social workers play a role in how these professionals provide services and interventions to individuals that require such services. Vairo (2010) suggested that the attitudes held by service providers and administrators could adversely impact the quality of services that are provided to individuals, particularly when individuals are mandated to receive services. Emphasizing the importance of recognizing that negative attitudes toward clients treatment can be detrimental when providing services, Vairo suggested that opportunities should be provided for service providers and administrators to examine their attitudes and how their attitudes might affect the provision of services.

Police officers' and social workers' attitudes toward social problems are shaped by occupational culture, professional and personal experience, and education and training. Attitudes are also shaped by world views. Embracing liberal, moderate, and conservative political ideologies among police officers and social workers can also contribute to somewhat strained working relationships.

The research that investigated differences in attitudes among police officers and social workers is examined next. The following studies were conducted in the area of child maltreatment and are presented to illustrate the differences in attitudes toward child maltreatment which may affect collaboration. Research has also investigated these differences in attitudes toward domestic violence (McMullan, Carlan, & Nored, 2010). Attitudes have been examined associated with many of the social problems discussed in this book that are the focus of police social work practice and collaboration.

In some studies, the samples did not include social workers but included social service or child protective workers. Other samples did not include social workers and were comprised of recruits or police officers only. Some studies administered case vignettes to police officers and social workers depicting child maltreatment and a series of responses toward such maltreatment.

It stands to reason that police officers' and social workers' attitudes toward child maltreatment, among other social problems, should be examined, and they are provided with consultation and other opportunities to explore these attitudes and their affects. These differences in attitudes may arise both formally during a case conference or informally while discussing cases consequently affecting collaboration and joint activities.

Social workers also hold attitudes toward police officers and law enforcement in general, which may affect police social work practice or police and social work collaboration, in addition to attitudes regarding a social problem. Conte, Berliner, and Nolan (1980) identified some of the attitudes held by police officers and social workers that affect collaboration in responses to child sexual assault more than 40 years ago. Their findings remain relevant for contemporary police social work practice. First, police officers' attitudes toward investigating child sexual assault cases were not favorable. Second, these attitudes include the view that police officers and social workers should not collaborate, perceptions of the lack of trust and guardedness, and attitudes held by both police officers and social workers that their functions are too dissimilar to establish collaborations.

In a study comparing attitudes among police officers and child protective workers using a case vignette depicting child sexual abuse, Kelley (1990) found police officers viewed offenders as more responsible for the abuse, whereas child protective workers viewed environmental factors as more responsible. Police officers' attitudes toward offenders included harsher punitive interventions such as incarceration, whereas child protective workers considered therapeutic interventions more than police officers.

Both police officers and social workers reported negative attitudes of anger toward an offender, and feelings of empathy toward the child's situation.

However, police officers reported more negative attitudes that were associated with revenge toward an offender, and were more ambivalent about providing interventions to children and families than were social workers. Social workers were more likely to express discomfort with the child's situation and providing interventions to the child and family (Cheung & Boutte-Queen (2000).

Trute, Adkins, and MacDonald (1992) also compared the attitudes of police officers and child protective workers toward child sexual abuse. The study was conducted in a rural community. The authors found that police officers' attitudes toward the seriousness of child sexual abuse were less than the attitudes of child protective workers and mental health practitioners. Police officers also viewed treatment as less helpful than child protective workers and mental health practitioners and were more likely to favor punishing the offender. Child protective workers held a broader view of the factors that contribute to child sexual abuse and reported that it occurs across socioeconomic statuses, whereas police officers were more limited in their attitudes concerning families that experience child sexual abuse.

Using pre-test and post-test vignettes administered to police recruits before and after mandatory child abuse training in a law enforcement training academy, Patterson (2007) found that after completing the training, recruits reported improved skills to intervene in child maltreatment cases, expressed more sympathy toward offenders, and increased knowledge about child maltreatment situations. Given Kelley's (1990) findings, it would be interesting to examine the effects of law enforcement academy training for recruits and how long improved skills, sympathy, and knowledge are retained after a recruit becomes a police officer.

Demographic differences between police officers and social workers

In 2015, 86% of social workers graduating from social work educational programs were female and 85% of social workers with graduate degrees (MSW) were female (Salsberg et al., 2017). Race and ethnicity were not reported. In 2016, approximately 12% of full-time police officers employed and local law enforcement agencies were female. Approximately 71% of these officers were white, and 27% were police officers of color (Hyland & Davis, 2019). Educational levels were not reported.

Bar-On (1995) suggested that the most important differences between police officers and social workers are gender identity and levels of education with gender being the visible difference since the majority of police officers are male and the majority of social workers are female resulting in gender-based differences in law enforcement and social work functions. Social work is characterized by a graduate degree, whereas law enforcement is not resulting in different functions based on education. Bar-On asserted that these differences could impede collaboration.

The role of police unions

Similar to unions representing other employees, the role of the police union is to support and protect union members, who are sworn police officers, in a variety of work-related, health-related, and other areas. Some police unions may be concerned about civilian law enforcement agency personnel performing what they perceive as police functions and tasks when these civilians perform service law enforcement functions. Indeed, unions have concerns about non-union members performing union members' tasks. In other words, unions may be concerned about the employment of police social workers. However, these critical issues are not insurmountable.

Ethical issues in police social work practice

Police social workers, as employees in law enforcement agencies, negotiate the agency environment, clients' needs, and ethical social work practice. Police social work employment in law enforcement agencies can present numerous ethical challenges for both experienced police social workers as well as those who are new to this specialized area of social work practice.

Maintaining confidentiality in law enforcement agencies has long been recognized as having the potential to raise ethical dilemmas that social workers must resolve. Among the most challenging ethical that arise are privacy and confidentiality, commitment to employers, and interdisciplinary collaboration. Each of these ethical issues is examined next.

Privacy and confidentiality

The social work ethical standard that identifies the importance of privacy and confidentiality (NASW Code of Ethics, 2021) is applicable to police social work practice in law enforcement agencies. Police social workers should review and adhere to these ethical standards. For instance, conflicts have been reported between law enforcement in hospitals regarding the confidentiality and privacy of patients' medical information. Policies and procedures are needed to resolve these ethical conflicts (Friesen, 2006). Similar policies and procedures exist between law enforcement and social service agencies. In addition, Curtis and Lutkus (1985) reported that police officers might be concerned about the ethical responsibility of police social workers to maintain confidentiality because of how it might affect an investigation or criminal charges.

While maintaining confidentiality in law enforcement agencies may be problematic for police social workers who are required to uphold the NASW Code of Ethics, little is known about police social work confidentiality. Curtis and Lutkus (1985) surveyed 41 police social workers employed in Illinois having an average of 3.8 years of police social work practice experience. The questionnaire asked police social workers to provide a definition of confidentiality, indicate whether confidentiality was mentioned during their sessions with clients and if so, at what point during the session did the topic of confidentiality arise, identify the types of client information they regarded as confidential, whether it was difficult to maintain confidentiality while employed in a law enforcement agency, and to indicate whether police officers requested confidential information about clients, among other important confidentiality concerns.

Curtis and Lutkus (1985) found that the primary factors affecting collaboration were years of police social work experience, whether the police social worker was employed by a law enforcement agency or a social service agency, and the size of the police social work unit. The results obtained using one vignette showed that police social workers with more years of police social work practice experience were more likely to disclose confidential information to police officers. When salaries were paid by a law enforcement agency, police social workers were more likely to disclose confidential information to officers than when salaries were not paid by a law enforcement agency. However, the larger the police social work unit, the more likely police social workers were to maintain client confidentiality.

Due to the crisis nature of police social work practice, an individual or family typically provides verbal consent to share confidential information. Therefore the release of information procedures is primarily verbal consent. As much as possible, the police social worker facilitates the referral process and connects individuals and families with other agencies by telephone so they can directly share private and confidential information with the agency themselves. It is also more meaningful for individuals and families if they can complete as much of the referral process as possible in a crisis. In this way, it increases the likelihood of follow-up by the client with the referral agency. Indeed, one of the goals of police social work practice is to connect individuals and families with ongoing services to reduce the need for future law enforcement contact. However, some situations do occur when a signed release of information is either required or the intervention allows sufficient time to obtain a signed release.

Police social workers should examine or develop policies and procedures regarding the confidential nature of any written report prepared by the police social worker and maintained by the law enforcement agency. In an effort to maintain privacy and confidentiality, some police social workers employed in law enforcement agencies retain minimal written documentation.

Law enforcement agencies identify a spokesperson who shares information with the public and media regarding a situation. Police social workers should not share information about a situation publicly, even though in many instances, neighbors and community members may already be aware of the situation that has occurred unless requested to do so by law enforcement and for a specific reason that is consistent with ethical practice. The law enforcement agency may depending on the status of the investigation, make information publicly available such as whether or not an arrest was made, the nature of any criminal charges, information about any deceased individuals as well as other information deemed relevant.

Social workers should assist other professionals with understanding their ethical obligation to maintain confidentiality. When clear and convincing reasons exist for sharing confidential information, it is acceptable for social workers to do so (NASW Code of Ethics, 2021).

While police social workers respond to family conflicts, suicide, and mental health crises, the information obtained from clients by the police social worker should be shared with first responders including law enforcement to provide an efficient intervention (Curtis & Lutkus, 1985).

Commitment to employers

The NASW Code of Ethics (2021) identifies the commitments that social workers should maintain toward an employer and the employing organization. Accordingly, police social workers employed in law enforcement agencies have an ethical responsibility to enhance agency policies and procedures associated with providing services, and follow the commitments made to the law enforcement agency. Police social workers should resolve conflicts regarding these commitments in an ethical manner.

Social justice

Social work practice is increasingly informed by theoretical frameworks that attend to social justice. These frameworks include the just practice framework, the structural approach, and critical social theories such as critical race theory, feminist theory, and post-structural theory, among others. The social work profession embraces a commitment to the value of social justice. The NASW Code of Ethics (2021) specifically identifies these social justice values as well as the social justice practice activities for the social work profession. Social justice practice activities include confronting social injustice, engaging in social change, enhancing equal opportunities, acquiring cultural competency and knowledge about oppression.

A relevant, and perhaps less identified, area of social justice ethical practice is the provision of services. The NASW Code of Ethics (2021) also identifies providing clients with information, services, and resources, and helping clients to engage in appropriate decision-making as ethical social justice practice. Robinson (2010) argued that law enforcement is consistent with social justice when emergency services are provided. This involves the service law enforcement function.

Law enforcement agencies are described as both consistent and inconsistent with social justice. Law enforcement agencies are consistent with social justice when police officers enforce laws, individuals' rights are protected, and community safety is achieved. The implementation of a Law Enforcement Code of Conduct and the provision of crime prevention and other emergency services are also consistent with social justice. Law enforcement agencies are inconsistent with social justice when police officers abuse their discretion, enforce laws that are biased, make arrests that are disproportionate among racial and ethnic groups, and conduct racial profiling (Robinson, 2010).

Despite these inconsistencies with social justice, law enforcement agencies do employ police social workers, and as mentioned, perform the service law enforcement function, which comprises the majority of tasks. In this way, law enforcement agencies are also consistent with social justice. Indeed, numerous host settings that employ clinical social workers may also be both consistent and inconsistent with social justice. Consequently, a major task for the social work professional is to understand the practice setting dynamics in order to adequately address social injustice and provide quality services.

Excessive use of force and inappropriate police officer conduct

Concerns among social workers about police brutality is not a new occurrence. More than 40 years ago, Ellis (1981) asked, "Where is social work?" (p. 511) in response to police brutality observing that the profession was notably absent from involvement. Ellis asked another question "What roles and functions should the social work profession assume in the immediate crisis of the excessive use of deadly force inflicted by police on Black citizens and their inner-city, minority neighbors?" (p. 511). To answer this question, Ellis suggested that the social work profession should involve its professional organizations in the development of a task force to address this issue, and local organizational chapters should collaborate with advocacy groups to develop policy initiatives to address police brutality. Roles for social workers who are members of congregations have also been proposed to address police brutality. These include consulting and education roles (Wilson & Wolfer, 2020).

Law enforcement experts are increasingly concerned about the lack of policies and procedures that direct police officers at the scene of police brutality incidents to intervene and report excessive use of force, and other inappropriate conduct by police officers. These experts also suggest that non-intervention is not consistent with law enforcement training.

The Georgetown Innovative Policing Program at Georgetown Law in collaboration with the Sheppard Mullin law firm developed the Active Bystander for Law Enforcement (ABLE) Project. ABLE is based on the work of Dr. Staub and colleagues together with the New Orleans Police Department. Their program is known as Ethical Policing Is Courageous (EPIC) Peer Intervention Program. The objectives of ABLE are to offer free training and technical assistance to law enforcement agencies to support peer intervention during incidents of excessive use of force and other inappropriate conduct by police officers (Georgetown Law, n.d.).

Police social workers as employees of law enforcement agencies, while not sworn police officers, should determine whether any such policies and procedures apply to them should they witness excessive use of force or other misconduct by a police officer(s). In other words, police social workers should determine whether, as civilians employees of the law enforcement agency, they are also required to report excessive use of force and other inappropriate a police officer conduct. In such instances, the policies and procedures for reporting as well as the reporting requirements should be understood.

Different attitudes held among police officers and social workers may also involve different attitudes toward the use of inappropriate language. Although a social worker often overheard police officers use the word "'darkie'" (Garrett, 2004, p. 86) when referring to people of color, the social worker did not attribute the use of this language to racism or discrimination. Instead, the social worker suggested this language was used a result of the law enforcement occupational culture (Garrett, 2004). The social worker did not report how this situation was handled. Seeking supervision is useful for assistance with addressing these types of situations which may arise in law enforcement agencies.

Funding

Funding to support police social work positions can be a challenging critical issue. More funding is needed to support expanded police social work practice roles in law enforcement agencies.

For instance, the Aurora Police Department, located in Illinois, no longer employs a police social worker due to budget cuts. Instead, the department collaborates with social service agencies and houses social workers who are employees of a social service agency to provide crisis intervention services (Crosby, 2019).

Since the 1970s, the Law Enforcement Assistance Administration (LEAA) initiative has supported social work positions in law enforcement (Lamin & Teboh, 2016). Given the size and scope of law enforcement agencies and community need for emergency services in response to social problems, current funding resources are insufficient. Calzolaio (2018) described the funding of a clinical social work position shared between two law enforcement agencies. While the funding may be renewed, the initial funding was awarded for only three years.

Social work safety

NASW (2020) reports that incidents of violence against social workers are increasing. Social workers visiting clients' residences may be especially exposed to violence. NASW supports passage of the proposed legislation titled *Protecting Social Workers and Health Professionals from Workplace Violence Act of 2019 (S. 2880/H.R. 5138)*. The provisions of the proposed legislation include $10,000,000 given each year throughout a five-year period to purchase safety and security equipment in agencies, to develop and implement safety training, and to provide services for social workers who have been injured.

The practice of social work is becoming increasingly more challenging as a result of verbal and physical assaults from clients during interviews in community-based agencies as well as during field visits. As a result of physical assaults, social workers have been seriously injured or killed. Those employed in criminal justice settings were identified as particularly at high risk. Additional settings include mental health, child welfare, and domestic violence shelters (NASW, 2013). Considering that this book highlights collaborations primarily in these areas and police social workers have more frequent contact with individuals and families in these areas, police social work safety is particularly relevant. As a result, establishing safety guidelines is essential.

Police social work safety, as well as the safety of social workers involved in collaborations with law enforcement, is an important issue. Situations can suddenly and unexpectedly become violent. For instance, it is possible that mediation interventions can be unsuccessful and result in an angry outburst. Disputes such as landlord and tenant disputes, and family disagreements can become violent. Since the crisis intervention is not occurring in an office or other private location, it may be that friends, family, and/or relatives arrive at the scene and become disruptive.

It is important to recognize that many of the situations which result in law enforcement contact, and subsequently police social work contact, involve individuals who are experiencing conflict. While conflict does not always involve violence resolving conflict can be unpredictable.

It is also important to recognize that the types of situations that police social workers address can be anxiety and anger-provoking themselves. For example, someone's child has been abused and the caregiver is learning this information for the first time or someone has been violently victimized by a stranger or family member.

NASW (2013) does support police officers providing a joint field visit with social workers when a social worker is involuntarily removing a child from caregivers or a caregiver is incapacitated. Further recommended guidelines for social work safety include 11 standards:

1. Agencies should promote safety and security for social workers.
2. Agencies should assume preventive approaches to social work safety and security.
3. Social workers' offices should be a safe and secure space.
4. Agencies should fully utilize the benefits and recognize the challenges of technology to enhance social worker safety and security.
5. When conducting home visits and interviews, social workers should be provided with cell phones to enhance safety and security.
6. Prior to entering the field to conduct visits and interviews a determination should be made about the level of risk the visit might have for safety and security.
7. Prior to transporting clients, a determination should be made concerning the level of risk the transport might have for safety and security.

8. A schedule of field visits should be made available to appropriate staff together with relevant information that could be needed should a safety or security issue arise.

9. Agencies should have established policies and procedures for social workers to report violence or verbal abuse.

10. Annual safety and security training should be provided to social workers.

11. These standards are also applicable to social work student interns (NASW, 2013).

Clearly, police social work safety issues should include establishing social work safety protocols prior to implementing the collaboration. When social workers and other collaboration partners provide emergency services without a law enforcement presence, the safety protocols should include procedures for requesting law enforcement at the scene when safety issues arise.

Moreover, when implementing an emergency response utilizing social workers and other collaboration partners without a law enforcement presence, it is necessary to collect and analyze data describing requests for law enforcement involvement. This is an important activity given that current collaborations are being established that do not include a law enforcement presence.

These data should describe how frequently a request for a police officer to come to the scene is made and identify the reasons for the request. For example, data were collected and analyzed in the fourth month of a pilot program implemented to respond to mental health crises without a police officer as a collaboration partner. The collaboration was established only between a social worker and a paramedic. The data showed that among the approximately 400 emergency responses that were provided during this period, all responses were provided without requesting a police officer at the scene (Enos, 2020).

Police legitimacy and police social work practice

Another critical issue in police social work practice that may concern the social work profession is that law enforcement agencies will use social work to increase police legitimacy in communities. Excessive use of force, police brutality, racial profiling, and other inappropriate police officer conduct affect community support for law enforcement. It may be perceived that law enforcement agencies employ police social workers as an approach to increase community perceptions of legitimacy because police social workers provide a range of social services to the public as employees and representatives of a law enforcement agency.

For example, Ankerfelt, Davis, and Futterer (2011) reported that the Joint Community Police Partnership was established in a diverse community in Brooklyn Park, Minnesota, to provide community policing initiatives such as problem-solving and other services such as sharing information as an approach to enhance police legitimacy.

Sunshine and Tyler (2003) pointed out that police legitimacy refers to the amount of community support given to law enforcement for policing roles and tasks. When law enforcement is perceived by the community to be legitimate, then support for their roles and tasks increases. When a community does not perceive the police as legitimate, there is less cooperation with law enforcement and less support for their roles and functions.

In response to an assertion that media coverage of a police brutality event in 2005 in Milwaukee led to a decrease in 911 calls and an increase in homicides, Zoorob (2020) analyzed data to determine whether these media reports of police brutality resulted in a decrease in 911 calls for emergency services, and whether homicide rate subsequently increased particularly in Black communities. The initial assertion suggested that as a result of media coverage, a lack of trust developed concerning requesting law enforcement services. However, Zoorob found that the data did not support these assertions and 911 calls did not decrease in Black communities, White communities, or the community overall. Zoorob's research illustrates the need for data to inform communities about the effects of excessive use of force and police brutality on police legitimacy as well as 911 calls for police services.

Public safety and public health

The criminal justice system addresses both public safety and public health issues. As a component of the criminal justice system, law enforcement is directly involved with public safety. Law enforcement also plays a key role in public health matters. In fact, police powers are afforded to law enforcement to intervene in public health matters.

Public safety

Addressing public safety issues can present challenges for police social workers and police social work collaboration. As the concept implies, public safety involves efforts to reduce victimization, fear of crime, and enhance community members' perceptions of safety. Social workers may focus on the offender and the offender's situation such as lack of mental health services, inadequate housing, unemployment, or lack of education, among social problems.

Social workers should also consider victimization and the effects of crime on the victims and survivors, communities, and society. This topic is the focus of Chapter 9. Because victimization can cause fear in communities' policies and practices that enhance public safety and reduce victimization should be well understood. Indeed, it is challenging to protect public safety and the individual rights of others. The sample law enforcement agency mission statements contained in Chapter 1 identify reducing fear of crime among the public as a public safety issue.

Public health

Although the criminal justice system, and in particular law enforcement, clearly addresses public safety issues, public health issues also come to the attention of law enforcement and the police social worker. Examples of public health issues include HIV and AIDS, the opioid epidemic, alcohol and substance abuse, mental health matters, and the Covid-19 pandemic, for example.

While the primary reason why individuals contact law enforcement may not be due to a public health issue, the police social worker upon conducting an assessment, is likely to determine that a public health issue also exists. This requires that police social workers have knowledge about public health community resources to provide referrals to individuals and families. Because many of these public health issues may require insurance or fees for service, it is necessary that the police social worker provide referrals that are low cost or no cost to meet community needs.

Social work practice skills

Given the critical issues discussed in this chapter, and the types of interventions police social workers provide, not only should police social workers be knowledgeable and skilled concerning ethical practice but they also must be comfortable and confident with the services they provide.

In other words, some social work practitioners may feel uncomfortable with this type of social work practices not only because of the law enforcement setting but they may also feel that providing a referral and crisis intervention are insufficient services for social problems that require longer term more in-depth interventions. Social workers may also have concerns that individuals may not follow up on a referral and continue to use law enforcement as an emergency service provider.

Chapter summary

This chapter examined numerous critical issues that arise in police social work practice, and police and social work collaboration. An understanding and ability to successfully address these critical issues is essential to the provision of services to individuals having law enforcement contact. This includes the skills to successfully resolve ethical dilemmas that arise. Ethical issues include privacy and confidentially, commitment to the law enforcement agency as an employer, and the practice of interdisciplinary collaboration. Ethical issues should be resolved in accordance with the NASW Code of Ethics.

This chapter has shown that the successful practice of police social work requires the ability to function in a host setting characterized by social control and authority, as well as the ability to negotiate the distinctive occupational functions and demographic differences between law enforcement and the social work profession all while maintaining a social work perspective.

Questions for discussion

1. What are some of the differences between police officers maintaining confidentiality in a law enforcement agency and police social workers maintaining confidentiality in a law enforcement agency based on the NASW Code of Ethics?
2. In what additional ways might gender identity differences between law enforcement and the social work profession affect interdisciplinary collaboration?
3. Based on the NASW Code of Ethics, what approach could a police social worker use to address differences in attitudes toward child maltreatment that arise between law enforcement officers and police social workers during collaboration?

Activities for further learning

1. Applying the ethical statements regarding interdisciplinary collaboration articulated in the NASW Code of Ethics, prepare a plan for resolving some of the ethical issues that might occur during interdisciplinary collaboration with law enforcement and other first responders.
2. Locate and read a published article or report describing police social work practice. Identify the social problem that is the focus of the practice. Based on what you read in the article or report, list the critical issues that you believe might arise applying the content discussed in this chapter.
3. Create a list of additional agencies characterized by social control that employ social workers. After completing your list, what are your views about social work employment in these agencies?

References

Ankerfelt, J., Davis, M., & Futterer, L. (2011). The Brooklyn Park, Minnesota, police's joint community-police partnership. *The Police Chief*, 78, 22–31.

Bar-On, A. (1995). They have their job, we have ours: Reassessing the feasibility of police-social work cooperation. *Policing and Society*, 5, 37–51.

Bronstein, L. R. (2003). A model for interdisciplinary collaboration. *Social Work*, 48(3), 297–306.

Cacciatore, J., Carlson, B., Michaelis, E., Klimek, B., & Steffan, S. (2011). Crisis intervention by social workers in fire departments: An innovative role for social workers. *Social Work*, 56(1), 81–88.

Calzolaio, S. (2018). *Franklin, Medway police will share clinician to aid in mental health-related calls*. Retrieved from https://www.milforddailynews.com/news/20181014/franklin-medway-police-will-share-clinician-to-aid-in-mental-health-related-calls

Cheung, M., & Boutte-Queen, N. M. (2000). Emotional responses to child sexual abuse: A comparison between police and social workers in Hong Kong. *Child Abuse & Neglect*, 24(12), 1613–1621.

Cole, G. F., & Smith, C. E., & DeJong, C. (2019). *The American system of criminal justice (16th ed.)*. Boston, MA: Cengage Learning, Inc.

Conte, J. R., Berliner, L., & Nolan, D. (1980). Police and social worker cooperation: A key in child sexual assault cases. *FBI Law Enforcement Bulletin, 49*, 7–10.

Cropp, D. (2012). The theory and practice of collaborations in law enforcement. *International Journal of Police Science & Management, 14*(3), 213–218.

Crosby, D. (2019). Police departments relying more on in-house social workers. Retrieved from https://www.chicagotribune.com/suburbs/aurora-beacon-news/opinion/ct-abn-crosby-police-counselors-st-0506-story.html

Curtis, P. A., & Lutkus, A. M. (1985). Client confidentiality in police social work settings. *Social Work, 30*(4), 355–360.

Ellis, A. L. (1981). Where is social work? Police brutality and the inner city. *Social Work, 26*(6), 511–514.

Enos, G. (2020). Crisis response in Denver progresses, with many other communities watching. *Mental Health Weekly, 30*(37), 1–6.

Friesen, R. K. (2006). Confidentiality, privacy, and public safety: Managing information disclosure disputes between hospitals and law enforcement agencies. *Conflict Resolution Quarterly, 24*(2), 131–147.

Garrett, P. M. (2004). Talking child protection: The police and social workers "working together." *Journal of Social Work, 4*(1), 77–97.

Georgetown Law (n.d.). *Active bystander for law enforcement (ABLE).* Retrieved from https://www.law.georgetown.edu/innovative-policing-program/active-bystandership-for-law-enforcement/

Hepworth, D. H., Rooney, R. H., Dewberry Rooney, G., Strom-Gottfried, K., & Larsen J. (2006). *Direct social practice: Theory and skills* (7th ed.). Belmont, CA: Thompson Higher Education.

Hyland, S. S., & Davis, E. (2019). *Local police departments, 2016: Personnel.* Washington, DC: U.S. Department of Justice, Office of Justice Programs, Bureau of Justice Statistics.

Krishnamurthy, M. (2016). *Why suburbs could use more police social workers.* Retrieved from https://www.dailyherald.com/article/20160201/news/160209974/

Lamin, S. A., & Teboh, C. (2016). Police social work and community policing. *Cogent Social Sciences, 2*(1), 1212636.

Lardner, R. (1992). Factors affecting police/social work inter-agency co-operation in a child protection unit. *The Police Journal, 65*(3), 213–228.

McMullan, E. C., Carlan, P. E., & Nored, L. S. (2010). Future law enforcement officers and social workers: Perceptions of domestic violence. *Journal of Interpersonal Violence, 25*(8), 1367–1387.

Moore, G. (1998). *Crisis management.* Retrieved from https://www.chicagotribune.com/news/ct-xpm-1998-06-07-9806070171-story.html

National Association of Social Workers (2013). *Guidelines for social work safety in the workplace.* Washington, DC: Author.

National Association of Social Workers (2021). *Code of ethics of the National Association of Social Workers.* Washington, DC: Author.

National Association of Social Workers (2020). Issue brief – Protecting social workers and health professionals from workplace violence act of 2019 (S. 2880/H.R. 5138). Retrieved from https://www.socialworkers.org/LinkClick.aspx?fileticket=_PaNxVmrZOg%3d&portalid=0

Patterson, G. T. (2007). An exploratory study assessing the effects of demographic characteristics on attitudes toward child abuse and neglect among police recruits. *Psychological Reports, 101*, 451–456.

Patterson, G. T. (2003). Police-social work collaboration in response to the World Trade Center attacks. *International Journal of Mass Emergencies and Disasters, 21,* 87–102.

Re, J. (2021). *Mental health response pilot program to launch this spring.* Retrieved from https://www.ny1.com/nyc/all-boroughs/news/2021/02/22/mental-health-response-team-pilot-launches-this-spring-in-central-and-east-harlem

Robinson, M. (2010). Assessing criminal justice practice using social justice theory. *Social Justice Research, 23,* 77–97.

Salsberg, E., Quigley, L., Mehfoud, N., Acquaviva, K. D., Wyche, K., & Silwa, S. (2017). *Profile of the social work workforce.* Retrieved from https://www.socialworkers.org/LinkClick.aspx?fileticket=wCttjrHq0gE%3d&portalid=0

Stuart, P. (2019). Social work profession: History. In *Encyclopedia of social work.* Retrieved From: https://oxfordre-com.proxy.wexler.hunter.cuny.edu/socialwork/view/10.1093/acrefore/9780199975839.001.0001/acrefore-9780199975839-e-623.

Sunshine, J., & Tyler, T. R. (2003). The role of procedural justice and legitimacy in shaping public support for policing. *Law & Society Review, 37*(3), 513–548.

Trute, B., Adkins, E., & MacDonald, G. (1992). Professional attitudes regarding the sexual abuse of children: Comparing police, child welfare and community mental health. *Child Abuse & Neglect, 16*(3), 359–368.

Vairo, E. (2010). Social worker attitudes toward court-mandated substance-abusing clients. *Journal of Social Work Practice in the Addictions, 10*(1), 81–98.

Vollmer, A. (April, 1919). *Writings, the policeman as social worker.* BANC MSS C-B 403. Berkeley, CA: The Bancroft Library, University of California.

WGME (2021). *Maine police departments will soon have social workers in-house.* Retrieved from https://www.chicagotribune.com/news/ct-xpm-1998-06-07-9806070171-story.html

Wilson, B. L., & Wolfer, T. A. (2020). Reducing police brutality in African American communities: Potential roles for social workers in congregations. *Social Work and Christianity, 47*(3), 66–84.

Zoorob, M. (2020). Do police brutality stories reduce 911 calls? Reassessing an important criminological finding. *American Sociological Review, 85*(1), 176–183.

5

SPECIALIST POLICE SOCIAL WORK PRACTICE

Chapter overview

The majority of literature that describes professional police social work practice is focused on the police social worker providing interventions to community residents who come to the attention of law enforcement. Much less literature describes police social work practice that includes providing training to recruits and police officers and counseling recruits, police officers, and their families. Similarly, less literature describes police social workers or professional social workers as consultants in law enforcement agencies. These roles are more often assumed by police psychologists and police psychiatrists. This situation occurs despite the fact that social work is recognized as a qualified service provider for law enforcement. This chapter examines these specialist police social work practice roles and discusses the preparation and skills police social workers require to perform these roles.

Introduction

The majority of the literature focused on police social work describes police social workers responding to social problems such as child abuse and neglect and interpersonal violence to assist community residents. Further, these police social workers are often employees of a law enforcement agency, although in some instances social workers who are not employees of law enforcement agencies also assist police officers with responding to community social problems.

The knowledge and skills required by police social workers for specialist practice are generally acquired through on-the-job training since it is unlikely that social workers will have either field practice experience or professional social work experience in a law enforcement agency. Whereas law enforcement

DOI: 10.4324/9781003132257-5

agencies are unique due to their paramilitary structure other host agencies in the criminal justice system, such as jails and prisons, employ correctional officers who wear uniforms, hold officer ranks, and follow a chain of command structure which is paramilitary.

Employment in these host agencies or providing interventions to employees in other agencies is a beneficial experience for some specialist police social work roles. As discussed in Chapter 3 not all law enforcement collaborations are formed with police social workers as collaboration partners. This occurs because social workers may be employed in community-based agencies, and therefore they will not professionally identify as police social workers. Furthermore, police social workers are typically employees in a law enforcement agency. For that reason when considering opportunities for specialist police social work roles these opportunities also apply to professional social workers not employed in law enforcement agencies. For example, a social worker employed in an Employee Assistance Program (EAP) providing counseling to a police officer would not identify as a police social worker.

In this chapter, the use of the term specialist police social work practice refers to the application of advanced social work practice skills to provide services to community residents, police officers and recruits, their families, and law enforcement agencies. This chapter first examines specialist services provided to community residents and second examines specialist services provided to police officers and recruits, their families, and law enforcement agencies. This chapter also examines how specialist practice is defined in the social work profession.

Specialist social work practice

In its standards that are used to accredit baccalaureate and master's degree social work educational programs, the Council on Social Work Education (CSWE) (2005) articulates the concept of specialized social work practice in the Educational Policy and Accreditation Standards (EPAS) in the following way: "Specialized practice builds on generalist practice, adapting and extending the Social Work Competencies for practice with a specific population, problem area, method of intervention, perspective or approach to practice. Specialized practice extends social work knowledge, values, and skills to engage, assess, intervene, and evaluate within an area of specialization."

Specialist police social work practice

The practice of police social work with law enforcement personnel, their families, and the law enforcement agency is specialized social work practice because of the population receiving services and the types of social problems addressed. Even the practice of police social work in a law enforcement agency providing services to individuals and families who have law enforcement contact and are referred by police officers is specialized social work practice.

The potential exists for numerous specialist areas of practice with law enforcement. These possibilities are in addition to assisting community residents with the commonly identified areas of domestic violence and mental health, for example, which come to the attention of law enforcement. Further, these specialist areas of practice involve both police social work practice and clinical social work practice. Clinical social workers represent the largest group of mental health and substance abuse practitioners in the United States. As of 2013, the Substance Abuse and Mental Health Services Administration (SAMHSA) identified 193,038 clinical social work practitioners, 95,545 psychologists, and 33,727 psychiatrists (SAMHSA, 2013). These figures show that more clinical social workers are mental health and substance abuse practitioners than psychologists and psychiatrists combined.

Among the three major groups of mental health practitioners (social workers, psychologists, psychiatrists) more social work hiring parity with psychologists and psychiatrists is needed in law enforcement agencies. Clinical social workers do not professionally identify as police social workers. However, clinical social workers assist police officers with responding to individuals experiencing mental health crises, suicidal ideation, and alcohol abuse (Calzolaio, 2018). Although police officers receive training in mental health and de-escalation techniques the training is not uniform among states (Plotkin & Peckerman, 2017). This underscores the need for assistance from clinical social workers.

Fewer descriptions report the hiring of clinical social workers in law enforcement agencies to provide services to the organization and police officers, although social workers are among the five professional groups identified as service providers in law enforcement agencies (social workers, counselors, psychologists, psychiatrists, and management consultants) (Schowengerdt, 1984). Clearly, social workers have not assumed these roles consistent with their numbers as mental health and substance abuse practitioners. The social work profession's more than 100-year history providing services to individuals who have law enforcement contact has committed less emphasis on these roles.

More specifically, expanded roles for social work practice in law enforcement agencies were identified nearly four decades ago and include: (1) assisting law enforcement agencies with selecting, screening, and evaluating police officer candidates; (2) providing stress management training, divorce, substance abuse, and suicide counseling for police officers; (3) providing consultation to administrative officers regarding officer job satisfaction and assistance with identifying topics for in-service officer training; (4) providing assistance with developing psychological profiles for offenders; and (5) assisting officers with hostage situations (Schowengerdt, 1984). Ellis (1981) expressed concern that inappropriate police officer candidates would be hired and recommended that social workers become involved in assessing candidates' mental health functioning.

The above roles are relevant for police social work practice. For instance substance abuse and suicide counseling for police officers require specialized knowledge and skills. Rouse et al. (2015) identified some of the suicide risk factors that are unique to law enforcement suicide. These factors included alcohol abuse and the lack of preparation among a police officer's peers to intervene when an officer is experiencing alcohol abuse.

All of the above practice areas must be provided within the scope of professional social work practice based on the National Association of Social Workers (NASW) Code of Ethics and state licensing regulations. For example, developing psychological profiles of offenders and conducting psychological evaluations of police officer candidates may not be feasible due to the lack of training, experience, and licensing regulations. However, utilizing the person-in-environment perspective together with conducting biopsychosocial assessments social workers can help to identify police officers experiencing work and personal stressors, substance abuse, suicidal ideation, and trauma.

Assuming these additional practice roles requires that social workers possess knowledge about law enforcement functions, occupational culture, training, and occupational policies and procedures. Equipped with this knowledge, and combined with the unique practice perspective and values of the profession and licensure, social workers can assume these roles.

Applying the CSWE (2005) definition of specialist social work practice to police social work practice is relevant in several areas. First, recruits, police officers, and their families are a unique population. Second, addressing the presenting problems of stress, domestic violence, and substance use, among others, requires specialized competencies. Third, interventions provided to law enforcement personnel, their families, and the law enforcement agency are varied and include counseling, relationship counseling, stress management interventions, training, and consultation. Fourth, police social work practice involves using practice approaches that combine law enforcement functions, law enforcement occupational culture, and diversity.

Further, CSWE (2005) articulates the role of research in specialized practice to enhance practice and services. The use of research is consistent with social workers' ethical responsibility to monitor and evaluate programs, policies, and interventions (National Association of Social Workers, 2021).

Finally, as the social work profession examines approaches to respond to 911 and 311 emergency and non-emergency calls for service without law enforcement accompaniment this also creates opportunities for specialized practice. In a study conducted in a large city located in the Northeast, Briar (1985) found that nearly 50% of 911 calls were not dispatched to police officers by the 911 operator. The calls that were not dispatched involved social service needs such as housing, requests for information, and missing persons and runaways. A total of 26% involved a request for information, and 22% were associated with victimization. Briar suggested that police social workers could assume roles that provide "communications center intake services" (p. 601) in which police social workers are employed as 911 operators to assist callers with social service needs, victimization, and resolving crises. As an alternative social workers could provide 24-hour assistance to 911 operators, or 911 operators can refer callers to police social workers. This approach could be used to ensure that 911 callers receive much-needed services and information.

Specialist police social work practice with police officers and recruits

As first responders police officers are the first to be called and to arrive at the scene of mass shooting and mass violence incidents, after an area has been secured police social workers can assist victims and survivors of mass violence (Patterson, 2003; Patterson & Telesco, 2004). Indeed, as a result of exposure to these traumatic events police officers themselves, as well as police social workers, may require specialized mental health services after responding to these traumatic incidents. Entire communities may experience trauma as a result of mass violence.

In law enforcement without effective interventions the effects of trauma has the potential to result in negative consequences for the recruit or police officer, their colleagues, community residents, and/or the law enforcement agency.

Specialist police social work practice with police officers involves providing interventions to officers to enhance their occupational and personal well-being. This includes addressing work and life stressful events, domestic violence, substance abuse, suicidal ideation, divorce, and financial problems, among numerous other presenting problems. Peer counseling, individual counseling, and group counseling are used to address these social problems. Police social work practice with police officers and recruits requires that police social workers possess specialized knowledge and skills regarding social problems and effective interventions, as well as knowledge about culture and diversity including law enforcement culture and attitudes toward these social problems and stressors.

When providing counseling and other mental health services to police officers, police social workers should be aware of the importance of confidentiality and its concern among police officers. Police officers may be concerned about how seeking mental health services may impact promotions and other opportunities. Further, the culture of law enforcement may embrace not utilizing mental health counseling services. Therefore police social workers should be skilled in helping police officers to understand the importance of seeking mental health services and sometimes the consequences of not seeking needed mental services. This may involve helping police officers to overcome any perceived stigma associated with seeking mental health services and counseling.

Certainly police officers have been identified as an occupational group at higher risk for developing mental and physical health problems. Work stress and law enforcement culture are the primary contributing factors to these risks. Both direct interventions such as counseling and indirect interventions such as stress management training should be provided. Combining these two types of interventions with motivational interviewing shows promise as a stress management intervention for police officers who are apprehensive regarding such interventions (Steinkopf, Hakala, & Van Hasselt, 2015).

Police officers also utilize the services of social workers in private practice or other social workers skilled in providing counseling. As mentioned elsewhere in the book, these social workers do not professionally identify as police social workers. The Supreme Court case *Jaffee v. Redmond* illustrates an example of a social worker providing counseling to a police officer. The basis for the Supreme Court case was a police officer-involved shooting. Mary Lou Redman, a police officer, witnessed Ricky Allen threatening to stab someone with a knife. Ricky Allen did not follow the officers' commands to put down the knife and was subsequently shot and killed. After the shooting and during pretrial discovery a representative for Ricky Allen, who filed a federal lawsuit asserting a violation of Ricky Allen's civil rights, received information that the police officer attended nearly 50 psychotherapy sessions with a clinical social worker (Colledge et al., 2000).

Although the focus of the Supreme Court case was psychotherapeutic privilege and confidentiality, and Colledge et al. (2000) focused on how the Supreme Court ruled in this case, the case also highlights the provision of social work counseling to police officers and the importance of confidentiality. In some instances, police officers are eligible for workers' compensation in response to mental injury resulting from the use of deadly force. In some jurisdictions, police officers may submit workers' compensation claims for mental and physical work–related injuries representing another area in which social workers should be knowledgeable (Patterson, 2010).

Specialist police social work practice with police officers and their families

In addition to specialist police social work practice with police officers and recruits, police social workers, and clinical social workers, also engage in specialist practice with police and their families together. This type of specialist practice involves working with families including children and adolescents, spouses, recruits, and police officers and their partners. Social work services are provided using group counseling, peer counseling, couples counseling, and family counseling. Openshaw (2009) suggested that support and education provided in a group setting can be beneficial for police officers and their partners.

Specialist police social work practice with law enforcement agencies

Opportunities exist for police social workers to provide services to a law enforcement agency. Consulting and training are reviewed next.

Consulting

Social workers, although not employees in law enforcement agencies, are hired as consultants to provide specific types of services. These services may include curriculum advisement, training, liaison between community groups and the law enforcement agency, program development, and/or program evaluation. To assume a consulting position requires specialized social work knowledge and skills including research, policy, and practice as well as an understanding of social problems and the role of law enforcement in responding to these social problems. As mentioned, Schowengerdt (1984) suggested that social work consultants can provide police officer candidate screening and perform other services provided by disciplines such as psychology.

Training recruits and police officers

There are many differences between providing training to police recruits who have no police experience and police officers who vary in their amount of years of police experience, rank, assignment, as well as the type of law enforcement work they performed as members of specialty units. Providing training to recruits and police officers requires an awareness of these differences.

Several models of law enforcement training academies also exist. Reaves (2016) reported that 48% of police recruits were trained in a "stress-based model" (p. 1), which refers to a military model that emphasizes physical and psychological stress. Another 18% were trained using a "nonstress model" (p. 1), which emphasizes academic coursework, physical activities, and a low-stress environment. In total, 34% of police recruits were trained in a law enforcement academy that combined both models and fewer recruits received training in academies that utilized primarily non-stress models.

In 2016, there were 15,322 city, county, sheriff's, state, and highway law enforcement agencies that employed 701,169 full-time police officers (Hyland, 2018). Between 2011 and 2013, 664 state and local law enforcement academies provided basic training to approximately 45,000 police recruits in each of these years. Thus, approximately 135,000 recruits received training over this three-year period. Academies provided approximately 840 hours or 21 weeks of training (Reaves, 2016). Reaves further reported that the majority of law enforcement training academies provided training in the following topics. The average number of hours of training provided is shown in parentheses:

- domestic violence (13 hours)
- mental illness (10 hours)
- sexual assault (6 hours)
- crimes against children (6 hours)
- gangs (4 hours)
- victim assistance (5 hours)
- hate crimes (3 hours)
- elder abuse (3 hours)
- human trafficking (3 hours).

As these data show, few hours of training are given to police recruits to assist them with addressing the social problems that comprise the law enforcement social service function. These topics are taught in a short block of time given that academy training consists of hundreds of hours. In summary, although police officers respond to social problems, recruits receive limited preparation during the academy training to respond to social problems, although such problems will comprise the majority of their duties as police officers.

Case Example

Training Police Recruits in a Law Enforcement Training Academy

A local police commissioner contacted the dean at a graduate school of social work to request assistance with training recruits on the topic of child maltreatment. The law enforcement agency has noticed an increase in responding to child maltreatment calls for service, particularly in immigrant communities.

When a faculty member is identified the commissioner plans to contact the state agency and seek the appropriate certification for the faculty member. A social worker providing training as a law enforcement training instructor should determine whether certification is required by a state agency or a regulating body that oversees law enforcement training.

After speaking with the dean at the school of social work one of the primary concerns was salary. It was negotiated that as a part of the faculty member's community service the faculty member would teach one less social work course and instead provide training at the law enforcement training academy. The faculty training was considered community service by the dean, who recognized the benefits to both the social work department and law enforcement agency. The police commissioner also regarded the faculty training as a benefit for the training academy to have an affiliation with an academic institution.

The next step was to identify a faculty member with practice skills in the topic area as well as possessing the ability to provide training in a law enforcement environment. After the dean identified the faculty member, the next step was to hold several meetings with the police commissioner, faculty member, and training academy staff to become familiar with the recruit class and training environment. The faculty member also toured the training academy.

Prior to beginning the training the faculty member was aware of the short block of time allotted for the training when compared to a semester-long course in an academic institution. The faculty member was surprised that the short amount of time appeared similar to the amount of time given in a continuing education course or a social service agency training, given that recruits perhaps had little experience with the topic.

On the first day of training upon entering the classroom to provide the training one of the recruits, identified as the recruit class leader, stood up and shouted a military command. At that point all of the recruits stood up and saluted the trainer who was informed beforehand to say "as you were" or "at ease." The entire recruit class then took their seats for the training to begin. The faculty member immediately noticed the differences between teaching in an academic classroom and training recruits. Among other things, the faculty member noticed the complete silence prior to beginning the training, whereas in an academic classroom numerous conversations occur at the same time that the instruction begins.

The faculty member was also informed in advance that when training police officers they do not stand and salute, and conversations may also occur when the training begins, unlike the recruit class training environment. The faculty member also observed when walking in a congested hallway with recruits the command "make way" was shouted and the recruits cleared the hallway by standing against the wall and allowing the instructor to pass. The faculty member compared this experience to going to a classroom in an academic environment and walking through hallways crowded with students. Clearly, these are very different procedures and experiences for social workers compared to providing academic instruction or training in a social service agency.

Once the training began it was essential for the social worker to ensure the training was relevant and delivered in a manner consistent with the role and functions of law enforcement. In other words, the social worker also included law enforcement tasks and functions in the training. An experienced police officer was present during the training to assist in these areas when needed.

In-service training is the term used to describe training that is provided to sworn police officers. The training may be provided in either a law enforcement training academy or an off-site location. For comparison with training recruits the following case example highlights the differences between recruits and police officers and implications for training. While the example shows the preparation and use of a standardized curriculum for training additional knowledge and skills will be needed when training police officers to use specific stress management interventions. Patterson, Chung, and Swan (2014) conducted a meta-analysis to examine the effectiveness of stress management interventions for both police officers and recruits. They found that stress management intervention training in law enforcement ranged from nutrition information and physical conditioning activities to Eye Movement Desensitization and Reprocessing. As first responders police officers respond to traumatic events and may themselves experience trauma and traumatic stress resulting in the need for them to seek stress management interventions.

Data are available which show that 81% of law enforcement training academies provided training in stress prevention and management, and when provided recruits received an average of 6 hours of training. More academies provided training in health and fitness, 96%, with an average of 49 hours of training out of approximately 840 hours total hours of recruit training (Reaves, 2016).

Case Example

Providing Stress Management Intervention
Training to Police Officers

Police officers have law enforcement experience, whereas a recruit in academy training to become a police officer does not. Consequently, police officers may have experienced some of the stressful and traumatic occupational events identified in the police stress literature, whereas recruits will not have such experiences. However, both police officers and recruits may have experienced stressful and traumatic life events. Accordingly a social worker assigned to provide stress management training to police officers or recruits should be prepared for stressful work and life events.

Although the social worker was given a curriculum used by the law enforcement agency to become more familiar with the topic the social worker employed skills taught in graduate social work education to search databases and retrieve information about law enforcement stress and coping strategies. The social worker conducted a review of the literature and noticed that the majority of the literature focused on samples of police officers with law enforcement experience as opposed to recruits. For example, the social worker examined several models and issues associated with training law enforcement officers (Anderson, Swenson, & Clay, 1995; Carlan & Nored, 2008; Chapin et al., 2008; Patterson, 2008).

The social worker also read the literature describing the types of stressful events police officers experience (Burke, Waters, & Ussery, 2007), physical health problems among police officers compared to the general population (Mumford, Taylor, & Kubu, 2015), traumatic stress (Violanti & Paton, 1999), effective stress management interventions provided to police officers (Burke & Cooper, 2016), and the types of coping strategies police officers use (Arble, Daugherty, & Arnetz, 2018).

Combined with knowledge of trauma theory and sources of trauma and its effects, the social worker felt prepared to provide the training. Preparation was further supplemented with information about law enforcement culture and police officers' attitudes toward stress management training. The stress management training was provided in an 8-hour block of time, similar to the Dallas Police Department Police Officer Course Curriculum (2018).

Employee assistance programs

EAPs are programs that provide a variety of services to employees in response to life and work-related events. These services include individual and family counseling, crisis intervention, legal assistance, referrals to address social problems such as legal matters, gambling, health issues, alcohol and substance use, domestic violence, and family problems including parenting issues, stress, and mental health needs.

Three types of EAPs have been described specifically for law enforcement. The first type is an EAP that is established and operated within a law enforcement agency. The second type is an EAP that is external to a law enforcement agency, and the third type is a combination of an EAP established in a law enforcement agency. In this type of EAP, peer police officers provide EAP services to police officers in combination with an EAP that is external to a law enforcement agency that also provides services to police officers. The later type of EAP enables police officers to receive services more rapidly and to receive these services from a peer familiar with law enforcement culture, functions, and tasks (Goldstein, 2006).

Donnelly, Valentine, and Oehme (2015) surveyed 934 police officers employed in a large southern state and found that 16.2% had previously utilized EAP services, and 56.4% were familiar with the types of EAP services available to police officers. Further, 33.4% of the officers reported they would consider the possibility of utilizing the EAP services to address personal experiences of domestic violence with their partners. They found no statistically significant differences between police officers who previously utilized EAP services and those who had not in terms of whether they experienced domestic violence, alcohol abuse, stress, or post-traumatic stress.

Preparation for specialist police social work practice

Preparation for specialist police social work practice includes educational opportunities and on-the-job training opportunities. When law enforcement agencies seek to employ experienced practitioners on-the-job training may be given less emphasis.

Social work education

CSWE publishes resources that describe the practice of advanced social work practice in areas that are applicable to specialist police social work practice. These areas are applicable for practice with individuals and families referred to police social workers by police officers, in addition to recruits, police officers, and their families, and law enforcement agencies.

The publication titled *Advanced social work practice in the prevention of substance use disorders* (CSWE, 2008) recognizes the advanced social work practice skills required to prevent substance use disorders among individuals, families, and agencies. The knowledge and skills outlined in the publication match the competencies taught in graduate social work programs and are relevant for specialized police social work practice. Substance abuse is a major area of police social work practice, particularly when co-occurring disorders are present and when providing interventions to police officers, recruits, and their families. The skills are also valuable for police social workers implementing substance abuse prevention interventions and strategies in law enforcement agencies.

Similar to the need for knowledge and skills to prevent substance use disorders, police social workers require knowledge and skills for trauma-informed practice. In their work in law enforcement agencies police social workers have contact with multiple individuals who have experienced traumatic events. CSWE (2012) also provides material regarding knowledge and skills for advanced practice in trauma that matches the competencies taught in graduate social work programs. The purpose of this publication is to outline essential competencies needed by social work students to provide trauma-informed services to individuals, families, groups, agencies, and communities. While intended for social work educational programs the material can also be invaluable for police social workers who provide interventions in each of these levels of practice. The following types of situations illustrate why a trauma-informed approach is necessary for police social work practice:

- Individuals and families referred by police officers to police social workers have experienced trauma as a result of violent victimization and other traumatic events. Among some individuals and families having law enforcement contact itself can be a traumatic situation.
- Police officers experience trauma events that are both personal and work related. Due to the nature of their work they are exposed to traumatic events, violence, and death.
- The families of police officers may also experience trauma.
- As a result of traumatic events experienced by the workforce, the law enforcement agency can benefit from utilizing a trauma-informed approach. Such an approach is applicable to the workforce as well as police officers applying a trauma-informed approach during their contacts with the public. In Chapters 1 and 2, LEAD was identified as a policing strategy in which police officers refer low-level offenders to trauma-informed services such as substance use treatment (LEAD National Support Bureau, n.d.). In this way, law enforcement agencies have begun to recognize the importance of providing trauma-informed services to individuals with law enforcement contact.

Social work credentials and licensure

Specialty police social work practice requires an MSW and years of experience in a substantive area of practice. Police social work practice must be performed within the scope of professional social work practice based on the NASW Code of Ethics and state licensing regulations. For example, developing psychological profiles of offenders and conducting psychological evaluations of police officer candidates may not be feasible due to the lack of training, experience, and licensing regulations that do not permit social workers to administer and score certain types of standardized instruments. However, utilizing a person-in-environment perspective together with conducting biopsychosocial assessments police social workers can help to identify police officers experiencing work and personal stressors, substance abuse, suicidal ideation, and trauma.

Professional development and continuing education

Although professional development opportunities that provide specific knowledge and skills for police social work practice are limited, numerous opportunities for professional development can be found that provide social workers interested in police social work with a foundation for professional practice. These topics include ethics; harm reduction approaches; trauma-informed care; risk assessment; co-occurring disorder; suicide and youth suicide; and cultural, racial, ethnic, religious, and gender identity, among many other topics.

The lack of sufficient professional development opportunities for preparation for police social work practice includes insufficient continuing education units (CEUs). Consequently, the abovementioned topics can be useful when offered as CEUs to enhance the ability of police social workers to provide services to community residents, address a variety of emergency crisis situations, and perform interdisciplinary collaboration.

CEUs are a necessary requirement to maintain social work state licensure. Social workers should consult with state licensing boards to determine the number of hours of CEUs required each year to maintain licensure. Examples of sources for seeking relevant CEUs include graduate social work programs that offer continuing education and professional organizations such as NASW. Licensed clinical social workers employed in the FBI completed CEUs to maintain both their clinical skills and state social work licensure (Federal Bureau of Investigation, n.d.).

Psychology was identified as a profession that is a provider of numerous law enforcement services. Board certification in police psychology is separate from state licensure as a psychologist (Corey et al., 2011). The American Board of Professional Psychology lists numerous Academies in the specialties of school psychology, forensic psychology, clinical psychology, and clinical health psychology. Among these specialties is the American Academy of Police & Public Safety Psychology. This Academy provides continuing education courses and other supports to enhance police and public safety psychology in the areas of assessment, research, and the practice of psychology in law enforcement agencies (American Board of Professional Psychology, n.d.). Further, police psychologists' involvement with law enforcement agencies includes intervening in hostage situations involving an armed individual (Rogers, 2020) and police officer selection (Davis & Rostow, 2002).

At the present time no such board certification exists for the practice of police social work. Moreover, a national specialized certification for police social work has not been established.

Chapter summary

The social work profession has a more than 100-year history of providing services to individuals who have law enforcement contact. This area of social work practice, known as police social work, has a clearly delineated scope of practice.

This chapter suggested that the time has come to expand police social work practice roles in law enforcement agencies. Some of these roles can be assumed by professional social workers who do not identify as police social workers. These expanded roles include providing training to recruits and police officers and counseling recruits, police officers, and their families. Providing consultation to law enforcement agencies represents another role that can be assumed by either police social workers or social workers.

Assuming these additional practice roles requires that police social workers possess knowledge about law enforcement functions, culture, training, and occupational policies and procedures. In this way, this type of practice is specialized social work practice. With that said the focus of this book is specialist social work practice. The social problems of child maltreatment, domestic violence, mental health, and substance abuse, for example, require specialized social work practice skills as well as the practice of police social work. Equipped with this knowledge, and combined with the unique practice perspective and values of the profession, police social workers can assist police officers and recruits, their families, and law enforcement agencies.

Questions for discussion

1. Have you previously considered police officers and their families as clients in need of social work services such as family counseling and mental health services?
2. Using a catalog listing of continuing education courses identify the courses you believe are most relevant for police social work practice as part of a plan for professional development.
3. Based on your social work educational program, academic courses, and field education experiences what additional learning and practice needs can you identify to prepare you for specialized police social work practice?

Activities for further learning

1. Prepare a list of practice areas that support identifying police social work as specialist social work practice.
2. Create a professional development plan for acquiring specialized social work practice skills to prepare you for police social work practice.
3. Create a professional development plan for training police officers and recruits. In addition to obtaining additional knowledge about a social problem that will be the focus of training be sure to include what additional information you would seek to provide the actual training in a law enforcement training academy.

References

American Board of Professional Psychology (n.d.). *Academies.* Retrieved from https://www.abpp.org/About/Academies.aspx

Anderson, W., Swenson, D., & Clay, D. (1995). *Stress management for law enforcement officers.* Englewood Cliffs, NJ: Prentice Hall.

Arble, E., Daugherty, A. M., & Arnetz, B. B. (2018). Models of first responder coping: Police officers as a unique population. *Stress and Health, 34*(5), 612–621.

Briar, K. H. (1985). Emergency calls to police: Implications for social work intervention. *Social Service Review, 59*(4), 593–603.

Burke, R. & Cooper, C. (Eds.). (2016). *Stress in policing: Sources, consequences and intervention.* Aldershot, UK: Gower Publishing Ltd.

Burke, R., Waters, J. A., & Ussery, W. (2007). Police stress: History, contributing factors, symptoms, and interventions. *Policing: An International Journal of Police Strategies & Management, 30*(2), 169–188.

Calzolaio, S. (2018). *Franklin, Medway police will share clinician to aid in mental health-related calls.* Retrieved from https://www.milforddailynews.com/news/20181014/franklin-medway-police-will-share-clinician-to-aid-in-mental-health-related-calls

Carlan, P. E., & Nored, L. S. (2008). An examination of officer stress: Should police departments implement mandatory counseling?. *Journal of Police and Criminal Psychology, 23*(1), 8–15.

Chapin, M., Brannen, S. J., Singer, M. I., & Walker, M. (2008). Training police leadership to recognize and address operational stress. *Police Quarterly, 11*(3), 338–352.

Colledge, D., Zeigler, F., Hemmens, C., & Hodge, C. (2000). What's up doc? Jaffee v. Redmond and the psychotherapeutic privilege in criminal justice. *Journal of Criminal Justice, 28*(1), 1–11.

Corey, D. M., Cuttler, M. J., Cox, D. R., & Brower, J. (2011). Board certification in police psychology: What it means to public safety. *The Police Chief, 78,* 100–104.

Council on Social Work Education (CSWE) (2005). *Educational policy and accreditation standards for Baccalaureate and Master's Social Work Programs.* Alexandria, VA: Council on Social Work Education. Retrieved from https://cswe.org/getattachment/Accreditation/Standards-and-Policies/2015-EPAS/2015EPASandGlossary.pdf.aspx

Council on Social Work Education (CSWE) (2008). *Advanced social work practice in the prevention of substance use disorders.* Alexandria, VA: Council on Social Work Education.

Council on Social Work Education (CSWE) (2012). *Advanced social work practice in trauma.* Alexandria, VA: Council on Social Work Education.

Dallas Police Department Police Officer Course Curriculum (2018). *Dallas police academy basic training curriculum.* Retrieved from https://dallaspolice.net/joindpd/Shared%20Documents/DPD%20Basic%20PO%20Course%20Curriculum%20-%207-9-18%20-%20MASTER.pdf

Davis, R. D., & Rostow, C. D. (2002). M-PULSE. *Forensic Examiner, 11*(11/12), 19–24.

Donnelly, E., Valentine, C., & Oehme, K. (2015). Law enforcement officers and employee assistance programs. *Policing: An International Journal of Police Strategies & Management, 38*(2), 206–220.

Ellis, A. L. (1981). Where is social work? Police brutality and the inner city. *Social Work, 26*(6), 511–514.

Federal Bureau of Investigation (n.d.). *Office for victim assistance.* Retrieved from http://www.fbi.gov/news/podcasts/inside/office-for-victim-assistance.mp3/view

Goldstein, D. B. (2006). Employee assistance for law enforcement: A brief review. *Journal of Police and Criminal Psychology, 21*(1), 33.

Hyland, S. (2018). *Full-time employees in law enforcement agencies, 1997–2016.* NCJ 251762. Washington, D.C.: U.S. Department of Justice, Office of Justice Programs, Bureau of Justice Statistics.

LEAD National Support Bureau (n.d.). Retrieved from https://www.leadbureau.org/

Mumford, E. A., Taylor, B. G., & Kubu, B. (2015). Law enforcement officer safety and wellness. *Police Quarterly, 18*(2), 111–133.

National Association of Social Workers (2021). *Code of Ethics of the National Association of Social Workers.* Washington, D.C.: National Association of Social Workers.

Openshaw, L. (2009). Police officers and their spouses. In A. Gitterman & R. Salmon (Eds.), *Encyclopedia of social work with groups* (pp. 228–230). New York: Routledge.

Patterson, G. T. (2003). Police-social work collaboration in response to the World Trade Center attacks. *International Journal of Mass Emergencies and Disasters, 21*, 87–102.

Patterson, G. T. (2008). A framework for facilitating stress management educational groups for police officers. *Social Work with Groups, 31*(1), 53–70.

Patterson, G. T. (2010). Mental stress and workers' compensation claims among police officers. *Journal of Workplace Rights, 14*(4), 441–455.

Patterson, G. T., Chung, I. W., & Swan, P. G. (2014). Stress management interventions for police officers and recruits: A meta-analysis. *Journal of Experimental Criminology, 10*(4), 487–513.

Patterson, G. T., & Telesco, G. A. (2004). Mass violence and law enforcement personnel. In L. Straussner & N. Phillips (Eds.), *Social work and mass violence* (pp. 117–125). Boston, MA: Allyn & Bacon.

Plotkin, M., & Peckerman, T. (2017). *The variability in law enforcement state standards: A 42-state survey on mental health and crisis de-escalation training.* New York: The Council of State Governments.

Reaves, B. A. (2016). *State and local law enforcement training academies, 2013.* NCJ 249784. Washington, D.C.: U.S. Department of Justice, Office of Justice Programs, Bureau of Justice Statistics.

Rogers, T. (2020). Into the night: A police psychologist presents a play-by-play of a barricaded subject/hostage situation. *Sheriff & Deputy, 72*(3), 56–58.

Rouse, L. M., Frey, R. A., Lopez, M., Wohlers, H., Xiong, I., Llewellyn, K., … & Wester, S. R. (2015). Law enforcement suicide: Discerning etiology through psychological autopsy. *Police Quarterly, 18*(1), 79–108.

Schowengerdt, G. C. (1984). Human service professionals for smaller departments. *The Police Chief, 51*, 29–31.

Steinkopf, B. L., Hakala, K. A., & Van Hasselt, V. B. (2015). Motivational interviewing: Improving the delivery of psychological services to law enforcement. *Professional Psychology: Research and Practice, 46*(5), 348.

Substance Abuse and Mental Health Services Administration (SAMHSA) (2013). *Behavioral health, United States, 2012.* Rockville, MD: Substance Abuse and Mental Health Services Administration.

Violanti, J. M., & Paton, D. (Eds.). (1999). *Police trauma: The psychological aftermath of civilian combat.* Springfield, IL: Charles C. Thomas.

6

POLICE: A MODEL FOR THE DEVELOPMENT, IMPLEMENTATION, AND EVALUATION OF POLICE SOCIAL WORK COLLABORATION

Chapter overview

This chapter introduces a model for developing, implementing, and evaluating police social work collaborations. The model referred to as POLICE and put forward by the author comprises a six-stage process – planning, organizing, listening, implementation, collecting data, and evaluation. This model is intended to provide guidance to advance these phases for police social work or police and social work collaboration that addresses any social problem(s). This model can be particularly useful when social workers are employed in social service agencies rather than law enforcement agencies and are committed to establishing a collaboration with a law enforcement agency. Throughout this book when social workers collaborate with law enforcement and are not employed in law enforcement agencies this is referred to as police and social work collaboration. Police social work, on the other hand, refers to the employment of a professional social worker within a law enforcement agency.

Establishing a collaboration with law enforcement is filled with unique challenges. These include evaluation challenges such as selecting appropriate outcome measures, use of random assignment, obtaining informed consent, confidentiality, and possessing data collection and data analysis skills. While an evaluation plan should be developed prior to implementing a collaboration, the initial steps also involve obtaining buy-in from key stakeholders. This chapter examines these issues. In subsequent chapters, a brief application of the POLICE Model is offered relevant to the chapter topic.

DOI: 10.4324/9781003132257-6

Introduction

The social work profession has a rich tradition of practice-informed research and research-informed practice. This implies that the practice of social work is based on research findings that demonstrate effective practice approaches and intervention outcomes. Likewise, the practice of social work informs research methods. As such, the relationship between practice and research is invaluable for developing, implementing, and evaluating police social work and police and social work collaborations. Existing research and evaluation knowledge can be applied to developing new collaborations or evaluating existing ones.

The most in-depth information describing the development and implementation of a police social work collaboration is provided in the book titled *The police-social work team: A new model for interprofessional cooperation: A university demonstration project in manpower training and development: Jane Addams School of Social Work, University of Illinois at Chicago Circle* written by Harvey Treger.

Treger's (1975) book is the first police social work collaboration resource that describes in detail the initial planning phase, objectives, implementation, and research methods used to identify the types of services provided. He described the development of the Police-Social Service Project (SSP) and its objectives. Four primary objectives of SSP were identified: (1) to divert individuals from further criminal justice system involvement after contact with law enforcement; (2) to create collaboration opportunities between law enforcement and social workers; (3) to reduce the number of individuals who become involved with the court and corrections components of the criminal justice system; and (4) to provide social services to low-level, non-violent offenders and offenders involved in victimless offenses following a law enforcement contact.

The SSP was implemented in the Wheaton, IL, and Niles, IL, police departments. Each SSP was comprised of two social workers. These social workers also provided supervision to several second-year MSW students. The SSP provided stipends for these interns whose internship consisted of at least 24 hours each week. Tuition was waived at the Jane Addams School of Social Work, University of Illinois. Overall, social workers and social work students provided assessment, 24-hour crisis services, both short-term and long-term individual and group counseling, and referrals to community-based agencies (Treger, 1975).

The content in this chapter is influenced by Treger's (1975) methods. Many of the approaches that he utilized to develop and implement the two police social work collaborations over a three-year period are elaborated upon in this chapter. Many communities are exploring options for providing an emergency response that does not include law enforcement. These collaborations are formed between social workers and other partners such as paramedics. While these types of collaborations are not the focus of this chapter the subject matter remains relevant even when law enforcement is not included as a collaboration partner. For instance, social workers have an ethical responsibility to monitor and evaluate newly implemented collaborations (National Association of Social Workers, 2021).

Police social work collaboration outcomes

One of the first issues to consider before implementing a police social work collaboration is to identify the type of social problem(s) that will be the focus of the collaboration. Once the social problem(s) has been identified the next major issue is to identify what the collaboration expects to accomplish. This will form the foundation for selecting collaboration outcomes. Accordingly, while the collaboration outcomes may change over time they should be determined prior to implementing the police social work or police and social work collaboration so that the goals of the collaboration can be clearly identified among stakeholders and can also be measured. In this way, it can be determined whether the collaboration outcomes have been achieved.

Outcomes appropriate for a police social work collaboration might include a reduction in repeat calls for police service, linking community residents with community-based services through referrals, or providing crisis intervention. CrimeSolutions defines and provides examples of primary and secondary outcomes and Tier 1 and Tier 2 outcomes for criminal justice programs. Primary outcomes are the main effects of a program associated with the criminal justice system or the provision of services such as victim services. Secondary outcomes are additional program effects such as reducing fear of crime or reducing substance use. Tier 1 outcomes are general outcomes such as mental health or victimization. Tier 2 outcomes are more clearly identified outcomes such as violent offenses as a type of crime or opioid use as a type of substance use (National Institute of Justice, Office of Justice Programs, (n.d.).

The following examples illustrate outcomes associated with social problems relevant for police social work collaboration. Sampson (2007) recommended outcomes for domestic violence police calls for service such as measuring the number of arrests made, how much time passed between an arrest and a conviction, the number of arrests in which the offender was convicted, and the number of domestic violence incidents in which both the victim and the offender were arrested. Additional outcomes included measuring the number of domestic violence victims that utilized referrals, the number of police calls for domestic violence, and the number of medical assessments provided.

In another example, CrimeSolutions identified three outcomes that were used in the Lethality Assessment Program (Oklahoma): repeat incidents of domestic violence and victimization, pursued an order of protection, and received domestic violence interventions (National Institute of Justice, Office of Justice Programs, 2016). While these outcomes are relatively easy to measure one noticeable feature about these outcomes is that they do not measure psychological or physiological outcomes.

Research methods

Different types of research methods can be used to either provide information about a police social work collaboration or to evaluate a collaboration. Hilton et al. (2020) summarized the following three research designs. First, pre-experimental designs do not include a control group or random assignment. These are described as the weakest type of research designs, although these designs do include measurement of pre-test and post-test outcomes. Second, quasi-experimental designs may include a comparison group, although research participants are not randomly assigned to the group. As a result, the two groups are not equivalent. While this design is more robust than a pre-experimental design because it includes a non-equivalent comparison group it is weaker than an experimental design due to the lack of random assignment. The third design is an experimental design. This design involves randomly assigning research participants to a control group and an experimental group. It provides the strongest evidence for collaboration effectiveness.

The POLICE Model

The purpose of introducing the POLICE Model, comprised of a six-stage process – planning, organizing, listening, implementation, collecting data, and evaluation – is to provide guidance to advance these phases for police social work or police and social work collaboration that addresses any social problem(s). Figure 6.1 presents this process beginning with the planning phase. The circular nature of the process suggests that upon completion of an evaluation of the collaboration the evaluation methods and data obtained may suggest a return to the planning phase to repeat earlier phases if necessary.

The focus of the POLICE Model introduced in this chapter is the development and implementation of new police social work collaborations. Application of the six stages is described next.

Planning

The planning phase is the initial phase in the process used for implementing a new police social work collaboration. Collaboration partners can jointly participate in meetings during the planning phase of the police social work collaboration. During this phase a major concern is whether the collaboration is feasible. Feasibility refers to the availability of funding, office space, training and supervision opportunities, safety concerns, and importantly having sufficient numbers of community residents with law enforcement contacts who experience a social problem(s) to make the collaboration worthwhile.

Treger (1975) described numerous concerns during the planning phase that needed to be addressed before the SSP could be implemented. These were: (1) having a shared interest in the SSP among collaboration partners; (2) obtaining

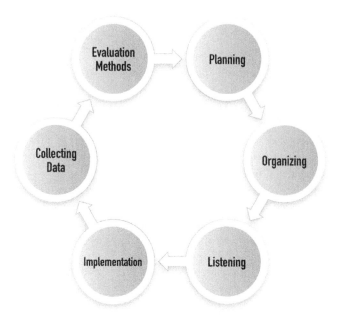

FIGURE 6.1   POLICE Model – a strategy for the development, implementation, and evaluation of police social work collaboration

community "buy-in" including financial support for the SSP; (3) having access to the types of clients articulated in the SSP goals; and (4) the provision of office space in the law enforcement agency for social workers.

Planning and subsequent phases of the POLICE Model should also include the involvement of community members affected by the social problem that the collaboration is intended to address. Community members bring a unique perspective that can be invaluable for avoiding problems before they arise. Community-based behavioral health agencies, particularly those agencies that may both refer to the collaboration and receive referrals from the collaboration, are also important to include in the POLICE Model. Similar to community residents, these agencies bring a unique perspective that can be invaluable for problems before they arise. Further, their input will be invaluable for developing referral protocols. This is a critical activity since law enforcement agencies provide crisis services and rely on community-based behavioral health and other agencies to receive referrals and provide services to individuals. Finally, these agencies should be familiar with the collaboration and its goals. One way is to achieve this is to establish memorandums of understanding.

Also during the planning phase the goals of the police social work collaboration, types of services that will be provided, and the population that will receive the services must be clearly articulated. In Chapter 8 second responder programs are examined as a police and social work collaboration response to domestic violence. Co-responder programs comprised of collaborations formed between police and mental health practitioners to respond to mental health crises are examined in Chapter 10. Each of these collaboration types responds to a single social problem. More than one type of social problem can be addressed in a police social work collaboration. Thus, consideration also needs to be given to the types of social problem(s) that will be the focus of the collaboration.

Law enforcement agencies may maintain data that can be used to identify the social problem(s) that will be the focus of the collaboration. Whereas community stakeholders and social service agencies may also maintain data or other information law enforcement agencies are a primary source for this data, given that they are first responders to specific types of community social problems. In many instances it may be that a law enforcement agency is the first to recognize the need for assistance with social problems and subsequently contacts social service providers for assistance.

Discussions held during the planning phase should focus on when the police social worker will respond and become involved during a law enforcement contact, and the duration of police social work services. Treger (1975) collected data that showed how much time elapsed after police officers made referrals to the police social workers and when services were provided. The majority of clients began to receive police social work services within two weeks after a referral was made (89.6%). This was followed by service provision within one week (75.8%), within five days (67.9%), and within two days (53.9%). The fewest clients received services the same day the police officer made a referral to the SSP (40.2%).

The author's police social work experience involved responding immediately to referrals and providing services. During the majority of instances police officers were still at the scene. Delays responding only occurred when police social workers were providing interventions on other calls. Thus, all police social work responses and interventions were provided the same day the referral was received. Many situations such as mental health crises, domestic violence, homelessness, and transportation needs, to mention a few situations, require an immediate response.

The planning phase also considers the duration of police social work services. Given that police social workers primarily provide crisis intervention and brief short-term counseling whether the collaboration will provide longer-term counseling that requires different intervention approaches is important to consider. Police social workers who immediately respond to referrals may be unable to carry a caseload. To illustrate, SSP data showed the majority of police social work services continued for more than four months (34.2%). Next, services were provided for less than one month (30.1%), 2–3 months (16.0%), and 3–4 months (10.0%). The shortest duration for services was 1–2 months (9.8%) (Treger, 1975). These data suggest that a police social worker carrying a caseload may experience conflicts if required to primarily respond to immediate referrals. The length of time required to provide each crisis response should also be considered. This has implications for the number of police social workers that should be hired. If police social workers only respond to crisis situations, there may be times when they are less busy, and the opposite can also occur in which the police social workers are very busy responding to crises.

Treger's planning activities as an example

Treger (1975) conducted a planning phase that involved meetings with local governmental officials including the mayor, city manager and city council members, social service agencies, and police chiefs. Joint presentations describing the SSP facilitated by social workers and police officers were provided to community stakeholders.

The planning phase should include creating drafts of documents that will be required to maintain records for the police social work collaboration. These documents will also be utilized during the data collection phase. Developing these documents should begin prior to collaboration implementation, although revisions may be necessary after collaboration implementation. Documents may require revisions or new forms may need to be created based on new and unanticipated requirements. This chapter identifies the types of documents Treger employed.

The planning phase requires consideration of numerous other factors. Importantly, funding and employment benefits for police social work positions and the types of positions that will be hired requires consideration from the onset. Police social work collaborations can include the use of full-time or part-time police social workers or a combination of full-time and part-time staff.

Planning to hire staff

Although written more than four decades ago, Treger (1975) described the most comprehensive positions to include in a police social work collaboration. These positions were:

- Professional social workers
- Second-year MSW social work interns
- Senior social workers
- Project director
- Secretary
- Full-time research associate
- Part-time research assistant
- Research consultant
- Faculty research advisor
- Police consultant
- Legal consultant
- Psychiatric consultant

- Professional-Technical Advisory Team
- Community-Citizens Advisory Committee (this committee was not established).

Organizing

The second phase of the POLICE Model is organizing. This involves performing tasks such as scheduling meetings, assigning workgroups, assigning tasks, and sharing information. Competent organizational skills are necessary given the different goals and missions among the agencies interested in establishing the collaboration.

There is a great deal of overlap between planning and organizing. This occurs during the process of organizing because the collaboration partners continue to be involved in the planning of the collaboration. Among social service and other agencies, collaboration partners should understand law enforcement functions. Such an understanding will facilitate workgroup and other meeting discussions. Likewise, the benefits and challenges of police social work practice should be openly shared with law enforcement to address concerns prior to implementing the collaboration.

During the organizing phase it may be determined that additional stakeholders should be included or that additional information about the collaboration is needed. Organizing in this regard involves collecting, organizing, and disseminating information among collaboration partners. Organizing also calls for an understanding of organizational culture and the ability to organize meeting spaces that include law enforcement, perhaps uniformed and armed. Efforts should be made to avoid agency hierarchy. Indeed, there is much to consider while organizing stakeholders for collaboration. Further, multiple meetings will need to be organized. The meeting agenda should be distributed prior to holding a meeting. During a meeting minutes should be taken to provide a record of meeting attendance, a summary of the discussion, and actions that are both planned and achieved.

Listening

Continuing to build on the first two phases, active listening is required throughout the POLICE Model. Given the occupational differences between law enforcement and social work active listening is essential. Moreover, even among different professional groups interested in the collaboration active listening is required. It is important to listen to each collaboration partner's concerns about establishing a collaboration so that these concerns can be addressed. It is important not only to address these concerns before implementing the collaboration but to continue this process once the collaboration is developed and implemented.

During discussions listening with the intent to understand each partner's roles, functions, challenges, and concerns about collaborating should be non-judgmental. Listening is a process that applies throughout each of the POLICE Model phases. The planning, organizing, and listening phases may take several months or more to accomplish. These phases will be followed by the implementation phase if it is determined that the collaboration is feasible.

Implementation

Following careful and successful planning, organizing, and listening phases the next phase is to begin implementation of the collaboration. During the previous phases numerous tasks have been completed. Some of these tasks include a completed review of established police social work and police and social collaborations, resolution of the major collaboration barriers, comprehensive discussions concerning collaboration benefits, and written protocols for providing referrals to police social workers, to mention but a few of the major tasks that should be completed.

The implementation phase involves the police social workers beginning to respond to calls for service and providing services based on the formal agreement established during prior phases. During this phase discrepancies may be observed between what was planned during the planning phase and the reality of responding to calls. Collecting data can be a useful activity for identifying these discrepancies.

Collecting data

Once the collaboration has been implemented collecting data is essential. Data are necessary to document who received services and why, to describe how the collaboration is operating, to provide information for stakeholders and funders, and for evaluation purposes. Furthermore, data can provide information to determine whether the collaboration goals established during the planning are being achieved. In addition to collecting outcome data, demographic data such as age, race, and ethnicity are useful types of data. Documenting the start and end times that police social work services are provided also provides useful information.

Forms are needed for data collection. Treger (1975) offers samples of the forms created for use in the SSP. These forms include: (1) a job description for a police social work position; (2) a set of written guidelines that provide instructions for police officers to identify the types of individuals and situations that are appropriate referrals to the SSP; (3) a biopsychosocial history form; (4) a consent form requiring a parental/guardian signature for adolescents to receive SSP services; (5) forms for adults to consent to receive voluntary services from the SSP as well as consent for deferred adult prosecution; (6) a consent form giving permission to the SSP and law enforcement agency to release confidential information; (7) a consent form to participate in group counseling services; and (8) a monthly statistics form that identifies the number of clients who received services, and the number of opened and closed cases each month. Numerous other forms are offered.

Evaluation

Social workers have an ethical obligation to monitor and evaluate programs as they are implemented as well as the policies and interventions associated with the program (National Association of Social Workers, 2021). Consequently, police social workers have an ethical responsibility to monitor and evaluate a newly implemented police social work collaboration. Implicit in this statement is the obligation to modify and improve the collaboration developed during the planning phase should the evaluation results show that the collaboration is not operating as intended. Further, the Code of Ethics does not prescribe a specific research method that should be used. This is the role of the police social worker to determine the most appropriate research method(s) that will be used to conduct the evaluation. In some instances, this may require the use of a research consultant.

Forming a control group using random assignment comprised of individuals who have law enforcement contact but do not receive social work services presents numerous ethical and other challenges. Fewer police social work collaboration evaluations include a control group using random assignment or, in other words, a randomized controlled trial. Although randomized controlled trials provide the strongest evidence of collaboration effectiveness less robust research designs can provide useful information.

Treger (1975) identified the research design used in the development and implementation of the SSP as "exploratory and descriptive" (p. 11). Exploratory research refers to activities intended to identify and define some phenomena, whereas descriptive research has the purpose of describing some phenomena (Hilton et al., 2020). As mentioned these are not the most robust research methods, although the methods can provide useful information regarding a police social work collaboration.

If the police social work collaboration has not yet been implemented it may be possible to collect pre-test and post-test data measuring collaboration outcomes. Among established collaborations data collection may only occur at one time point which is after police social work services have been provided. Quantitative outcomes are typically measured. One advantage of using quantitative outcomes is the ease with which they can be measured.

Qualitative outcomes, which are comprised of words instead of numbers, although not often measured, can provide valuable information. For example, asking an individual in what ways the police social work collaboration was helpful or not helpful for them and their situation. Because the responses will be varied identifying and summarizing the themes found among qualitative outcomes can be challenging.

Putting it all together

Putting all of the above concepts together can be summarized in several steps: (1) identify the social problem(s) that will be addressed; (2) identify the goal(s) of the collaboration; (3) identify the outcomes that will be measured; (4) implement the collaboration; and (5) collect and analyze the data that will be used to evaluate the collaboration. The collaboration data can be used for a variety of purposes, one of which is to modify and improve the collaboration, if needed, based on the data. Another use is to determine which days of the week and times the collaboration is most likely to be utilized.

Chapter summary

This chapter introduced a model for developing and implementing police social work collaborations. The model includes the following phases: (1) planning, (2) organizing, (3) listening, (4) implementation, (5) collecting data, and (6) evaluation. As this chapter has shown numerous important issues need to be considered before implementing a police social work collaboration. The type of social problem(s) that will be addressed, the goals of the collaboration, and obtaining funding and buy-in from stakeholders are among the most critical decisions. Once these decisions have been made the phases contained in the POLICE Model can be helpful for developing and implementing the collaboration. Although this chapter focused on police social work collaboration with law enforcement many communities are exploring the use of collaborations that do not include law enforcement.

Questions for discussion

1. Is it necessary to collect quantitative and qualitative data to evaluate a police social work collaboration? Identify some of the challenges associated with collecting these data.
2. In what ways is monitoring and evaluating a police social work collaboration consistent with the NASW Code of Ethics? Be sure to include the specific language contained in the NASW Code of Ethics in your answer.
3. What are your thoughts about using less robust research methods to develop, implement, and evaluate a police social work collaboration?

Activities for further learning

1. Locate a published description of a police social work or police and social work collaboration. Does the description include the collaboration outcomes? If not, what outcomes might be included in a list of possible outcomes based on the collaboration description?

2. Locate a published evaluation study of a police social work or police and social work collaboration. What type of research design did the author(s) use? Did the author(s) identify the reasons for choosing the research design?
3. Describe an approach you would use to chair a meeting with key stakeholders as part of the organizing phase of the POLICE Model. Prepare a script to invite key stakeholders.

References

Hilton, T. P., Fawson, P. R., Sullivan, T. J., & DeJong, C. R. (2020). *Applied social research: A tool for the human services* (10th ed.). New York: Springer Publishing Company, LLC.

National Association of Social Workers (2021). *Code of ethics of the National Association of Social Workers.* Washington, D.C.: National Association of Social Workers.

National Institute of Justice, Office of Justice Programs (2016). *Program profile: Lethality assessment program (Oklahoma).* Retrieved from https://crimesolutions.ojp.gov/ratedprograms/495

National Institute of Justice, Office of Justice Programs. (n.d.). *Glossary.* Retrieved from https://crimesolutions.ojp.gov/about/glossary#O

Sampson, R. (2007). *Domestic violence.* Problem-Oriented Guides for Police Problem-Specific Guides Series Guide No. 45. Washington, D.C.: U.S. Department of Justice, Office of Community Oriented Policing Services.

Treger, H. (1975). *The police-social work team: A new model for interprofessional cooperation: A university demonstration project in manpower training and development: Jane Addams School of Social Work, University of Illinois at Chicago Circle.* Springfield, IL: Charles C. Thomas Publisher.

7

CHILD MALTREATMENT

Chapter overview

As mandated reporters of child maltreatment both police officers and social workers are required to recognize and report such cases to child protective officials. Police officers can additionally criminally charge caretakers and others with endangering the welfare of a child or other offenses, whereas social workers do not have such authority. This chapter describes the role of law enforcement and social work in child welfare. The chapter acknowledges that police and social work collaborations are among the most common types of police and social work collaborations. Further, this chapter summarizes the differences between child abuse and neglect and identifies the unique knowledge and skills that police officers and social workers require when addressing child maltreatment.

Each state enacts statutes that define child abuse and neglect. The purpose of this chapter is not to cover all child maltreatment laws enacted in each state but rather to illustrate some of the important similarities and differences. The activities for further learning and questions for discussion located at the end of the chapter provide suggestions to search for information relevant to a particular state.

Introduction

Child maltreatment is one of the major social problems that are the focus of police and social work collaboration. A body of literature describes the benefits and challenges found among these collaborations, which are international in scope. Collaborations have been identified in numerous countries. Collaboration partners include social work and other partners such as child protective workers, health and mental health professionals, courts, and educators.

DOI: 10.4324/9781003132257-7

Multiple sources of data describe the size and scope of child maltreatment in the United States. These sources provide information about the rates of different types of child maltreatment and include the U.S. Department of Health and Human Services, Administration for Children Services, Centers for Disease Control and Prevention, National Center of Health Statistics, Office of the Assistant Secretary for Planning and Evaluation, and the Administration for Children and Families and Children's Bureau (Child Trends, 2019). The legal definition of child maltreatment is not uniform among states, although states define four types of child maltreatment: physical abuse, sexual abuse, neglect (i.e., educational neglect, medical neglect), and emotional maltreatment (Child Trends, 2019).

According to the most recent estimates, in 2017 approximately 674,000 substantiated cases of child maltreatment occurred in the United States, representing a rate of 9 children every 1,000 children. This figure represents a decline from previous years. Rates of child maltreatment were higher in previous years. To illustrate, between 1990 and 1994 cases of child maltreatment that were substantiated or indicated increased from 861,000 to 1,032,000, representing a rate of 15 children every 1,000 children. The rate began to decrease between 1994 and 1999 when child maltreatment cases decreased to 829,000, representing a rate of 15 children every 1,000 children (Child Trends, 2019).

Data also show the characteristics of children who were included among these child maltreatment cases. In 2017, more instances of child maltreatment occurred among younger children than older children, with children three years old and younger experiencing the highest instances of child maltreatment. American Indian, non-Hispanic black, and multi-race children experienced higher incidences of child maltreatment than children of other races and ethnicities (Child Trends, 2019).

Police officers and social workers are mandated to report suspected child maltreatment to child protective authorities. As mandated reporters both groups require training to identify and report child maltreatment and employ emergency interventions to protect the safety of children. Moreover, some types of child maltreatment are always a criminal offense and require that law enforcement file criminal charges against a parent(s), guardian(s), or individual(s) accused of maltreatment. Although social workers are mandated reporters they cannot file criminal charges against offenders. Only police officers can file any criminal charges against offenders.

Child maltreatment is one of the most common types of collaboration formed between police and social workers. Child welfare agencies that are authorized to investigate child maltreatment employ child protective workers, and these agencies have also formed collaborations with law enforcement. In most instances these child protective workers are not professional social workers.

Indeed, the protection of children is an area of social work practice in which social workers can make significant contributions such as participating in joint interviews to reduce the trauma of children recounting their experiences numerous times to both law enforcement for criminal prosecution and social workers for treatment needs. Clearly, law enforcement cannot provide the necessary treatment to address the long-term effects of child maltreatment. However, by immediately responding to and identifying cases of child maltreatment law enforcement can provide referrals to ensure that these services are provided in a timely manner. Ensuring that interventions are provided in a timely manner can begin the process of addressing the long terms effects of child maltreatment and ending the maltreatment. Collaborating with social workers and other service providers is a significant approach to achieving these objectives.

Child abuse and neglect defined

The legal definition of child maltreatment is not uniform among states, although states define four types of child maltreatment: physical abuse, sexual abuse, neglect (i.e., educational neglect, medical neglect), and emotional maltreatment (Child Trends, 2019). A definition of child abuse and neglect is necessary among police officers and social workers to identify what behaviors to report. As the following definitions demonstrate child maltreatment has serious consequences primarily focused on caregivers.

Child Welfare Information Gateway (2019) provides the federal definition of child abuse and neglect:

> Federal legislation lays the groundwork for State laws on child maltreatment by identifying a minimum set of actions or behaviors that define child abuse and neglect. The Federal Child Abuse Prevention and Treatment Act (CAPTA), as amended and reauthorized by the CAPTA Reauthorization Act of 2010, defines child abuse and neglect as, at a minimum, "any recent act or failure to act on the part of a parent or caretaker which results in death, serious physical or emotional harm, sexual abuse or exploitation (including sexual abuse as determined under section 111), or an act or failure to act which presents an imminent risk of serious harm."
>
> *42 U.S.C. 5101 note, § 3*

> Additionally, it stipulates that "a child shall be considered a victim of 'child abuse and neglect' and of 'sexual abuse' if the child is identified, by a State or local agency employee of the State or locality involved, as being a victim of sex trafficking (as defined in paragraph (10) of section 7102 of title 22) or a victim of severe forms of trafficking in persons described in paragraph (9)(A) of that section" (42 U.S.C. § 5106g(b)(2)). Most Federal and State child protection laws primarily refer to cases of harm to a child caused by parents or other caregivers; they generally do not include harm caused by other people, such as acquaintances or strangers. Some State laws also include a child's witnessing of domestic violence as a form of abuse or neglect.
>
> *Reprinted with permission* Child Welfare Information Gateway (2019). *What is child abuse and neglect? Recognizing the signs and symptoms.* Washington, D.C.: U.S. Department of Health and Human Services, Children's Bureau.

Types of child maltreatment

Child maltreatment is a general term used to describe child abuse and neglect. Distinct types of child abuse and neglect are defined in state legislation. Child Welfare Information Gateway (2019) identifies and defines the different types of child abuse and neglect as well as identifying a few of the differences among state definitions. These are described as follows:

> Within the minimum standards set by CAPTA, each State is responsible for providing its own definitions of child abuse and neglect. Most States recognize four major types of maltreatment: physical abuse, neglect, sexual abuse, and emotional abuse. Additionally, many States identify abandonment, parental substance use, and human trafficking as abuse or neglect. While some of these types of maltreatment may be found separately, they can occur in combination.

Physical abuse

> Physical abuse is a nonaccidental physical injury to a child caused by a parent, caregiver, or other person responsible for a child and can include punching, beating, kicking, biting, shaking, throwing, stabbing, choking, hitting (with a hand, stick, strap, or other object), burning, or otherwise causing physical harm.

Child neglect

> Neglect is the failure of a parent or other caregiver to provide for a child's basic needs. Neglect generally includes the following categories:

> - Physical (e.g., failure to provide necessary food or shelter, lack of appropriate supervision)
> - Medical (e.g., failure to provide necessary medical or mental health treatment, withholding medically indicated treatment from children with life-threatening conditions)
> - Educational (e.g., failure to educate a child or attend to special education needs)
> - Emotional (e.g., inattention to a child's emotional needs, failure to provide psychological care, permitting a child to use alcohol or other drugs)

Sexual abuse

> Sexual abuse includes activities by a parent or other caregiver such as fondling a child's genitals, penetration, incest, rape, sodomy, indecent exposure, and exploitation through prostitution or the production of pornographic

materials. Sexual abuse is defined by CAPTA as "the employment, use, persuasion, inducement, enticement, or coercion of any child to engage in, or assist any other person to engage in, any sexually explicit conduct or simulation of such conduct for the purpose of producing a visual depiction of such conduct; or the rape, and in cases of caretaker or interfamilial relationships, statutory rape, molestation, prostitution, or other form of sexual exploitation of children, or incest with children."

42 U.S.C. § 5106g(a)(4)

Emotional abuse

Emotional abuse (or psychological abuse) is a pattern of behavior that impairs a child's emotional development or sense of self-worth. This may include constant criticism, threats, or rejection as well as withholding love, support, or guidance. Emotional abuse is often difficult to prove, and, therefore, child protective services may not be able to intervene without evidence of harm or mental injury to the child (Prevent Child Abuse America, 2016).

Abandonment

Abandonment is considered in many States as a form of neglect. In general, a child is considered to be abandoned when the parent's identity or whereabouts are unknown, the child has been left alone in circumstances where the child suffers serious harm, the child has been deserted with no regard for his or her health or safety, or the parent has failed to maintain contact with the child or provide reasonable support for a specified period of time. Some States have enacted laws – often called safe haven laws – that provide safe places for parents to relinquish newborn infants. Information Gateway produced a publication as part of its State Statutes series that summarizes such laws.

Parental substance use

Parental substance use is included in the definition of child abuse or neglect in many States. Related circumstances that are considered abuse or neglect in some States include the following:

- Exposing a child to harm prenatally due to the mother's use of legal or illegal drugs or other substances
- Manufacturing methamphetamine in the presence of a child
- Selling, distributing, or giving illegal drugs or alcohol to a child
- Using a controlled substance that impairs the caregiver's ability to adequately care for the child.

Human trafficking

Human trafficking is considered a form of modern slavery and includes both sex trafficking and labor trafficking. Sex trafficking is recruiting, harboring, transporting, providing, or obtaining someone for a commercial sex act, such as prostitution, pornography, or stripping. Labor trafficking is forced labor, including drug dealing, begging, or working long hours for little pay (Child Welfare Information Gateway, 2018a). Although human trafficking includes victims of any sex, age, race/ethnicity, or socioeconomic status, children involved in child welfare, including children who are in out-of-home care, are especially vulnerable.

(2018) Reprinted with permission Child Welfare Information Gateway (2019). *What is child abuse and neglect? Recognizing the signs and symptoms.* Washington, D.C.: U.S. Department of Health and Human Services, Children's Bureau.

To illustrate the types of child maltreatment reported most often, in 2017 more instances of child neglect were reported than any other type. Seven children every 1,000 children were reported as victims of child neglect, whereas two children every 1,000 were reported for physical abuse, one child every 1,000 children was reported for sexual abuse, and one child every 1,000 children was reported as a victim of emotional abuse (Child Trends, 2019).

As Table 7.1 further illustrates, child neglect was the most often reported type of child maltreatment in both 1990 and 2017. While reported instances of sexual abuse and physical abuse decreased in 2017 compared to 1990, reports of child neglect increased from 49% in 1990 to 75% in 2017 (Child Trends, 2019).

Substantiated and indicated child maltreatment cases

Because an instance of child maltreatment victimization is reported to child protective authorities does not mean that sufficient evidence exists to support victimization. As mentioned, mandated reporters are required to report any of the above types of child maltreatment. However, child protective authorities after investigating these reports may find insufficient evidence to support child maltreatment. In general, child maltreatment reports are either substantiated or indicated by child protective authorities. "Substantiated cases are those in which an allegation of maltreatment or risk of maltreatment was supported or founded according to state law or policy. Indicated cases are those in which an allegation of maltreatment or risk of maltreatment could not be substantiated, but there was reason to suspect maltreatment or the risk of maltreatment" (Child Trends, 2019).

TABLE 7.1 Percentage of reported child maltreatment by type in 1990 and 2017

Year	Child neglect	Sexual abuse	Physical abuse
1990	49%	17%	27%
2017	75%	9%	18%

While states identify and define different types of child abuse and neglect, different terminology is also used among states to describe substantiated and indicated child maltreatment cases. Terms used among states to identify substantiated cases include "unfounded," "not indicated," or "unconfirmed." Terms used to identify indicated cases include "founded" and "confirmed" (Child Welfare Information Gateway, 2018b).

Domestic violence and child maltreatment

All states do not recognize incidents when children witness domestic violence as child abuse or neglect (Child Welfare Information Gateway, 2019). Suggesting that children who witness domestic violence are at risk for child maltreatment, Norman (2000) acknowledged that some states do not define children who witness domestic violence as child maltreatment, and child protective services may not investigate such cases unless the child has been injured. Norman urges for more collaboration and collaborative training to address these issues.

The role of law enforcement in response to child maltreatment

The role of law enforcement in child maltreatment involves responding to, intervening including mandated reporting, and investigating instances of child maltreatment. Clearly, based on the definitions and types of child abuse and neglect identified by Child Welfare Information Gateway (2019), a law enforcement response to child abuse and neglect is essential because some types are illegal and violate state and federal statutes. Child maltreatment also requires further criminal justice system involvement from the courts and corrections components.

Child maltreatment training provided to police officers tends to have a minimal focus on the stages of child development and child issues. The training is dominated by the criminal types of child sexual abuse with less training time allotted to other forms of child maltreatment such as physical abuse and neglect, which may not be a crime. These other forms are also among the often reported types of child maltreatment (Portwood, Grady, & Dutton, 2000). Regardless of whether the type of child maltreatment is a crime law enforcement is mandated to report all types of child maltreatment defined in their jurisdiction to child protective officials. Police recruits receive this training prior to becoming a sworn police officer (Patterson, 2007).

Endangering the welfare of a child and child endangerment

Law enforcement officers can file charges against an individual suspected of child maltreatment. These charges are classified by different terms among different states and are articulated in state statutes. For example, in California the one term used for a child maltreatment criminal charge is child endangerment. It is defined in California Penal Code 273a – Child Endangerment Law. Because this legislation refers only to a criminal charge of child endangerment it is different from California Penal Code 273d, which defines child abuse (Shouse Law Group, A.P.C., 2021). Another example is found in New York State law, which defines one type of child maltreatment criminal charge as endangering the welfare of a child. This charge is defined in New York Penal Law 260.10 and is classified as a Class A misdemeanor (New York State Senate, n.d.).

Office of juvenile justice and delinquency prevention

The Office of Juvenile Justice and Delinquency Prevention (OJJDP) (2020) reports that between 2017 and 2019 approximately $195 million dollars were provided to federal, state, and tribal law enforcement agencies as well as agencies that prosecute cases of child maltreatment that involve missing, abducted, and exploited children. During each of these years the funding provided to law enforcement increased over the previous year. OJJDP described three programs that support the role of law enforcement in child maltreatment. These programs include the following.

The National Center for Missing & Exploited Children

The National Center for Missing & Exploited Children maintains resources to assist law enforcement with responding to situations that involve missing and exploited children. These resources include a 24-hour missing children hotline, the Child Victim Identification Program that assists law enforcement with identifying children who appear in pornography, and Team Adam, which provides an emergency response to assist law enforcement with helping families.

The AMBER Alert Program

The AMBER Alert Program is activated after law enforcement has found that a child has been abducted and is in a dangerous situation. The program publically disseminates information about the abduction through cell phones, billboard signs, media, and other means.

The Internet Crimes Against Children Program

The Internet Crimes Against Children Program is a coalition of 61 distinct task forces formed among law enforcement and agencies that prosecute exploitation of children on the internet. The task forces are responsible for investigating and arresting offenders.

Police social work collaboration in response to child maltreatment

The following case example offers the benefits of police social work collaboration. It illustrates how a police social worker can assist law enforcement with a child maltreatment situation in response to children left home alone. Police social workers can provide an immediate response to the scene, report the child maltreatment to child protective services, facilitate the emergency placement of the children, and provide transportation.

Case Example

Police Social Work Response to Child Maltreatment Involving Unsupervised Children

A neighbor contacted 911 after noticing that three children across the street appeared to be at home unsupervised. A police officer first visited the home of the three children and interviewed the children to determine how long they had been left alone without parental supervision. The police officer determined from the children that their ages were 7, 5, and 2 years old, and they had been home alone for several hours. Next, the police officer spoke with the neighbor who called 911 and several other neighbors to obtain additional information that might be useful for locating the parent.

The children did not have a phone number to contact their father and told the officer that he had gone to the store several hours ago. They stated this was not the first time their father left them home alone. The 7 year old told the officer he is watching his two brothers and that he has watched them previously while their father was away.

While the officer was conducting the investigation the father returned. By this time the officer had already contacted the police social worker for assistance with placing the children in an emergency placement. Both the police officer and the police social worker are mandated reporters, so either one could report this incident to child protection authorities. It was determined that the police social worker would report this incident.

The police social worker coordinated with the after-hours child protection hotline worker to seek an emergency out-of-home placement for the three children. The emergency out-of-home placement consisted of temporary placement with a relative. Child protection services planned to follow up with a home visit with the mother, relatives, and children the following morning. The police social worker transported the three children to the relative's home and conducted an assessment in the home. The police social worker also facilitated contact by telephone between the after-hours child protection worker and the family's relative.

In some jurisdictions officially recognized child maltreatment collaborations between police and social workers do not exist. Consequently, police and social workers conduct independent investigations, may obtain different information, and have independent contacts with children and families. Child protective services may also not allow workers to share information with law enforcement. In these instances police officers and social workers have established informal collaborations (Cross, Finkelhor, & Ormrod, 2005).

Six goals of collaborations formed between police and social workers in response to child maltreatment have been identified: (1) to reduce the need for medical examinations where appropriate, (2) to enhance assessments and evidence that can be used for court proceedings and case planning, (3) to utilize a trauma-informed approach that recognizes the trauma experienced by children and families, (4) to reduce the need to conduct multiple interviews in which children and families are required to give an account of the abuse, (5) to improve collaboration and information sharing between law enforcement, social work, and child protective workers with the goal of enhancing services and interventions provided to children and families, and (6) to clarify the unique roles among law enforcement, social work, and child protective workers (Findlay, 1991).

Police officers and social workers also collaborate to interview and investigate child sexual abuse victims, which are videotaped (Fielding & Conroy, 1992). Police officers and social workers conduct these collaborative interviews and investigations with child sexual abuse victims utilizing approaches that are consistent with law enforcement and social work training (Cheung, 1997).

Police officers, social workers and child protection workers respond to child sexual abuse cases and provide services to child victims (Cheung & Boutte-Queen, 2000; Kelley, 1990). However, police officers and social workers do not report the same attitudes toward child sexual abuse (Trute, Adkins, & MacDonald, 1992), and attitudes can affect the provision of services and interventions (Vairo, 2010). Because these dissimilar attitudes can affect collaboration it is important to recognize these differences.

Waterhouse and Carnie (1991) found that police officers had more law enforcement experience than social workers had professional practice experience, and 90% of police officers had experience conducting child sexual abuse investigations, whereas 45% of social workers had investigating experience. Among social workers, 55% were conducting their first sexual abuse interview investigation. Social workers viewed their role as assessing risks and identifying instances of sexual abuse, whereas police officers viewed their role as collecting evidence, arresting the offender, and preparing documents for court proceedings. Challenges affecting the collaboration included police officers' concerns that social work interventions negatively affect the evidence obtained during investigative interviews, information obtained during an investigation not being shared in a timely manner, role conflict associated with investigating a criminal offense and conducting a risk assessment, and lack of experience.

However, collaborating can also provide positive experiences for police officers and social workers. Conte, Berliner, and Nolan (1980) reported that police officers increased their understanding of the interventions social workers provide to children and families, and social workers gained an increased understanding of the role of law enforcement in sexual abuse cases.

Indeed, when police officers and social workers collaborate on child maltreatment cases the differences in their roles come into view. Garrett (2004) interviewed police officers and social workers to examine their views toward their roles in child maltreatment collaborations. Police officers viewed the law enforcement agency as the primary agency conducting the investigation. Social workers perceived that they assumed more of a law enforcement perspective as opposed to a social work perspective in their approach to their work with children and families. These perceptions highlight the different expectations, values, behaviors, and conflicts that can arise when police officers and social workers partner in child maltreatment collaborations. Additionally, less than optimal communication, training, and decision-making among police officers and social workers can negatively affect collaboration functioning (Lardner, 1992).

Child protective services

A police social worker, as an employee of a law enforcement agency, is different from a child protective worker who is an employee of a state or county child protective services agency. Child protective services agencies are either operated by a state, county, or a combination of state and county oversight. The 2001 National Study of Child Protective Services Systems and Reform Efforts identifies the differences found among state- and county-operated agencies (Child Welfare Information Gateway, 2018c). Among other tasks, these agencies operate a hotline for reporting child maltreatment, receive and investigate child maltreatment cases, and provide interventions. As mandated reporters police officers and social workers report suspected instances of child maltreatment to child protective services agencies.

Similar to the challenges that arise when police officers and social workers collaborate, these challenges have also been observed when police officers and child protective workers collaborate. Some of the challenges to collaboration include the different tasks and functions between law enforcement and child protective workers, holding different world views, and length and depth of prior training and experience responding to child maltreatment cases including utilization of approaches to child maltreatment investigations. These are organizational factors that can be resolved by implementing policies to address these differences (Cross et al., 2005).

Child and family treatment agencies

Child and family treatment agencies provide a variety of services to children and families to meet their needs in response to child maltreatment, adoption, foster care, and other family situations. Services offered include parenting skills training, family counseling, child care, preventive services, and residential services, among many others. Police officers, police social workers, and social workers employed in these settings may have collaborative involvement to meet the needs of children and families. Consequently, they should be familiar with the types of agencies and services provided as well as each other's roles.

POLICE Model application

As this chapter has shown organizational differences between law enforcement and child protective workers arise when collaborating on child maltreatment cases. Because these organizational differences can be resolved through implementing policies intended to address them (Cross et al., 2005), phases of the POLICE Model can be useful in this regard. Professional differences can also arise when law enforcement, police social workers, and professional social workers collaborate on child maltreatment cases. The organizing phase emphasized the ability to understand organizational culture and organize different agencies for joint meetings. The listening phase emphasized the use of active listening. These phases can be useful for policy development. Further, the evaluation phase includes social workers' ethical obligation to monitor and evaluate policies. Thus, it is inadequate to only develop and implement collaboration policies; they must also be evaluated.

Chapter summary

Child maltreatment was identified as one of the most common types of collaboration formed between police and social workers. As mandated reporters both police officers and social workers are required to identify and report child maltreatment to child protection authorities. Such reporting requires knowledge and skills regarding what types of behaviors to report. This chapter identified and described the federal definition and types of child maltreatment to illustrate the knowledge needed. The roles of law enforcement, child protection workers, and social workers were also examined.

Questions for discussion

1. State why some incidents of child abuse and neglect (such as child sexual abuse, trafficking, and abduction) are always a crime, whereas other types of incidents are not always a crime.
2. What are the major differences between child abuse and child neglect?
3. What are the differences and similarities between the roles of law enforcement and social work in response to child maltreatment?

Activities for further learning

1. Given that each state defines child maltreatment differently locate and identify how your state defines the various types of child maltreatment discussed in this chapter.
2. Locate your local child abuse reporting hotline contact information. Summarize the protocols for using the hotline to report cases of child maltreatment.
3. Prepare a script that you could use at the beginning of your work with clients to inform them that as a social worker you are a mandated reporter and that confidentiality cannot be maintained in instances of child maltreatment.

References

Cheung, K. F. M. (1997). Developing the interview protocol for video-recorded child sexual abuse investigations: A training experience with police officers, social workers, and clinical psychologists in Hong Kong. *Child Abuse & Neglect, 21*(3), 273–284.

Cheung, M., & Boutte-Queen, N. M. (2000). Emotional responses to child sexual abuse: A comparison between police and social workers in Hong Kong. *Child Abuse & Neglect, 24*(12), 1613–1621.

Child Trends (2019). *Child maltreatment.* Retrieved from https://www.childtrends.org/indicators/child-maltreatment

Child Welfare Information Gateway (2018a). *Human trafficking: Protecting our youth.* Retrieved from https://www.childwelfare.gov/pubPDFs/trafficking_ts_2018.pdf

Child Welfare Information Gateway (2018b). *Review and expunction of central registries and reporting records.* Washington, D.C.: U.S. Department of Health and Human Services, Children's Bureau. Retrieved from https://www.childwelfare.gov/pubPDFs/registry.pdf

Child Welfare Information Gateway (2018c). *State vs. county administration of child welfare services.* Washington, D.C.: U.S. Department of Health and Human Services, Children's Bureau.

Child Welfare Information Gateway (2019). *What is child abuse and neglect? Recognizing the signs and symptoms.* Washington, D.C.: U.S. Department of Health and Human Services, Children's Bureau.

Conte, J. R., Berliner, L., & Nolan, D. (1980). Police and social worker cooperation: A key in child sexual assault cases. *FBI Law Enforcement Bulletin, 49,* 7–10.

Cross, T. P., Finkelhor, D., & Ormrod, R. (2005). Police involvement in child protective services investigations: Literature review and secondary data analysis. *Child Maltreatment, 10*(3), 224–244.

Fielding, N. G., & Conroy, S. (1992). Interviewing child victims: Police and social work investigations of child sexual abuse. *Sociology, 26*(1), 103–124.

Findlay, C. (1991). Joint police and social work investigations in child abuse: A practice example from Central Scotland. *Children & Society, 5*(3), 225–231.

Garrett, P. M. (2004). Talking child protection: The police and social workers "working together." *Journal of Social Work, 4*(1), 77–97.

Kelley, S. J. (1990). Responsibility and management strategies in child sexual abuse: A comparison of child protective workers, nurses, and police officers. *Child Welfare* (LXIX, 1), 43–51.

Lardner, R. (1992). Factors affecting police/social work inter-agency co-operation in a child protection unit. *The Police Journal*, *65*(3), 213–228.

New York State Senate (n.d.). *Section 260.10 endangering the welfare of a child.* Retrieved from https://www.nysenate.gov/legislation/laws/PEN/260.10

Norman, J. (2000). Should children's protective services intervene when children witness domestic violence?. *Trauma, Violence, & Abuse*, *1*(3), 291–293.

Office of Juvenile Justice and Delinquency Prevention (OJJDP) (2020). *Child protection: Law enforcement – in-focus-law-enforcement.* Retrieved from https://ojjdp.ojp.gov/publications/in-focus-law-enforcement.pdf

Patterson, G. T. (2007). An exploratory study assessing the effects of demographic characteristics on attitudes toward child abuse and neglect among police recruits. *Psychological Reports*, *101*, 451–456.

Portwood, S. G., Grady, M. T., & Dutton, S. E. (2000). Enhancing law enforcement identification and investigation of child maltreatment. *Child Abuse & Neglect*, *24*(2), 195–207.

Prevent Child Abuse America (2016). *Fact sheet: Emotional child abuse.* Retrieved from http://www.preventchildabuse.org/images/docs/emtionalchildabuse.pdf

Shouse Law Group, A.P.C. (2021). *Penal Code 273a PC – Child Endangerment – California.* Retrieved from https://www.shouselaw.com/ca/defense/penal-code/273a/

Trute, B., Adkins, E., & MacDonald, G. (1992). Professional attitudes regarding the sexual abuse of children: Comparing police, child welfare and community mental health. *Child Abuse & Neglect*, *16*(3), 359–368.

Vairo, E. (2010). Social worker attitudes toward court-mandated substance-abusing clients. *Journal of Social Work Practice in the Addictions*, *10*(1), 81–98.

Waterhouse, L., & Carnie, J. (1991). Research note social work and police response to child sexual abuse in Scotland. *The British Journal of Social Work*, *21*(4), 373-379.

8

DOMESTIC VIOLENCE

Chapter overview

Often considered the most dangerous types of police calls for service, domestic violence is a social problem requiring a law enforcement response that includes both the law enforcement function and the service law enforcement function. The law enforcement function is necessary due to mandatory or pro-arrest law enforcement policies and procedures that include the arrest of offenders, and the service law enforcement function is necessary to provide support and interventions focused on safety for victims. The focus of this chapter is police social work and police and social service collaboration and the role of law enforcement in domestic violence victimization. This chapter also examines the collaboration that occurs between social service workers and social workers employed in domestic violence shelters and victim assistance programs. The various types of domestic violence incidents that result in law enforcement contact are also reviewed.

This chapter summarizes information that shows no uniform definition of domestic violence exists among the 50 states. As such, the purpose of reviewing this material is not to examine definitions within each state but rather to illustrate that law enforcement and law enforcement collaboration tasks while similar also vary among states. The questions for discussion and activities for further learning located at the end of this chapter include suggestions to search for information relevant to a specific state.

Introduction

In the United States, between 2006 and 2015 an average of 1.3 million incidents of non-fatal domestic violence occurred in each of these years. Non-fatal domestic violence incidents include violence that is classified as serious such as rape

DOI: 10.4324/9781003132257-8

or sexual assault, robbery, and aggravated assault, as well as simple assault. The offender was identified as an intimate partner, an immediate family member, or a relative. Among these 1.3 million annual victimizations approximately 56% were reported to law enforcement. When police officers responded to the scene a police report was written in 78% of these instances. Further, among the victimizations reported to law enforcement a criminal complaint was signed among 48% of these incidents, and either charges were filed against the offender or the offender was arrested in 39% of these instances either at the scene or when police officers provided follow-up interventions. The offender was arrested at the scene in 23% of these domestic violence incidents. Finally, when victims were seriously physically injured and signed a criminal complaint either the offender was arrested or criminal charges were filed in 89% of these instances (Reaves, 2017).

In general, these findings suggest that a law enforcement response does not always result in an arrest or criminal charges being filed against the offender. The above statistics illustrate the significant role of law enforcement in responding to domestic violence. But then again these statistics also suggest that between 2006 and 2015 of the approximately 1.3 million victimizations that occurred law enforcement was not contacted in 44% of these instances.

Reaves (2017) reports the statistics describing the number of incidents of domestic violence victimizations were obtained from the National Crime Victimization Survey (NCVS), which is a voluntary self-report questionnaire. Therefore victims completed the NCVS, which asked if an individual experienced criminal victimization, reported the crime to law enforcement, provided the reasons for reporting or not reporting, and described the characteristics of the crime and offender and their experiences with law enforcement and the criminal justice system.

It is important to note that these statistics do not include the number of fatal domestic violence incidents. Further, all victims of domestic violence did not contact law enforcement when a domestic violence incident occurred. These statistics provide important implications for both law enforcement and victim service providers. For example, without a criminal police report a victim of domestic violence cannot receive state compensation. However, without having a criminal police report the victim can still request an order of protection in some states.

A note about terminology

The term *domestic violence* continues to be the used term among police officers and in law enforcement agencies (Sampson, 2007). Further, the term domestic violence refers to "… any violence between intimate partners …" (Kelley & Johnson, 2008, p. 478), and Kelley and Johnson indicate the term has generally been used among victim advocates to refer to the violence that occurs when males commit violence against women. The term *gendered violence* has been used to refer to crimes such as domestic and sexual violence and child sexual assault, in which the majority of offenders are male and the majority of victims are female (Miller, Hefner, & Iovanni, 2020).

In a review of terms used throughout numerous states, Child Welfare Information Gateway (2018) found that commonly used terms were: "domestic assault," "domestic battery," "domestic abuse," or "assault against a family or household member" (p. 3). Among law enforcement and criminal justice practices and procedures and federal data collection the term domestic violence is often used. As a case in point, the title of Reaves' (2017) special report is *Police response to domestic violence, 2006–2015*. Throughout this chapter and the book, the terms domestic violence, intimate partner violence, and interpersonal violence are used interchangeably.

Definitions of domestic violence

The definition of domestic violence varies depending on the context in which the term is used. A clinical or behavioral definition is "a pattern of assaultive and/or coercive behaviors, including physical, sexual, and psychological attacks, as well as economic coercion, that adults or adolescents use against their intimate partners" (Schechter & Edelson, 1999).

> The U.S. Department of Justice defines domestic violence as "A pattern of abusive behavior in any relationship that is used by one partner to gain or maintain power and control over another intimate partner. Domestic violence can be physical, sexual, emotional, economic, or psychological actions or threats of actions that influence another person. This includes any behaviors that intimidate, manipulate, humiliate, isolate, frighten, terrorize, coerce, threaten, blame, hurt, injure, or wound someone."
>
> *Office of Violence Against Women, U.S. Department of Justice (2017)*

It stands to reason that if the term domestic violence includes a clinical definition it should also include a legal definition used to identify law violations. "In criminal laws, domestic violence may be defined as 'any criminal offense involving violence or physical harm or threat of violence or physical harm' committed by one family or household member against another" (Child Welfare Information Gateway, 2018, p. 3).

The definition of domestic violence varies among states based on state statutes. State statutes include (1) civil laws, (2) child abuse and reporting and child protection laws, (3) criminal laws, and (4) an identification of individuals who are included in state definitions. The following two examples representative of California and Florida illustrate how state statutes vary among states.

California
Current Through August 2017

Defined in Domestic Violence Civil Laws Citation: Fam. Code §§ 6203; 6320

For purposes of this act, 'abuse' means any of the following:

- Intentionally or recklessly causing or attempting to cause bodily injury
- Sexual assault
- Placing a person in reasonable apprehension of imminent serious bodily injury to that person or to another
- Engaging in any behavior that has been or could be enjoined pursuant to § 6320

Abuse is not limited to the actual infliction of physical injury or assault. The court may issue an ex parte order enjoining a party from molesting; attacking; striking; stalking; threatening; sexually assaulting; battering; harassing; telephoning, including, but not limited to, making annoying telephone calls as described in § 653m of the Penal Code; destroying personal property; contacting, either directly or indirectly, by mail or otherwise; coming within a specified distance of; or disturbing the peace of the other party; and, in the discretion of the court, on a showing of good cause, of other named family or household members.

Defined in Child Abuse Reporting and Child Protection Laws

This issue is not addressed in the statutes reviewed.

Defined in Criminal Laws Citation: Penal Code § 273.5

Any person who willfully inflicts corporal injury resulting in a traumatic condition upon a victim described in the section below is guilty of a felony.

As used in this section, the term 'traumatic condition' means a condition of the body, such as a wound or external or internal injury, including, but not limited to, injury as a result of strangulation or suffocation, whether of a minor or serious nature, caused by a physical force. For purposes of this section, 'strangulation' and 'suffocation' include impeding the normal breathing or circulation of the blood of a person by applying pressure on the throat or neck.

Persons Included in the Definitions Citation: Fam. Code § 6211; Penal Code § 273.5

In civil law: 'Domestic violence' is abuse perpetrated against any of the following persons:

- A spouse or former spouse
- A cohabitant or former cohabitant, as defined in § 6209
- A person with whom the respondent is having or has had a dating or engagement relationship

- A person with whom the respondent has had a child, where the presumption applies that the male parent is the father of the child of the female parent under the Uniform Parentage Act
- A child of a party or a child who is the subject of an action under the Uniform Parentage Act, where the presumption applies that the male parent is the father of the child to be protected
- Any other person related by consanguinity or affinity within the second degree

In criminal law: Section 273.5(a) shall apply if the victim is or was one or more of the following:
- The offender's spouse or former spouse
- The offender's cohabitant or former cohabitant
- The person to whom the offender is engaged or someone with whom the offender has, or previously had, an engagement or dating relationship
- The mother or father of the offender's child

Holding oneself out to be the spouse of the person with whom one is cohabiting is not necessary to constitute cohabitation as the term is used in this section.

Reprinted with permission Child Welfare Information Gateway (2018). *Definitions of domestic violence.* Washington, D.C.: U.S. Department of Health and Human Services, Children's Bureau.

The California state statutes are now compared and contrasted by describing the statutes enacted in Florida. Notice that the four Headings are the same whereas the content contained in each heading explaining the state definitions are different.

Florida
Current Through August 2017

Defined in Domestic Violence Civil Laws Citation: Ann. Stat. § 741.28

'Domestic violence' means any assault, aggravated assault, battery, aggravated battery, sexual assault, sexual battery, stalking, aggravated stalking, kidnapping, false imprisonment, or any criminal offense resulting in physical injury or death of one family or household member by another family or household member.

Defined in Child Abuse Reporting and Child Protection Laws
This issue is not addressed in the statutes reviewed.

Defined in Criminal Laws
This issue is not addressed in the statutes reviewed.

Persons Included in the Definitions Citation: Ann. Stat. § 741.28
'Family or household member' means the following:

- Spouses or former spouses
- Persons related by blood or marriage
- Persons who are presently residing together as if a family or who have resided together in the past as if a family
- Persons who are parents of a child in common regardless of whether they have been married
- With the exception of persons who have a child in common, the family or household members must be currently residing or have in the past resided together in the same single dwelling unit.

Reprinted with permission Child Welfare Information Gateway (2018). *Definitions of domestic violence.* Washington, D.C.: U.S. Department of Health and Human Services, Children's Bureau.

To point out one major difference when comparing and contrasting the statutes enacted in California with those enacted in Florida, while both states do not have legislation that defines domestic violence in child abuse reporting and child protection laws, California defines a "traumatic condition" injury in criminal law whereas in Florida no definition exists in criminal law.

Types of domestic violence

As we have reviewed, uniform terms are not used to refer to domestic violence. Similarly, uniform definitions are not used among states to identify domestic violence. Although the characteristics and types of domestic violence are well documented definitions vary based on how the term is being used.

Several conceptualizations of domestic violence exist. For instance, Kelly and Johnson (2008) identified four types of domestic violence: (1) *Coercive Controlling Violence* is characterized by coercion and control, emotional abuse, and physical violence perpetrated by one partner toward another. This is the most common of the four types observed in law enforcement; (2) *Situational Couple Violence* refers to violence among partners that is not characterized by power and control; (3) *Violent Resistance* refers to situations in which victims and survivors, both males and females, use violence themselves to end the violence perpetrated against them by a partner; and (4) *Separation-Investigated Violence* occurs in the absence of a history of abuse or violence or coercive control. This type of violence typically follows a separation such as a divorce.

Although Kelly and Johnson (2008) identified coercive controlling violence as the most common form of domestic violence that comes to the attention of law enforcement it is important to keep in mind that the other types of domestic violence also come to the attention of law enforcement. The other types of domestic violence; situational couple violence, violent resistance, and separation-investigated violence are also subject to mandatory arrest and other law enforcement policies. Victims of these types of domestic violence also require victim services.

Case Example

Parent and Child Relationship as Domestic Violence

Mrs. R, the 43-year-old mother of Samantha, dialed 911, stating that she had a verbal and physical argument with her 21-year-old daughter. During the argument her daughter punched her in the head, although she was not injured. The argument began when Mrs. R told Samantha that she would no longer tolerate her not doing her chores, not contributing to household expenses, and causing an increase in electric and food bills. She has been unhappy with these living arrangements for some time and today decided to confront her daughter.

Mrs. R told the officer when she provided suggestions to Samantha about contributing to the household expenses the discussion escalated and became an argument. Samantha left the home before police arrived, and therefore she was not arrested. Only Mrs. R was interviewed by police. Mrs. R was given a Domestic Incident Report (DIR) documenting the criminal charge of harassment. The report also documented the allegations, and Mrs. R was encouraged to obtain a warrant for Samantha's arrest. She was also given documentation describing the role of law enforcement, the courts, and information summarizing state laws pertaining to domestic violence. The documentation included telephone and online resources for victims. State law mandated police officers to give the documentation to victims.

Finally, Mrs. R was given the contact information of a victim service provider. Because Mrs. R was the victim of a crime the criminal police report was forwarded to the victim service unit, which is embedded in the law enforcement agency as a specialty unit and staffed with civilian employees.

As this case example illustrates incidents of domestic violence that occur between parents and their children are also categorized as domestic violence. Even among these situations victims are encouraged to seek a warrant for the arrest of their child. Consequently, law enforcement officers also respond to situations in which domestic violence is not always perpetrated by an offending partner in an intimate partner relationship.

The law enforcement function (i.e., making an arrest or investigating a domestic violence offender) was not applicable in this case example. However, the service law enforcement function includes a wide variety of interventions such as the provision of information and referrals was applicable.

The role of law enforcement in response to domestic violence

Domestic violence police calls for service are common in law enforcement (Sampson, 2007). These calls for service are also among the most challenging calls for police officers, even in the absence of violent behavior. Three explanations summarize police officers' attitudes toward domestic violence calls.

First, officers are concerned about their safety since the possibility for physical intervention may exist. Second, officers are concerned about the length of time required to provide interventions during domestic violence calls. Third, officers perceive that the interventions provided to both victims of domestic violence and offenders may not be effective and result in future violence or future calls for police service (Reuland, Morabito, Preston, & Cheney, 2006).

In general, the goal of a law enforcement response to domestic violence is to enhance the safety of the victim and encourage a victim to contact law enforcement in the future should another domestic violence incident occur, to provide a prompt response to the scene, and to reduce future incidents of domestic violence and police calls for service (Reuland, Morabito, Preston, & Cheney, 2006). The role of law enforcement in response to domestic violence also involves both the law enforcement function (i.e., investigating and arresting offenders, enforcing orders of protection) and the service law enforcement function (i.e., providing information and interventions to victims).

Levens and Dutton (1980) identified the following process for a law enforcement response to domestic violence. First, 911 is called and the 911 operator screens the call to determine if a police officer should be dispatched to the scene. Either a police officer is dispatched to the scene or the 911 operator makes a determination that a police officer is not needed in this instance. If an officer is not needed and therefore not dispatched to the scene the 911 operator provides information, and a referral if necessary. Second, if a police officer is dispatched to the scene the law enforcement interventions options provided include (a) documenting the call as unfounded, (b) providing mediation, (c) utilizing a collaboration partner, (d) providing a referral to a social service agency, (e) providing crisis intervention, and/ or (f) arresting the offender. When referrals are provided to either a social service agency, the court system, or a collaboration partner the police officer subsequently receives feedback information related to the outcome of the referral.

When domestic violence victimization occurs the 911 call is not always made by someone at the scene such as the victim, offender, or another individual. In some instances neighbors or witnesses call 911. For example, witnesses may have overhead a loud disagreement and call 911. Furthermore, in some instances when police are called to an incident of domestic violence victimization physical violence may not have occurred, whereas in other instances violence may have occurred with physical injuries or a fatality. Although these incidents also receive a law enforcement response in the absence of evidence that physical violence has occurred or that a law has been violated, police officers may be limited to interventions such as providing referrals. The following case example exemplifies these instances.

Case Example

A Neighbor Calls 911

Neighbors living in an apartment building heard shouting coming from next door between a couple which appeared to be escalating. The neighbors could not see the dispute but clearly heard shouting and called 911. Two police officers arrived at the apartment, where the shouting was heard since the neighbors knew the apartment number.

After speaking with the couple the police officers learned that the couple did not have a history of domestic violence and were having a loud dispute over an unpaid bill. They were surprised to see two police officers at their door. After learning more about this incident the police officers asked the couple if they were willing to speak with a police social worker. The couple agreed and accepted the referral.

When seen by the police social worker the couple stated they did not feel the need for ongoing relationship counseling but were interested in exploring options to address the unpaid bill with the assistance of the police social worker. Mediation was provided with each partner speaking one at a time and proposing their solutions to the unpaid bill. The police social worker reframed each proposal until the couple agreed upon two proposals they planned to use. They were appreciative of the assistance provided by the police department, although still dismayed that a neighbor called 911.

The New York State Division of Criminal Justice Services (DCJS) website publicly provides information about the role of law enforcement in New York State in response to domestic violence incidents. The online materials also make available information about the role of family court and criminal court in response to interpersonal violence. This information is contained in the New York State Standardized Domestic Incident Report (DIR). The information is required to be given to a victim at the scene of a domestic violence incident. For example, domestic violence victims are provided with a description of six tasks associated with the role of law enforcement:

1. to provide safety interventions
2. to provide information about the role of criminal and family courts
3. to provide medical interventions for victims and children
4. to provide assistance with securing personal items from the victim's residence
5. to provide the victim with a copy of the police report
6. to inform victims a criminal complaint can be filed against the offender in criminal court (New York State Division of Criminal Justice Services, 2020). For a victim, obtaining a copy of a criminal police report is necessary to apply for and receive services from State victim services such as compensation. These services are discussed in greater detail in Chapter 9.

Additional information contained in the DIR includes contact information for the New York State 24 Hour Domestic and Sexual Violence Hotline, the Victim Information and Notification Everyday (VINE), and the Statewide Automated Victim Information and Notification (SAVIN-NY). The DIR contains guidance for police officers with instructions for completing the DIR. Police officers are prompted to conduct private interviews with victims of domestic violence alone, if possible, provide victims with a copy of the Victim Rights Notice and a copy of the DIR. Finally, the DIR also includes suggested phrases for police officers to use when assessing previous domestic violence victimization and perceptions of the victim's safety and offering the victim assistance with safety planning and other interventions. Police officers are instructed that they are not mandated to arrest each individual when dual complaints are made. Officers are required to identify the primary aggressor. Any conclusions made about whether a victim will appear in court and cooperate with court proceedings cannot provide a basis for arresting the offender (New York State Division of Criminal Justice Services, 2020).

Because law enforcement plays such a prominent role in responding to incidents of domestic violence victimization it is imperative that police officers not only receive training that provides skills to intervene but also includes knowledge about the dynamics of domestic violence. Perhaps the most well-known model used to understand domestic violence is the Power and Control Wheel. This model places the concepts of power and control at the center of physical and sexual violence and also includes economic and physical abuse. The type of behaviors observed in these relationships include inappropriately using children such as threatening to seek custody of the children; coercion and threatening behaviors; minimizing, denying, and blaming; and isolation, intimidation, and exploiting male privilege by assuming all head of household responsibilities (Pence & Paymar, 1993).

As discussed in Chapter 5, between 2011 and 2013, 664 state and local law enforcement academies provided basic training to approximately 45,000 police recruits during each of these years. The total recruit training consisted of approximately 840 hours or 21 weeks of training time. The average number of hours devoted to domestic violence was 13 hours (Reaves, 2016).

Unquestionably, specialized training that includes knowledge and skills required to provide law enforcement interventions during a response to domestic violence is needed. Law enforcement collaborations with police social workers, professional social workers, and social service workers can also be useful in this regard. One example of a specialized skill involves conducting a risk assessment to assess the level of risk for future domestic violence victimization.

Risk assessment

A complete discussion of the validity, reliability, and use of standardized risk assessment instruments in law enforcement and social work practice is beyond the scope of this book. Similarly, the administration procedures, scoring, and interpretation scores for these instruments are also beyond the scope of this book. Standardized risk assessment instruments should demonstrate robust validity and reliability in order to have confidence in the results that are obtained when the instrument is administered.

Validity refers to whether a standardized risk assessment instrument can "... measure the variable it is intended to measure ..." (Hilton, Fawson, Sullivan, & DeJong, 2020, pp. 130–131). In other words a standardized instrument intended to measure the risk for future domestic violence victimization should correctly predict these incidents and not unrelated incidents.

Hilton, Pham, Jung, Nunes, and Ennis (2021) reported that the validity of standardized risk assessment instruments for domestic violence is typically determined after the instrument has been administered to a sample. These data are subsequently examined to determine whether offenders became repeat offenders or whether the offender was found guilty of the offense.

Reliability means that a standardized risk assessment instrument has "... the ability to yield consistent results each time it is applied" (Hilton et al., 2020, p. 134). In other words, when a police officer administers a standardized risk assessment instrument for domestic violence victimization similar results should be obtained among different officers who administer the same instrument.

The purpose of the following presentation is to call attention to the fact that standardized risk assessment instruments are used by police officers to predict repeat incidents of domestic violence. The most commonly administered standardized instruments in law enforcement are also identified.

In order to provide an effective law enforcement domestic violence victimization response numerous considerations for training exist. These include training officers to administer valid and reliable standardized risk assessment instruments and to distinguish between domestic offenses and other types of offenses (Kebbell, 2019).

The first standardized risk assessment instruments developed to assess a female victim's risk for future domestic violence victimization were developed in North American in the 1990s. These instruments were initially developed for use in clinical practice and probation departments and then were subsequently used by domestic violence victims' advocates to implement safety planning for high-risk domestic violence victims. After these initial uses law enforcement agencies began to utilize these instruments to assess individuals at risk for future domestic violence victimization. The majority of studies investigating the utility of these instruments have been conducted by instrument creators, utilizing small samples that predominantly consisted of white male domestic violence offenders (Turner, Medina, & Brown, 2019).

Graham, Sahay, Rizo, Messing, and Macy (2021) conducted a systemic review to examine the validity, reliability, and feasibility of administering standardized risk assessment instruments most likely to be used by law enforcement, social work, and other first responders to domestic violence. Instruments administered to assess risk of domestic violence victimization as well as instruments used to assess risk of homicide were included in the review. Given that police officers administer these instruments at the scene of domestic violence incidents, together with performing other law enforcement tasks, examining the feasibility of administration is an important endeavor. Graham et al. found that among

43 studies, a total of 18 risk assessment instruments for both domestic violence and intimate partner homicide were identified. Only one study examined the feasibility of administering these instruments during a domestic violence incident, although approximately half of the studies examined the validity and reliability of the instruments. The majority of the studies were conducted in English and in North America. Among their conclusions was a recommendation that more research is needed to assess the validity, reliability, and feasibility of administering these instruments with diverse populations such as female offenders, LGBTQ, and same-sex couples.

Instead of requiring police officers to administer standardized instruments an external agency can provide risk assessments for law enforcement. Hilton et al. (2021) described the use of the Integrated Threat and Risk Assessment Centre (ITRAC) in Canada to determine whether examining police reports alone, without interviewing offenders and victims, could identify individuals at high risk for future domestic violence victimization. The ITRAC employs threat assessors to conduct assessments. Hilton et al. found the domestic violence incidents referred to the ITRAC were assessed as high-risk domestic violence situations which supported the ITRAC's assessment based only on documentation contained in police reports.

They also asserted that the most frequently investigated standardized risk assessment instruments used for assessing repeat domestic violence victimization are: (1) the Ontario Domestic Assault Risk Assessment (ODAR) (Hilton, Harris, & Rice, 2010; Hilton, Harris, Rice, Lang, Cormier, & Lines, 2004) and (2) the Spousal Assault Risk Assessment Guide (SARA) (Kropp, Hart, Webster, & Eaves, 1995; Kropp & Hart, 2000). Further, they identify the SARA as comprised of a "family of tools" (p. 159), which include: (a) the SARA Version 3 (SARA-V3) (Kropp & Hart, 2015) and (b) the Brief Spousal Assault Form for the Evaluation of Risk (B-SAFER) (Kropp, Hart, & Belfrage, 2010; Kropp & Hart, 2004).

Likewise, Graham et al. (2021) reported that the most widely researched standardized risk assessment instruments for domestic violence are: (1) the ODARA, (2) the Danger Assessment (20-item Revised Version) (DA), (3) the SARA, the Domestic Violence Screening Instrument-Revised (DVSI-R), and (4) the Spouse Violence Risk Assessment Inventory (SVRA-1).

While it is important to know which of these instruments has strong empirical support, it is also important to know which instruments are used most often. Turner et al. (2019) suggested that the most commonly used instruments are: (1) the SARA, (2) the Domestic Violence Screening Inventory (DVSI) (Williams & Houghton, 2004), and (3) the ODAR.

The use of standardized risk assessment instruments for domestic violence is not unique to American law enforcement agencies. Turner et al. (2019) reported the use of the Domestic Abuse, Stalking and Honour Based Violence (DASH). The DASH instrument is the most widely used standardized risk assessment instrument utilized by law enforcement agencies in the U.K. However, they found that when police officers administered the DASH to assess high-risk repeat victimization or repeat incidents of domestic violence, the instrument did not accurately predict these incidents. The authors attributed these findings to the possibility that the questions contained in the instrument are not appropriate risk factors for domestic violence or the possibility that the challenges associated with administering the instrument at the scene produced poor results.

Police officers can also administer standardized risk assessment instruments to determine the type of interventions to provide at the scene of a domestic violence incident. For instance, police officers administered risk assessment instruments to assess the significant factors used to inform decisions about whether to arrest an offender or transport the victim to a shelter or other safe location (Nesset, Bjørngaard, Nøttestad, Whittington, Lynum, & Palmstierna, 2020).

Mandatory arrest policies and procedures

During the 1970s and 1980s law enforcement agencies began to change their approach to domestic violence. Law enforcement agencies began to adopt mandatory arrest and pro-arrest policies when responding to incidents of domestic violence (Hamilton, Harris, & Powell, 2019). Durfee and Goodmark (2020) summarized the differences between mandatory arrest law enforcement policies, pro-arrest policies, and discretionary arrest policies. Mandatory arrest policies refer to a requirement that police officers arrest an offender when evidence has shown that the offender perpetrated domestic violence. Pro-arrest policies encourage police officers to arrest the domestic violence offender, although an arrest is not required even though the evidence shows that an individual was a victim of domestic violence. Finally, discretionary arrest policies refer to police officers using their discretion to make a decision to arrest a domestic violence offender even in the absence of a warrant for an arrest. In this way, police officers use their discretion to determine whether or not to arrest the offender. Recall that discretion refers to a police officer's ability to make choices regarding how to resolve a situation.

Durfee and Goodmark (2020) counted the inconsistencies found among these domestic violence arrest policies in 39 states that were examined in 2016. They counted 18 states that implemented mandatory arrest policies, 6 states with pro-arrest policies, and 15 states with discretionary arrest policies. They observed that police officers made arrests more often in states that have enacted mandatory arrests policies and arrested an offender more often when a victims' injuries were noticeable. Their results demonstrate that as of 2016 law enforcement policies and procedures toward domestic violence were not uniform among states.

Types of signed complaints

Table 8.1 shows the average number of signed criminal complaints about domestic violence that did not result in fatalities that were reported to law enforcement

TABLE 8.1 Signed criminal complaints obtained in non-fatal domestic violence victimizations reported to police, 2006–2015

Type of domestic violence victimizations	Average annual numbers of victimizations reported to police	Percent resulting in signed complaint
All victimizations	728,255	48%
Intimate partner	492,186	52%
Other relation	236,069	40%
Serious violence★	266,267	56%
Intimate partner	176,193	60%
Other relation	90,074	47%
Simple assault	461,988	44%
Intimate partner	315,993	48%
Other relation	145,995	36%

Notes: Other relation includes immediate family (except spouses) and other relatives.

★ Includes rape or sexual assault, robbery, and aggravated assault.

Reprinted with permission Reaves, B. A. (2017). *Police response to domestic violence, 2006–2015.* NCJ 250231. Washington, D.C.: U.S. Department of Justice, Office of Justice Programs, Bureau of Justice Statistics.

between 2006 and 2015. In the table the term intimate partner is used to refer to current or former spouses, boyfriends, and girlfriends (Reaves, 2017). As the table shows, the highest percentage of domestic violence victimization over the 2006–2015 period was serious violence perpetrated by an intimate partner (60%). The most frequent type of domestic violence victimization that resulted in a signed complaint from the victim was serious violence which includes rape or sexual assault, robbery, and aggravated assault (56%). The least frequent type of domestic violence victimization that resulted in a signed complaint from the victim was simple assault perpetrated by another relation (36%) (Reaves, 2017).

Case Example

Law Enforcement Response to Domestic Violence

Shirley told the police officers that although she is not married to her child's father because he is the father of her 8-year-old daughter she did allow him to come into her home and visit with his child. She allowed the visit despite a history of violence in their relationship and having an order of protection against him in the past. The order of protection is no longer valid. She is afraid of the offender and told the officers that she had an order of protection against him in the past but dropped the order to allow the offender to visit his child.

During the visit the child's father became argumentative with Shirley accusing her of having a new relationship and introducing her new partner to his daughter. He then became violent, putting his hands around her neck and choking her so that she could not breathe. Next he hit her face, pushed her on the bed, and began to choke her again.

Once again making it difficult for her to breathe. Shirley was able to free herself and lock herself and her daughter in another room.

After several hours she felt that he had calmed down enough so that she and her daughter could come out of the room. When she came out several hours later he once again became violent and took some of her possessions such as her cell phone, handbag containing credit cards, identification, and cash. When she tried to stop him he pushed her to the floor and left her apartment. She immediately telephoned 911 requesting assistance.

The two police officers noticed that Shirley appeared to have bruises on her face where she was hit and her neck where she was choked. The police officers took pictures of her face and neck. Shirley repeatedly told the officers she was afraid to call 911 because she thought he would return to the apartment and become even more violent knowing that she called the police.

One of the police officers searched for outstanding warrants and found the perpetrator had an outstanding warrant for violating a previous order of protection. The victim stated that although she is afraid, because this has been an ongoing situation and because she has given him numerous opportunities she would like to sign a criminal complaint. She provided the officer with a signature on the supporting deposition.

An officer completed a DIR charging the offender with assault and larceny. The police officer also provided the victim with written information explaining available assistance and resources available for victims of domestic violence. The documentation also included a 24-hour domestic and sexual violence hotline telephone number, the court telephone number, and information for victim's assistance.

This case example illustrates the dilemma for many victims of domestic violence who have children in common with an offender. The victim wanted her child to have a relationship with the father, although he is abusive and violent. The example further illustrates the trauma a child may experience witnessing domestic violence.

Types of domestic violence criminal charges

During calls for service that involve domestic violence victimization police officers charge offenders with several types of offenses. In New York State the types of offenses most often charged in response to domestic violence incidents are publically available on the Division of Criminal Justice Services website. These offenses are categorized into three areas: (1) family offenses (i.e., aggravated family offense, attempted assault, harassment, strangulation, and identify theft); (2) often committed offenses (i.e., coercion, assault, aggravated cruelty to animals, endangering the welfare of a child, and menacing); and (3) other offenses (i.e., criminal use of a firearm, rape, computer tampering, and kidnapping first- and second-degree) (New York State Division of Criminal Justice Services, 2020). Further, perpetrators of domestic violence do not have the right to gun ownership (National Coalition Against Domestic Violence, 2016).

Law enforcement interventions

A law enforcement response to domestic violence victimization includes the provision of a number of interventions. These include safety planning, transportation to a safe location, providing information about the criminal justice system and resources, investigating and arresting offenders, and providing emotional support and referrals.

Enforcing orders of protection

Victims of domestic violence may obtain court orders of protection against an offender. When an offender violates the order of protection and law enforcement is contacted police officers respond to enforce the order of protection.

Why some victims of domestic violence do not contact law enforcement

When victims of domestic violence were asked in the NCVS why they did not report domestic violence victimization to law enforcement, 32% reported wanting to maintain their privacy, 21% reported wanting to protect the offender from law enforcement, 20% perceived the offense and victimization as a minor situation and therefore did not report it to law enforcement, and 19% reported they afraid the offender would retaliate if law enforcement was contacted (Reaves, 2017).

The role of social work in response to domestic violence

There are no uniform policies and procedures for addressing domestic violence among states or among law enforcement agencies. Consequently, providing services to victims of domestic violence requires that social workers comprehend relevant law enforcement policies and procedures to address domestic violence. Other relevant knowledge is also needed.

The ecological model is a promising model for use by social workers to address domestic violence because it focuses on both individual and environmental factors. Individual factors include relationship issues and environmental factors include community and societal influences (Wilson & Webb, 2018). When working with partners and families the ecological model should consider factors such as race and ethnicity, culture, religious and gender identity, social class, and employment (Hepworth, Rooney, Dewberry Rooney, Strom-Gottfried, & Larsen, 2006).

Davis, Weisburd, and Taylor (2008) described the use of social workers in second responder programs. The results of their research are included in CrimeSolutions. The National Institute of Justice (NIJ) maintains CrimeSolutions, which is a clearinghouse. The website provides information that summarizes the quality of evidence that exists for criminal justice programs or practices. The goal is to disseminate information concerning "what works," "what doesn't," and "what's promising." The clearinghouse also includes a rating classification scheme for criminal justice programs and practices. The scheme considers the strength of the evidence demonstrating effectiveness and, based on the evidence, classifies a program or practice as either "Effective," "Promising," or "No Effects" (Office of Justice Programs, National Institute of Justice, 2020a). "Effective" is the highest rating indicating an effective program or practice, whereas "No Effects" implies an ineffective program or practice.

CrimeSolutions (Office of Justice Programs, National Institute of Justice, 2020b) identifies the purpose and types of services provided in second responder programs, which began to emerge in the 1980s. The purpose of the programs is to reduce future incidents of domestic violence victimization and connect victims with support services. The types of services offered by the programs include home visits, providing information concerning legal options such as seeking an order of protection and information about domestic violence, making a safety plan including domestic violence shelter referrals, and providing referrals to community-based social service agencies for additional services such as counseling and job training. CrimeSolutions rates second-responder programs as "No Effects" for reducing future domestic violence victimization.

Social workers can also administer and score standardized risk assessment instruments used to assess risk of domestic violence and homicide. Social workers should be aware of the strengths and limitations of these instruments and how to make use of the scores to advise law enforcement with recommendation (Messing & Thaller, 2015).

Police and social work collaboration in response to domestic violence

Police officers and social workers collaborate in response to respond domestic violence victimization (Ward–Lasher, Messing, & Hart, 2017). Placing social workers in law enforcement agencies to collaborate with police officers can provide an effective domestic violence response (Hamilton, Harris, & Powell, 2019). The majority of sheriff's departments and local and state police departments have implemented specialized domestic violence units comprised of social workers or counselors and detectives. The social workers and counselors provide liaison assistance to officers, investigate domestic violence cases, collaborate with domestic violence service providers, assist victims, and provide training to police officers, victims, and community residents (Reaves, 2017).

The most effective law enforcement collaborations enhance victim's safety and domestic violence victim services. The least effective law enforcement collaborations did not reduce future incidents of domestic violence and police calls for repeat domestic violence when these were identified as the collaboration goals. Further, police officers felt supported knowing that social workers also identified concerns about victims' safety when victims did not leave a domestic violence situation even after information, interventions, and resources were provided (Reuland, Morabito, Preston, & Cheney, 2006). It should also be noted that social workers recognize a victim's right to self-determination. In social work practice this refers to an individual's right to make choices and determine solutions to their problems (Hepworth et al., 2006).

Police officers also collaborate with victim advocates and respond to domestic violence victimization. Law enforcement and domestic violence agencies collaborate in programs known as the Lethality Assessment Program (LAP) (Dutton, Tamborra, & Pittman, 2019).

Specific victims of domestic violence

Women are the largest group of victims of domestic violence reported to law enforcement. However, they are not the only population to experience domestic violence victimization. Although referred to as the LGBTQ community, this community is comprised of different groups with unique experiences with the criminal justice system, and in particular law enforcement. Purposely exploring only the attitudes of the LGBQ community and not the transgender toward the criminal justice system, including law enforcement, Nadal, Quintanilla, Goswick, and Sriken (2015) reported gender identity, race, and discrimination intersect to affect perceptions of law enforcement. These perceptions may negatively affect victims of domestic violence readiness to contact law enforcement.

A relationship exists between changing societal attitudes and marriage equality legislation and increased arrests among same-sex partners (Addington, 2020). However, dual arrests made by police officers during a domestic violence response can result in both the offender and the victim receiving an order of protection and can have negative consequences, particularly among LGBTQ victims of domestic violence. A dual arrest has the potential to negatively affect victim safety, housing, and employment opportunities and reduce the possibility of contacting law enforcement in the future for assistance with domestic violence victimization. Often dual arrests are made due to the lack of information about LGBTQ victims and homophobia among police officers and in courts that issue mutual orders of protection (Andreano, 2020).

Franklin, Goodson, and Garza (2019) asserted that the important role of law enforcement in response to domestic violence applies to same-sex and heterosexual partners. This role is essential for ensuring victim safety, encouraging victims to seek future assistance if needed, and arresting the offender. Their research findings show that an arrest was made less often among same-sex partners than heterosexual partners. They attributed these findings to a law enforcement response that is based on knowledge concerning heterosexual domestic violence dynamics resulting in a biased response for same-sex partners. Franklin et al. recommend that law enforcement training should include content on the dynamics of domestic violence among same-sex partners in order to improve the law enforcement response.

In contrast, although Durfee and Goodmark (2020) found that among crimes reported to law enforcement that occurred in 39 states, same-sex partners were arrested for domestic violence at approximately the same rate as heterosexual partners. However, an arrest was made more often among male same-sex partners than female same-sex partners. Taken together, these study results suggest that specialized knowledge and skills are needed among all law enforcement collaboration partners that respond to domestic violence.

Additional specific populations that require specialized knowledge and skills among all law enforcement collaboration partners include persons living with disabilities, older adults, juveniles, and undocumented immigrants, to mention a few populations.

Domestic violence community-based service providers

In this chapter it was discussed that police officers in New York State are required to provide victims of domestic violence with contact information to access resources. Because this is a statewide requirement most of the information is statewide information. Police officers should also be familiar with local community-based service providers. These providers include emergency shelters, counseling programs, and victim assistance hotlines, among others.

POLICE Model application

Given the important role of law enforcement in assisting victims of domestic violence with receiving services it is imperative to ensure that collaborations are functioning effectively and efficiently. Situations may arise where domestic violence victim service providers may not be in agreement with the procedures taken by law enforcement. Although the collaboration has already been implemented the planning, organizing, and listening phases of the POLICE Model can be useful for discussing and resolving these differences.

Chapter summary

This chapter examined the use of terminology to describe domestic violence. Definitions and types of domestic violence were reviewed in connection to the critical role of law enforcement when responding to incidents of domestic violence. The law enforcement role encompasses mandatory, pro-arrest, and discretionary arrest policies and procedures and the administration of standardized risk assessment instruments to assess the potential for future violence. Co-responder models and other law enforcement collaborations have been implemented to provide services to victims of domestic violence. Victim service providers, the focus of the next chapter, provide interventions to victims of domestic violence as well as victims of other types of crime.

Questions for discussion

1. What are some of the reasons why Coercive Controlling Violence is the most common type of domestic violence observed by law enforcement?
2. What are your thoughts about the utilization of standardized risk assessment instruments in law enforcement to assess future risks for domestic violence?
3. What are your thoughts about mandatory arrest policies utilized in law enforcement?

Activities for further learning

1. Locate and summarize the content that should be included in a safety plan for a victim of domestic violence. Use this content to develop a simulated safety plan for an adult victim with children of domestic violence.
2. Search and locate a standardized risk assessment instrument and the instructions for administering the instrument to assess future risk for domestic violence. Prepare a summary of the specific population(s) for whom it is appropriate to administer the instrument, and provide the details describing the reliability and validity of the instrument if it is available.
3. Prepare a list of community resources such as emergency shelters and hotline telephone numbers available in your community to assist victims of domestic violence.

References

Addington, L. A. (2020). Police response to same-sex intimate partner violence in the marriage equality era. *Criminal Justice Studies, 33*(3), 213–230.

Andreano, J. (2020). The disproportionate effect of mutual restraining orders on same-sex domestic violence victims. *California Law Review, 108*(3), 1047–1074.

Child Welfare Information Gateway (2018). *Definitions of domestic violence.* Washington, D.C.: U.S. Department of Health and Human Services, Children's Bureau.

Davis, R. C., Weisburd, D., & Taylor, B. (2008). Effects of second responder programs on repeat incidents of family abuse: A systematic review. *Campbell Systematic Reviews, 4*(1), 1–38.

Durfee, A., & Goodmark, L. (2020). Domestic violence mandatory arrest policies and arrests for same-sex and opposite-sex intimate partner violence after legalization of same-sex marriage in the United States. *Criminal Justice Studies, 33*(3), 231–255.

Dutton, L. B., Tamborra, T. L., & Pittman, M. (2019). Police officers' and victim advocates' perceptions of the Lethality Assessment Program. *Criminal Justice Policy Review, 30*(7), 1023–1042.

Franklin, C. A., Goodson, A., & Garza, A. D. (2019). Intimate partner violence among sexual minorities: Predicting police officer arrest decisions. *Criminal Justice and Behavior, 46*(8), 1181–1199.

Graham, L. M., Sahay, K. M., Rizo, C. F., Messing, J. T., & Macy, R. J. (2021). The validity and reliability of available intimate partner homicide and reassault risk assessment tools: A systematic review. *Trauma, Violence, & Abuse, 22*(1), 18–40.

Hepworth, D. H., Rooney, R. H., Dewberry Rooney, G., Strom-Gottfried, K., & Larsen J. (2006). *Direct social practice: Theory and skills* (7th ed.). Belmont, CA: Thompson Higher Education.

Hilton, T. P., Fawson, P. R., Sullivan, T. J., & DeJong, C. R. (2020). *Applied social research: A tool for the human services* (10th ed.). New York: Springer Publishing Company LLC.

Hilton, N. Z., Pham, A. T., Jung, S., Nunes, K., & Ennis, L. (2021). Risk scores and reliability of the SARA, SARA-V3, B-SAFER, and ODARA among Intimate Partner Violence (IPV) cases referred for threat assessment. *Police Practice and Research, 22*(1), 157–172.

Hamilton, G., Harris, L., & Powell, A. (2019). Policing repeat and high-risk family violence: Police and service-sector perceptions of a coordinated model. *Police Practice and Research*, 22(1), 1–16.

Hilton, N. Z., Harris, G. T., & Rice, M. E. (2010). *Risk assessment for domestically violent men: Tools for criminal justice, offender intervention, and victim services*. Washington, D.C.: American Psychological Association.

Hilton, N. Z., Harris, G. T., Rice, M. E., Lang, C., Cormier, C. A., & Lines, K. J. (2004). A brief actuarial assessment for the prediction of wife assault recidivism: The Ontario domestic assault risk assessment. *Psychological Assessment, 16*(3), 267–275.

Kebbell, M. R. (2019). Risk assessment for intimate partner violence: How can the police assess risk?. *Psychology, Crime & Law, 25*(8), 829–846.

Kelly, J. B., & Johnson, M. P. (2008). Differentiation among types of intimate partner violence: Research update and implications for interventions. *Family Court Review, 46*(3), 476–499.

Kropp, P. R., & Hart, S. D. (2000). The Spousal Assault Risk Assessment (SARA) guide: Reliability and validity in adult male offenders. *Law and Human Behavior, 24*(1), 101–118.

Kropp, P. R., & Hart, S. D. (2004). *The development of the brief spousal assault form for the evaluation of risk (B-SAFER): A tool for criminal justice professionals*. Ottawa, Ontario, Canada: Department of Justice Canada.

Kropp, P. R., & Hart, S. D. (2015). *SARA-V3: User manual for version 3 of the spousal assault risk assessment guide*. Proactive Resolutions.

Kropp, P. R., Hart, S. D., & Belfrage, H. (2010). *Brief spousal assault form for the evaluation of risk (B-SAFER), Version 2: User manual*. Vancouver, British Columbia, Canada. Proactive Resolutions.

Kropp, P. R., Hart, S. D., Webster, C. D. & Eaves, D. (1995). *Manual for the spousal assault risk assessment guide* (2nd ed.). Vancouver: The British Columbia Institute on Family Violence.

Levens, B. R., & Dutton, D. G. (1980). *The social service role of police: Domestic crisis intervention*. Ottawa, Ontario, Canada: Communication Division, Ministry of the Solicitor General of Canada.

Messing, J. T., & Thaller, J. (2015). Intimate partner violence risk assessment: A primer for social workers. *The British Journal of Social Work, 45*(6), 1804–1820.

Miller, S. L., Hefner, M. K., & Iovanni, L. (2020). Practitioners' perspectives on using restorative justice with crimes of gendered violence. *Contemporary Justice Review, 23*(1), 65–90.

Nadal, K. L., Quintanilla, A., Goswick, A., & Sriken, J. (2015). Lesbian, gay, bisexual, and queer people's perceptions of the criminal justice system: Implications for social services. *Journal of Gay & Lesbian Social Services, 27*(4), 457–481.

National Coalition Against Domestic Violence (2016). *Domestic violence and firearms.* Retrieved from http://ncadv.org/files/Gun%20Fact%20Sheet.pdf

Nesset, M. B., Bjørngaard, J. H., Nøttestad, J. A., Whittington, R., Lynum, C., & Palmstierna, T. (2020). Factors associated with police decisions on immediate responses to intimate partner violence. *Journal of Interpersonal Violence, 35*(15–16), 2993–3010.

New York State Division of Criminal Justice Services (2020). *2020 Dir form – Full Dir – New victim rights 02-06-2020.pub – dir.pdf.* Retrieved from https://www.criminaljustice.ny.gov/ojis/documents/dir.pdf

Office of Justice Programs, National Institute of Justice (2020a). *About Crime Solutions.* Retrieved from CrimeSolutions, https://crimesolutions.ojp.gov/about

Office of Justice Programs, National Institute of Justice (2020b). *Second Responder Programs.* Retrieved from CrimeSolutions, https://crimesolutions.ojp.gov/ratedpractices/12

Office of Violence Against Women, U.S. Department of Justice (2017). *Domestic violence.* Retrieved from https://www.justice.gov/ovw/domestic-violence

Pence, E., & Paymar, M. (1993). *Education groups for men who batter: The Duluth model.* New York: Springer.

Reaves, B. A. (2016). *State and local law enforcement training academies, 2013.* NCJ 249784. Washington, D.C.: U.S. Department of Justice, Office of Justice Programs, Bureau of Justice Statistics.

Reaves, B. A. (2017). *Police response to domestic violence, 2006-2015.* NCJ 250231. Washington, D.C.: U.S. Department of Justice, Office of Justice Programs, Bureau of Justice Statistics.

Reuland, M., Morabito, M. S., Preston, C., & Cheney, J. (2006). *Police-community partnerships to address domestic violence.* Washington, D.C.: US Department of Justice, Office of Community Policing Services.

Sampson, R. (2007). *Domestic violence.* Problem-Oriented Guides for Police Problem-Specific Guides Series Guide No. 45. Washington, D.C.: U.S. Department of Justice, Office of Community Oriented Policing Services.

Schechter, S., & Edelson, J. (1999). *Effective intervention in domestic violence and child maltreatment cases: Guidelines for policy and practice* (122–123). Reno, NV: National Council of Juvenile and Family Court Judges.

Turner, E., Medina, J., & Brown, G. (2019). Dashing hopes? The predictive accuracy of domestic abuse risk assessment by police. *The British Journal of Criminology, 59*(5), 1013–1034.

Ward-Lasher, A., Messing, J. T., & Hart, B. (2017). Policing intimate partner violence: Attitudes toward risk assessment and collaboration with social workers. *Social Work, 62*(3), 211–218.

Williams, K. R., & Houghton, A. B. (2004). Assessing the risk of domestic violence reoffending: A validation study. *Law and Human Behaviour, 28*, 437–455.

Wilson, M. H., & Webb, R. (2018). Social work's role in responding to intimate partner violence. *Social Justice Brief.* Retrieved from https://www.socialworkers.org/LinkClick.aspx?fileticket=WTrDbQ6CHxI%3d&portalid=0

9
VICTIMS OF CRIME

Chapter overview

Hot spot policing strategies combined with law enforcement functions such as making arrests focus on crime prevention and reduction. Policing strategies such as community-oriented policing and the service law enforcement function can focus on collaboration and providing interventions to victims of crime. Victims of crime require information, assistance with court proceedings, assistance to help them cope with reactions to victimization, referrals, and other types of victim assistance. As an approach to provide assistance to victims of crime law enforcement agencies collaborate with social workers and victim service providers (VSPs). Victim services are provided by internal law enforcement units and external independent agencies. This chapter provides an overview of the role of law enforcement and law enforcement collaboration specific to assisting victims of crime.

Introduction

So important is the need to recognize victims of crime and available services that the National Crime Victims' Rights Week is held each year in April. Providing assistance to victims of crime is one of the most common types of police and social work and social service collaboration. Collaboration partners possess specialized knowledge and skills to provide victim support services.

The number of victims of violent crime, not including simple assault, increased from 1.1 million in 2015 to 1.4 million in 2018, before decreasing to 1.2 million in 2019 (Morgan & Truman, 2020). Morgan and Truman obtained these data from the National Crime Victimization Survey (NCVS), which identifies violent crime as rape or sexual assault, robbery, aggravated assault, domestic

DOI: 10.4324/9781003132257-9

violence, intimate partner violence, stranger violence, violent crime involving injury, and violent crime involving a weapon. The NCVS is the largest self-report crime survey administered in the United States. The survey also measures whether respondents reported these crimes to law enforcement.

The NCVS does not include self-reported violent crime victimization such as murder, non-negligent manslaughter, burglary, and other crimes against commercial businesses. These violent crimes are instead measured in the Uniform Crime Report (UCR), which measures crime reported by law enforcement agencies as opposed to crimes reported by victims, which is the case with the NCVS (Morgan & Truman, 2020). The differences in measurement approaches highlight the need to understand how criminal victimization rates are determined.

Slocum (2018) found that overall prior law enforcement contacts did not influence a victim's decision to report recent victimization. However, among Blacks and poor individuals if police officers initiated the law enforcement contact or victims perceived the prior law enforcement contact as unwarranted they were less willing to report certain types of victimization. Slocum suggests these findings imply the need consider victims' perceptions of fairness in order to increase victims' willingness to report certain types of victimization.

A note about terminology

Referring to victims of interpersonal violence, Ward-Lasher, Messing, and Hart (2017) reported that criminal justice practitioners use the term *victim* to refer to a victim of interpersonal violence, whereas domestic violence advocates use the term *survivor*. Throughout this chapter the term victim is used. Victim is a term identified in the name of some organizations that provide services, compensation funds, the NCVS, and criminal police reports, for example. It is also used to refer to victim assistance providers.

Defining a victim

Oudekerk, Warnken, and Langton (2019) identified the definition of a victim provided in the National Census of Victim Service Providers (NCVSP):

> A victim was a person who received assistance from a victim service provider (VSP) due to concerns about past, ongoing, or potential crimes or abuse. Victims included persons directly harmed or threatened by crimes or abuse and family or household members of the harmed or threatened persons.
>
> *Reprinted with permission* Oudekerk, B. A., Warnken, H., & Langton, L. (2019). *Victim service providers in the United States, 2017.* NCJ 252648. Washington, D.C.: U.S. Department of Justice, Office of Justice Programs, Bureau of Justice Statistics.

Also included in the NCVSP is a definition of the term services, referring to those that are typically provided by a VSP (Oudekerk et al., 2019):

> Services included any efforts to assist victims; to promote their safety, security, or recovery; to help them participate in the criminal justice system; or to meet other victim needs.
>
> *Reprinted with permission-* Oudekerk, B. A., Warnken, H., & Langton, L. (2019). *Victim service providers in the United States, 2017.* NCJ 252648. Washington, D.C.: U.S. Department of Justice, Office of Justice Programs, Bureau of Justice Statistics.

Defining a witness

According to the Cambridge Dictionary a witness is defined as: "A person who sees an event happening especially a crime or an accident: Police are appealing for witnesses to the crime to come forward, According to (eye) witnesses, the robbery was carried out by two teenage boys" (Cambridge University Press, 2021).

As we shall see later in this chapter both victims and witnesses of violent crime may experience behavioral, psychological, or physiological reactions to the crime. Further, both victims and witnesses may be eligible for compensation and other services.

Reactions to crime victimization

In addition to experiencing physical injuries, victims and witnesses may also experience a range of behavioral, psychological, and/or physiological reactions. Further, they may experience loss that involves the loss of a family member or close friend or financial or property loss. These reactions arise based on whether the crime is a violent or non-violent crime as well as other factors such as previous victimization.

Typically reactions and loss to violent crime have received the most attention. Regardless of the type of crime victims of crime may be in need of a variety of services from a VSP. These interventions may require medical, psychological, financial, or other interventions. In order to provide the necessary interventions to address loss and reactions, law enforcement collaborations with VSPs have been established.

Behavioral reactions

Examples of behavioral reactions experienced can include increased smoking, drinking, substance use, or missed workdays. These reactions are often accompanied by underlying psychological or physiological reactions.

Psychological reactions

Examples of psychological reactions experienced by victims and witnesses of crime can include anxiety, depression, or panic attacks. Experiences such as having one's life threatened, being injured, domestic violence victimization, or using ineffective coping strategies are risk factors for posttraumatic stress disorder (American Psychiatric Association, 2013).

Physiological reactions

Examples of physiological reactions experienced by victims and witnesses of crime can include body pains, increased heart rate, and high blood pressure.

The following case example shows how a witness of violence can experience both loss and reactions after witnessing a violent crime. It also demonstrates how a police social worker can respond immediately to the scene and provide support services as well as refer the witness to a VSP.

Case Example

A Witness' Crime Reactions and Crisis Interventions

Mr. H drove his partner home after taking her out to dinner on a date. While parked outside her home her ex-partner suddenly appeared and shot Ms. C in her head, killing her immediately as she sat in the car. Mr. H described a horrifying scene to the police officers upon their arrival and requested assistance with contacting her family to tell them what happened, thinking it would be better if they were informed by him rather than the police officers. The inside of the car and Mr. H were covered in blood from the shooting.

As a police officer interviewed Mr. H to obtain required information regarding the crime the officer asked Mr. H if he would be willing to speak with a police social worker. He agreed, and after the criminal police report was completed Mr. H spoke with the police social worker.

He was provided with emotional support, assistance with contacting his partner's family members, and a referral to a VSP.

In the days that followed crime, Mr. H noticed he was experiencing difficulty eating and sleeping, having nightmares re-experiencing the murder, feeling anxious, and experiencing headaches. He also continually thought about what he could have done differently to prevent the murder of Ms. C. He felt victimized and helpless. Although it appeared that Mr. H was not an intended victim of the shooting he did witness it.

Mr. H recognized that it was Ms. C's ex-partner and at the scene informed police that he knew her ex-partner. He expressed anger that she was murdered and pleaded with police to locate and arrest him. He further stated that he is willing to testify at trial because he wants to seek justice.

Types of victim services

Some services that are available for victims of crime are also available for witnesses. Each state operates programs funded by the Federal Victims of Crime Act (VOCA) (Office for Victims of Crime, n.d.a). The process for receiving victim services from a state program begins with a victim filing a claim either electronically or by mail. VSPs also assist victims with filing a claim. Information describing available services and eligibility and applications are available on state programs' websites. For example, in New York State a claim can be filed by a victim who is an innocent victim of a crime, meaning that the victim was not involved in offending or criminal behavior that resulted in victimization, a relative of a victim of crime, or a Good Samaritan who meets eligibility requirements. The compensation provides for "out-of-pocket" payments, in which either no insurance exists or no coverage by insurance or no other sources of financial support are available (New York State Office of Victim Services, 2021).

In Georgia, among the services described for a victim or witness of a violent crime are compensation for lost income, assistance with seeking court-ordered restitution, and obtaining a memorial sign for a victim of an impaired driver. Other types of benefits such as forensic medical examinations are also described on the website. Importantly, a witness of a violent crime may be eligible for services (Georgia Criminal Justice Coordinating Council, 2021).

The Office for Victims of Crime (n.d.a) website provides a list and contact information for VOCA-funded Victim Assistance Programs and Victim Compensation Programs available in each state. The Office for Victims of Crime, Office of Justice Programs (n.d.) provides an internet resource that is invaluable for locating VOCA-funded information available in each state (Office for Victims of Crime, n.d.b). Services and compensation are two separate types of assistance provided to victims of crime.

The types of services provided to victims of crime are also defined in federal legislation. The Federal Victims' Rights and Restitution Act (VRRA) identifies the following services that are available to victims of crime:

- To be informed of the place where they may receive medical and social services
- To be informed of public and private programs available for counseling, treatment, and other support services
- To receive reasonable protection from a suspected offender and persons acting in concert with or at the behest of the suspected offender
- To know the status of the investigation of the crime, to the extent it is appropriate and will not interfere with the investigation
- To have personal property being held for evidentiary purposes maintained in good condition and returned as soon as it is no longer needed for evidentiary purposes (Department of Justice, 2021).

As these federal legislative provisions demonstrate victims are required to receive information about medical, social and support services, counseling, and treatment available from both public and private providers.

Victim rights

Each state also identifies the rights of victims of crime. The National Crime Victim Law Institute (2013) makes these laws available for each state. The rights of victims of crime are also defined in Federal legislation. The VRRA also identifies the following Federal rights given to victims of crime. Some of these rights include:

- The right to be reasonably protected from the accused
- The right to reasonable, accurate, and timely notice of any public court proceeding, or any parole proceeding, involving the crime or of any release or escape of the accused
- The right not to be excluded from any such public court proceeding, unless the court, after receiving clear and convincing evidence, determines that testimony by the victim would be materially altered if the victim heard other testimony at that proceeding
- The right to be reasonably heard at any public proceeding in the district court involving release, plea, sentencing, or any parole proceeding
- The reasonable right to confer with the attorney for the government in the case
- The right to full and timely restitution as provided in law
- The right to proceedings free from unreasonable delay
- The right to be treated with fairness and with respect for the victim's dignity and privacy
- The right to be informed in a timely manner of any plea bargain or deferred prosecution agreement (Department of Justice, 2021).

As part of comprehensive victim services, victims should also be informed of their rights. Law enforcement collaboration partners should understand these rights and make them available to victims of crime. Importantly, victims have the right to be heard in court, which may involve a victim impact statement.

Special victims of crime

Similar to other collaborations formed with law enforcement, collaborations implemented to provide services to victims of crime require that all collaboration partners have specialized knowledge and skills. Such knowledge and skills are necessary to provide interventions in response to different types of victimization. The following examples illustrate this need.

Victims of hate crimes

As a unique type of crime victims of hate crimes require additional specialized knowledge and skills. The Federal Bureau of Investigation (FBI) provides the following definition of a hate crime: "The UCR Program defines a hate crime as a committed criminal offense which is motivated, in whole or in part, by the offender's bias(es) against a: race, religion, disability, sexual orientation, ethnicity, gender, gender identity. For UCR Program purposes, even if the offenders are mistaken in their perception the victim was a member of a certain group, the offense is still a bias crime because the offender was motivated by bias. The most common hate crimes reported to the data collection are destruction/damage/vandalism, intimidation, and simple assault" (FBI, n.d.a).

Police social workers and victim assistance providers, using knowledge and skills assisting victims, can also provide interventions and referrals that are relevant for each of the above identities. A list of community-based service providers should also be maintained to assist victims having the above identities with counseling and other services.

It is essential that collaboration partners be knowledgeable about community-based resources to provide appropriate referrals. Lacking knowledge about community-based resources can negatively affect victims receiving needed services (Vinton & Wilke, 2014).

Victims of elder abuse

Laws to protect older adults from elder abuse have been enacted in Federal legislation and legislation in all states, as well as the District of Columbia. These laws protect older adults from psychological, physical, and sexual abuse; financial exploitation; abandonment; and neglect (Department of Justice, n.d.). As a specialized population of victims, police social workers and victims service providers must not only be knowledgeable and skilled concerning victimization of this population, but they must also be knowledgeable and skilled concerning the State reporting requirements for reporting these incidents to adult protective services (APS).

Victims of natural disasters, critical incidents, and mass violence

Although the focus of this chapter is victims of crime and law enforcement collaboration with VSPs, police social workers may also be called upon to assist law enforcement with providing a response to natural disasters and critical incidents. A natural disaster can be a severe storm and a critical incident can involve a school bus crash with child fatalities or a building explosion or collapse. These latter incidents may or may not occur as a result of a crime.

Law enforcement responds to these events assisting victims and survivors and conducting an investigation. Police social workers with knowledge and skills assisting victims can assist victims and law enforcement at the scene of these incidents.

The above situations are likely to involve large numbers of victims. Similarly, mass violence incidents also involve numerous victims. Mass violence incidents can include a shooting, bombing, use of a vehicle to cause injuries, or other types of situations. Police social workers can also assist law enforcement at the scene of these situations.

Victims of community violence

Both victims and witnesses are exposed to community violence in a variety of forms. This exposure can include becoming a direct victim of community violence such as being the unintended victim of a shooting to witnessing or hearing gunfire. Gang violence and exposure to media reports covering community violence are additional examples. Exposure to such events has a cumulative effect on experiences of trauma. Throughout the country law enforcement agencies have established collaborations with community stakeholders to prevent and reduce community violence.

The role of law enforcement in victim assistance

In 2017, 1,886, or 15% of all U.S. law enforcement agencies, maintained a specialized victim service unit (Oudekerk et al., 2019). Wilson and Segrave (2011) identified three types of law enforcement–based victim service models found among U.S., U.K., Australian, and Canadian law enforcement agencies. The first type of victim service model is victim services units which are "a specialized unit within a police organization dedicated to assisting victim of crime" (p. 484). The second model type is the "Dedicated Liaison Officer" which is "... defined as police personnel being charged with specific responsibility for victims of crime (either directly or indirectly) who are dispersed throughout the organization" (p. 485). The third type of victim service model emphasizes referrals to crime VSPs involving "front-line police being utilized to connect with community-based and government services outside the police organization" (p. 486).

Whether a police officer refers a victim of crime to a VSP inside or outside of the law enforcement agency interventions may still be necessary at the scene of the victimization. The following example highlights the role of law enforcement in providing information and referrals and beginning a criminal investigation.

Case Example

A Law Enforcement Response to Victims of Crime

John was leaving a relative's home during daylight hours. He was in the process of unlocking and getting into his car when a male wearing a face mask held a gun to his head and stole his wallet, cell phone, and car keys. The suspect then drove away, stealing his car. John was unhurt but emotionally distressed following this victimization. He went back inside his relative's home, and after telling them what just occurred the relative called 911. Although it seemed to John as though half an hour had passed before the police officer arrived, the officer arrived within five minutes.

The police officer was aware and acknowledged John's emotional distress while completing a criminal police report that required information such as a description of the suspect, the time the victimization occurred, and a description of John's property that was stolen. John told the officer the situation happened so suddenly that he was unable to get a good description of the suspect. As a result the description he gave the officer was vague.

All law enforcement agencies do not maintain a VSP as a specialty unit within the law enforcement agency. Accordingly, upon giving John a copy of the criminal police report documenting his victimization the police officer encouraged John to contact the local non-profit VSP. John was also informed that he would receive a telephone call providing him with information for a lead police officer to contact about the investigation and his property. John asked the officer numerous questions about whether he would get his car returned, how the investigation would proceed, and what information should be provided to his cell phone company. The officer provided John with information about what typically happens with stolen cars and property based on previous cases.

The Federal Bureau of Investigation Victims Services Division

Although the primary function of the FBI is to investigate Federal crimes the FBI maintains resources for victims of crime (see https://www.fbi.gov/resources/victim-services). The types of federal crimes investigated by the FBI for which victim services are provided include violent crime; white-collar crime; health care, telemarketing, mortgage, and internet fraud; computer intrusion; identity theft; cybercrimes; child sexual exploitation; crimes against children; crimes committed in Indian country; domestic and international terrorism; civil rights violations such as hate crimes; and human trafficking (FBI, n.d.b).

The FBI has operated a Victims Services Division (VSD) since 2001. The VSD provides crisis intervention and referrals to victims of crime investigated by the FBI. Since its inception the VSD has assisted more than two million victims. The VSD includes numerous specialized victim services programs has to meet the needs of specific victims of crime: (1) The Terrorism and Special Jurisdiction program, (2) The Child Pornography Victim Assistance Program, (3) The Child Victim Services Program, (4) The Victim Services Response Team, and (5) Crisis response canines (FBI, n.d.c). Licensed social workers and clinical social workers are employed as victim specialists (FBI, n.d.d).

The role of social work in victim assistance

Victims of Crime A Social Work Response: Building Skills to Strengthen Survivors is a resource for the social work profession that contains workshop training materials to instruct social workers and social work students to provide services to victims of crime. The resource materials include a trainers' manual, participant manual, and a video discussion guide, among other items (Office for Victims of Crime, Office of Justice Programs, n.d.).

The primary goal of the workshop is to prepare social workers to provide interventions to adult victims of violent crime. Early in the workshop facilitators are encouraged to ask participants if they have been a victim of a crime, to describe the type of crime and whether they reported it to law enforcement.

The workshop materials identify the biopsychosocial effects of violent crime victimization, the need to understand the issues associated with victimization among specific populations such as immigrants, the elderly, and racial, ethnic, and religious groups. Additional topics include crime victims' rights, victim impact statements, and types of interventions provided to crime victims (Danis, 2006). An example describing a social worker assisting a victim with going to a law enforcement agency to speak with police regarding victimization is provided. The example is important for police and social work collaboration focused on victim assistance.

The role of victim assistance providers

In 2017 approximately 12,200 VSPs operated nationwide. VSPs are non-profit and for-profit, governmental and tribal, and situated in health care and educational organizations as well as other types of organizations (Oudekerk et al., 2019). Most VSPs employ counselors and social workers to assist victims of crime with filing a victim compensation claim, transportation, court accompaniment, crisis intervention and counseling, referrals, and advocacy. VSPs utilize different procedures and policies for collaboration with law enforcement.

POLICE Model application

In-house and external VSPs were discussed in this chapter. Whether or not a victim service provided is located within a law enforcement agency, similar to suggestions for application of the POLICE Model in Chapter 8, VSPs may not be in agreement with the procedures taken by law enforcement. As this chapter has demonstrated law enforcement provides necessary services for victims of crime. Consequently, collaborations established with VSPs should function effectively and efficiently. The planning, organizing, and listening phases of the POLICE Model can be useful for resolving any modifications that are required.

Chapter summary

Collaboration with VSPs is among the most well-developed law enforcement collaborations. This chapter reviewed the roles of law enforcement, social work, and victim assistance providers when assisting victims of crime. This chapter also reviewed two of the primary data collection methods used to measure crime. Definitions of a victim, witness, and victim services were provided. Additionally, this chapter reviewed the rights of crime victims, common reactions to criminal victimization and witnessing a crime, and types of victim services that may be required. Because some of the information presented in this chapter is based on federal legislation VSPs are encouraged to locate and retrieve information concerning local victim service assistance within specific communities.

Questions for discussion

1. Among the three types of law enforcement–based victim service models discussed in this chapter which type(s) do you believe has the most potential to reach and service the most victims of crime, and why?
2. Do you believe that victims of non-violent crimes and/or low-level crimes require victim services? Why or why not?
3. What types of specialized treatment or services might a victim or witness of a crime require as a result of their behavioral, psychological, or physiological reactions to the crime?

Activities for further learning

1. Locate the office of victim services for your state. Also, locate the procedures for filing a claim and the forms that a victim of crime should use to receive crime victim compensation or other needed victim services.
2. Does your local law enforcement maintain a specialized unit to assist victims of crime?
3. What type of services are provided to victims of crime in your community? Develop a listing of the services and VSPs.

References

American Psychiatric Association (2013). *Diagnostic and statistical manual of mental disorders* (5th ed.). Arlington, VA: American Psychiatric Association.

Cambridge University Press (2021). *Witness*. Retrieved from https://dictionary.cambridge.org/us/dictionary/english/witness

Danis, F. (2006). *Introductory workshop on crime victims' rights and services trainer's manual.* Retrieved from https://ovc.ojp.gov/sites/g/files/xyckuh226/files/assist/NASW_Kit/pdf/01_trainer_manual.pdf

Department of Justice (2021). *Rights of victims*. Retrieved from https://www.justice.gov/enrd/rights-victims

Department of Justice (n.d.). *State elder abuse statutes.* Retrieved from https://www.justice.gov/elderjustice/elder-justice-statutes-0

Federal Bureau of Investigation (FBI) (n.d.a). *Hate crime statistics.* Retrieved from https://www.fbi.gov/services/cjis/ucr/hate-crime

Federal Bureau of Investigation (FBI) (n.d.b). *FBI victim assistance program.* Retrieved from BI_VAP_brochure-1.pdf

Federal Bureau of Investigation (FBI) (n.d.c). Victim services. Retrieved from https://www.fbi.gov/resources/victim-services

Federal Bureau of Investigation (FBI) (n.d.d). *Office for victim assistance.* Retrieved from https://www.fbi.gov/audio-repository/news-podcasts-inside-office-for-victim-assistance.mp3/view

Georgia Criminal Justice Coordinating Council (2021). *Georgia Crime Victims Compensation Program.* Retrieved from http://crimevictimscomp.ga.gov/for-victims/

Morgan, R. E., & Truman, J. L. (2020). *Criminal victimization, 2019.* NCJ 255113. Washington, D.C.: U.S. Department of Justice, Office of Justice Programs, Bureau of Justice Statistics.

National Crime Victim Law Institute (2013). *Victims' rights law by state.* Retrieved from https://law.lclark.edu/live/news/23544-victims-rights-law-by-state

New York State Office of Victim Services (2021). *Victim compensation claim application.* Retrieved from https://ovs.ny.gov/sites/default/files/general-form/victim-compensation-claim-application-feb-2021.pdf

Office for Victims of Crime (n.d.a). *Help for victims.* Retrieved from https://ovc.ojp.gov/help-for-victims/help-in-your-state

Office for Victims of Crime (n.d.b). *State support.* Retrieved from https://ovc.ojp.gov/states

Office for Victims of Crime, Office of Justice Programs (n.d.). *Victims of crime a social work response: Building skills to strengthen survivors.* Retrieved from https://ovc.ojp.gov/sites/g/files/xyckuh226/files/assist/NASW_Kit/welcome.html

Oudekerk, B. A., Warnken, H., & Langton, L. (2019). *Victim service providers in the United States, 2017.* NCJ 252648. Washington, D.C.: U.S. Department of Justice, Office of Justice Programs, Bureau of Justice Statistics.

Slocum, L. A. (2018). The effect of prior police contact on victimization reporting: Results from the police-public contact and national crime victimization surveys. *Journal of Quantitative Criminology, 34*(2), 535–589.

Vinton, L., & Wilke, D. J. (2014). Are collaborations enough? Professionals' knowledge of victim services. *Violence Against Women, 20*(6), 716–729.

Ward-Lasher, A., Messing, J. T., & Hart, B. (2017). Policing intimate partner violence: Attitudes toward risk assessment and collaboration with social workers. *Social Work, 62*(3), 211–218.

Wilson, D., & Segrave, M. (2011). Police-based victim services: Australian and international models. *Policing: An International Journal of Police Strategies & Management, 34*(3), 479–496.

10

MENTAL HEALTH

Chapter overview

Responding to mental health crises is a common service law enforcement function. The purpose of this chapter is to examine the role of law enforcement when responding to mental health crises and the varied approaches utilized by law enforcement agencies to provide this response. These approaches include the use of police social workers or mental health practitioners or the implementation of CIT and co-responder models. The chapter first provides a brief historical overview of the care of individuals living with mental illness and the relationship between their care and the criminal justice system. Presently, emphasis is placed on decriminalizing or diverting individuals living with mental illness away from the criminal justice system. Because police calls for service involve responding to mental health crises and collaboration with mental health practitioners it is necessary that police officers have the knowledge and skills to respond to these crises. Indeed, law enforcement has had a prominent role throughout the history of the care of individuals living with mental illness.

Second, different types of mental illness are examined including co-occurring disorders. This chapter also discusses the role of specialty trained police officers in responding to mental health crises. Finally, this chapter concludes with the national guidelines for behavioral health and mental health crises developed by the Substance Abuse and Mental Health Services Administration (SAMHSA). These guidelines recommend limiting law enforcement involvement when providing a mental health crisis response unless a law enforcement presence is necessary for safety reasons.

DOI: 10.4324/9781003132257-10

Introduction

According to the National Institute of Mental Health (NIMH) (2021) mental illness is a common disorder in the United States. Accessing emergency mental health treatment can involve calls to the 911 operator and police calls for service. In 2017, the Boston Police Department received 5,953 calls to respond to individuals experiencing a mental health crisis (Morabito, Savage, Sneider, & Wallace, 2018). Although these calls only represented 0.87% of the total calls received by the Boston Police Department that year the figure does show that a law enforcement response was requested in nearly 6,000 mental health emergencies.

Often during these police calls for service law enforcement requires assistance from other emergency services and mental health practitioners. Law enforcement interventions can take on many forms such as including a mental health practitioner at the scene of the mental health crisis, providing transportation to a psychiatric emergency hospital department, mediation, providing a referral to a community-based mental health agency, or an arrest.

A unique situation may arise in which mental health practitioners including social workers employed in community-based mental health agencies may be reluctant to contact law enforcement for assistance with a client experiencing a mental health crisis. This reluctance arises due to concerns about law enforcement possibly using excessive force or other inappropriate approaches toward a client. In these instances it is important to assess the reasons why interventions provided by law enforcement may be needed and perhaps explore alternative options for addressing the crisis. Having an understanding of law enforcement interventions, and even assisting with these interventions when possible, can be beneficial for clients.

An overview of mental health and the criminal justice system

During the colonial period individuals living with mental illness were incarcerated in jails and prisons. Toward the end of the colonial period incarcerating individuals living with mental illness, instead of providing mental health treatment, ended as a result of the prison reform movement. From 1820 to 1970 the movement was influential in the creation of psychiatric hospitals in which individuals living with mental illness were hospitalized. Beginning in 1970 the process of deinstitutionalization began to occur, during which time individuals were discharged from psychiatric hospitals to live within communities. This period is characterized by insufficient community-based mental health treatment and as a consequence individuals were reincarcerated. Following deinstitutionalization the criminalization of individuals living with mental illness began to occur in which individuals were increasingly more involved with the criminal justice system than the mental health system. The present period is marked by decriminalization, in which the criminal justice system and mental health system are more integrated to ensure diversion to the mental health system (Lee & Cain, 2020).

The present period of decriminalization involves efforts among all of the components of the criminal justice system to divert individuals living with mental illness into the mental health system. Law enforcement, as a first responder to individuals experiencing a mental health crisis, provides interventions focused on diversion. These interventions include the use of specialty-trained police officers and models of collaboration with mental health practitioners.

Types of mental illness

Because law enforcement responds to calls for service that involve mental illness police officers require knowledge about the different types of mental illness. The National Institute of Mental Health (NIMH) identified two types of mental illness: (1) any mental illness (AMI) and serious mental illness (SMI).

Any mental illness

AMI is a mental, behavioral, or emotional disorder that results in either no impairment in functioning or mild, moderate, or severe impairment in functioning. When impairment is severe the type of mental illness is classified as SMI.

Serious mental illness

SMI is also a mental, behavioral, or emotional disorder, although as noted SMI is characterized by severe impairment in functioning affecting one or more areas of an individual's life. In 2019, approximately 51.5 million U.S. adults aged 18 and older were living with AMI. Among these individuals 23 million received mental health services. Also in 2019, approximately 13.1 million U.S. adults aged 18 and older were living with SMI, of which 8.6 million received mental health services (NIMH, 2021).

Clearly, as these figures show a large number of individuals living with AMI and SMI in 2019 did not receive mental health services. Although not all individuals who do not receive mental health services will have law enforcement contact many will have contacts with law enforcement.

Co-occurring disorders

Police officers also require an understanding of co-occurring disorders and interventions and how to assess these disorders during a mental health crisis response. A co-occurring disorder refers to an individual living with both a mental health disorder and a substance use disorder (Minkoff & Cline, 2005; SAMHSA, 2020a). Importantly, the types of mental health disorders that should be diagnosed together with the substance use disorder are not specified in order to determine that a co-occurring disorder exists (SAMHSA, 2020a). However, SAMHSA reports that among individuals who received medication-assisted treatment (MAT) the most often observed mental health disorders included anxiety and mood disorders, schizophrenia, bipolar disorder, and post-traumatic stress disorder, among others. Among the types of substances used to identify a substance use disorder most frequently reported substances were alcohol, opioids, stimulants, and prescription drugs, among others.

In addition to possessing knowledge concerning co-occurring disorders knowledge about an individual's level of functioning, support system, available community-based treatment providers, and interventions to treat the co-occurring disorder are also necessary (Minkoff & Cline, 2005). Although many communities have the capacity to provide treatment for individuals living with co-occurring disorders, Dupont and Cochran (2000) described situations in which police officers transported individuals in crisis to a mental health provider only to learn that substance abuse was the primary disorder. The police officers then transported the individual to a substance use provider, or vice versa.

The role of law enforcement agencies in mental health crises

One perspective regarding the role of law enforcement agencies responding to mental health crises suggests that all patrol officers can provide this response without receiving specialized training. This perspective further suggests that it is easy to provide patrol officers with the knowledge and skills necessary to provide an effective mental health crisis response. This approach has the result of decreasing the need for specialty-trained police officers and specialized law enforcement units (Fyfe, 2000). Another perspective proposed that providing specialized training and employing police officers with specialized skills to respond to mental health crises can benefit individuals in crisis and the law enforcement agency, although such specialization may be inconsistent with law enforcement (Dupont & Cochran, 2000).

Indeed, police officers require training to provide the knowledge and skills to understand mental hygiene law and mental hygiene arrest procedures, utilize appropriate de-escalation techniques effectively, and provide appropriate referrals that divert individuals into mental health treatment. As suggested this also requires knowledge about mental illness, substance use, co-occurring disorders, mental health treatment including MAT, and medications prescribed to treat mental illness.

Training law enforcement officers alone is an inadequate approach to address mental health crises. Numerous alternative models have been proposed that would eliminate the role of law enforcement. Because a law enforcement presence can exacerbate the trauma experienced by an individual experiencing a mental health crisis, and mistrust of law enforcement among communities of color, stakeholders in Chicago, IL, are exploring several alternative options, most of which eliminate the presence of police officers: (1) the use of an emergency telephone number exclusively for mental health crises comprised of a paramedic and mental health practitioner response; (2) forming a collaboration between law enforcement, mental health practitioners, and paramedics, (3) providing CIT training to more police officers; and (4) establishing mobile crisis teams comprised of paramedics and nurses or social workers. However, city officials plan to maintain the presence of law enforcement as part of the mental health crisis response (Sweeney & Gorner, 2020).

While the primary providers of a law enforcement response for individuals experiencing a mental health crisis involve state and local law enforcement agencies, the U.S. Government Accountability Office (GAO) (2018) examined the mental health response provided by federal law enforcement officers and agents employed in the Department of Homeland Security (DHS) and the Department of Justice (DOJ). While the DHS and DOJ agents and officers respond to mental health crises less frequently than state and local law enforcement agencies as part of their work they are also likely to provide a mental health crisis response. Therefore, the GOA conducted a study to identify the primary obstacles experienced among federal officers while providing a mental health crisis response. The study results identified the following obstacles were: (1) conducting an assessment to determine if the individual in crisis has a mental illness, (2) establishing a relationship with the individual, (3) providing an intervention with few community-based resources available, and (4) providing a mental health crisis response to individuals who have been seen during previous incidents.

In response to these findings the DHS and DOJ are reviewing agency policies, training, and current interventions (GAO, 2018). It is likely that some of the same obstacles experienced by federal law enforcement officers are also experienced by officers employed in state and local law enforcement agencies.

Specialized mental health training for law enforcement

Plotkin and Peckerman (2017) found inconsistencies in law enforcement standards among states for mental health and crisis de-escalation training provided to recruits. Based on the results of a 42 state survey they found that standards were primarily developed for recruits in academy training with fewer standards developed for police officer training. Mental health and crisis de-escalation training was categorized as either knowledge or as skill-building topics. The topics taught most often that were associated with knowledge included learning the signs and symptoms of mental illness, state laws defining involuntary commitment, mental disorders such as schizophrenia and mood disorders, and suicide. Knowledge topics such as the types of medications prescribed for mental illness, substance abuse, and co-occurring disorders were taught less often. The most frequently taught skills topics included non-verbal communication, officer safety, and active listening. Less training time was given to developing skills for conflict management and mediation and identifying behaviors associated with mental illness.

Types of law enforcement mental health collaborations

Finn (1989) described numerous early models of collaboration implemented in the 1980s between law enforcement agencies and mental health providers. Since Finn's early descriptions many more law enforcement and mental health provider collaborations have been implemented.

Deane, Steadman, Borum, Veysey, and Morrissey (1999) surveyed 174 law enforcement agencies located in cities with a population of more than 10,000 residents in 1996. Their purpose was to identify the types of collaborations law enforcement agencies implemented to respond to mental health crises. Among the 174 law enforcement agencies that responded to their survey, the majority ($n = 96$, 55%) reported that the agency had not implemented a collaboration or specialized mental health response for individuals experiencing a mental health crisis. Seventy-eight agencies reported implementing collaborations that were categorized as three types: (1) six agencies (3%) implemented a "police-based specialized police response" in which specialty-trained police officers responded to mental health crises; (2) 20 (12%) law enforcement agencies reported implementing a "police-based specialized mental health response" in which mental health practitioners are civilian employees of the law enforcement agency; among these 20 agencies 8 agencies utilized social workers and 12 agencies utilized other mental health practitioners such as psychologists; and (3) 52 (30%) law enforcement agencies reported utilizing a "mental-health-based specialized mental health response" primarily utilizing mobile crisis teams. Overall, their results showed that among law enforcement agencies that have implemented collaborations to respond to mental health crises, the majority of agencies that did establish collaborations utilized mobile crisis teams.

Steadman, Deane, Borum, and Morrissey (2000) compared three models of law enforcement and mental health collaborations. These models included a response provided by civilian law enforcement employees referred to as community service officers, a team of specialty-trained police officers, and a mobile crisis unit. Kisely, Campbell, Peddle, Hare, Pyche, Spicer, and Moore (2010) examined the use of such teams in Nova Scotia, Canada. The mobile crisis teams were comprised of police officers and a mental health practitioner. Data were collected both before the implementation of the mobile crisis team and after the team was implemented. Kisely et al. found after the mobile crisis team was implemented police officers' time at the scene of a mental health crisis decreased, and increased requests for services were received from individuals experiencing mental crises, their families, and community-based mental health providers.

Law enforcement and mental health collaborations appear to be widely implemented, although recent controversial law enforcement responses to a mental health crisis, most of which did not utilize a collaboration model, have been reported. Nevertheless when police officers collaborate with mental health practitioners to respond to mental health crises challenges that affect the collaboration also arise. These challenges include the lack of communication between collaboration partners both before and after a mental health crisis response and professional conflicts that arise between collaboration partners and behavioral health providers (Hollander, Lee, Tahtalian, Young, & Kulkarni, 2012).

Several types of law enforcement collaborations with mental health practitioners have been implemented. Two types of collaborations are perhaps the most widely implemented – Crisis Intervention Teams (CITs) and co-response teams. These collaborations are examined next.

Crisis Intervention Teams

The CIT or the Memphis Police CIT was developed following the shooting and death of a black man by white police officers in Memphis, TN, in 1987. He experienced a mental illness and was armed with a knife when police officers arrived. Upon arrival at the scene police officers ordered him to drop the knife, although he did not do so. Following his death a task force comprised of law enforcement, mental health practitioners, National Alliance on Mental Illness (NAMI), university and hospital administrators, and church leaders was formed to create a specialized intervention for a law enforcement response to mental health crises (University of Memphis, n.d.a.). The task force created the Memphis Police Department CIT, subsequently referred to as the Memphis Model. The goals of CIT are to function as a police-based first responder intervention for individuals and families experiencing a mental health crisis and connect individuals with community-based behavioral health providers. These goals are intended to divert individuals living with mental illness from jail and further criminal justice system involvement. CIT police officers are patrol officers who have received specialized training and are deployed on every shift alongside other patrol officers also performing patrol duties. When a call for a mental health crisis is received the specialty-trained CIT police officers are dispatched to the scene of the crisis alongside other patrol officers. In this way, a timely response is provided. Specialty trained police officers perform tasks such as assessment, de-escalation, and referral to community-based behavioral health providers (University of Memphis, n.d.b.).

Mental Health First Aid (n.d.) identified CIT and Mental Health First Aid for Public Safety as the most well-known law enforcement interventions for responding to mental health crises. The 8-hour Mental Health First Aid for Public Safety training for police officers focuses on understanding mental health disorders and suicide and using the necessary skills to provide crisis intervention during a mental health crisis response. Numerous recommendations are provided for Mental Health First Aid and CIT. First, as a best practice approach Mental Health First Aid should be combined with CIT to create an integrated mental health response. Second, Mental Health First Aid training should be provided to all police officers in a law enforcement agency including veteran officers as well as recruits. Third, the knowledge and skills acquired in Mental

Health First Aid training are not intended to be implemented as an alternative to CIT.

The following case example illustrates a mental health crisis response provided by a police social worker who assists with other types of police calls for service, not just mental health crises. The example shows how an individual experiencing a mental health crisis is linked with services at the scene by providing emergency mental services as well as providing follow-up with family members.

Case Example

A Police Social Work Response to a Mental Health Crisis

Two police officers responded to a family's request for assistance with a family member experiencing a mental health crisis. The family members stated that Mr. B became aggressive when he did not take his medication as prescribed and had been drinking alcohol and using drugs. He had also pushed and shoved around a few items of furniture in the home, although he did not physically harm any family members. When police arrived he was shouting, pacing in the home, and threatening to physically harm individuals in the home. Family members were more concerned about Mr. B's welfare and less concerned about his threatening behaviors.

The police officers separated Mr. B from his family, with one officer speaking with Mr. B and the other officer speaking with family members in different rooms. Each officer's assessment of the situation supported transportation to the hospital psychiatric emergency department. As part of their intervention the officers also contacted the police social worker to arrive at the scene. Driving an unmarked police vehicle the social worker arrived at the scene approximately 15 minutes after being contacted by the police officers.

The police social worker, with the police officers present, first interviewed Mr. B and then his family. An assessment supported the police officers' assessment indicating that Mr. B required emergency psychiatric evaluation and treatment. The police social worker informed the family of the procedures that would take place and assisted the officers with informing Mr. B that he would be transported to the hospital emergency department for care and observation.

Applying knowledge and experience with responding to mental health crises, the police social worker contacted the psychiatric assignment officer at the hospital emergency department by telephone to consult in advance of his arrival, informing staff that Mr. B will be transported to the hospital. The psychiatric assignment officer agreed that Mr. B should be seen for further evaluation and treatment. A police officer requested an ambulance and Mr. B was transported to the hospital psychiatric emergency department. The police officers and police social worker also traveled to the hospital and consulted in person with the emergency staff sharing information from the scene.

One week later the police social worker contacted the family for follow-up and was informed that Mr. B was hospitalized overnight after the crisis, stabilized, and prescribed new medication. The family members stated that the crisis situation had been resolved. Mr. B returned to live with his family after discharge from the hospital. The family was encouraged to contact police and the police social worker again in the future should the need arise. They were also encouraged to continue to utilize outpatient mental health treatment.

CIT has been implemented in law enforcement agencies for a longer period of time than co-responder teams, which are a more recent development. CIT has also been implemented in more law enforcement agencies than co-responder teams (Morabito, Savage, Sneider, & Wallace, 2018). Moreover, co-responder teams have been the subject of less research than CIT (Koziarski, O'Connor, & Frederick, 2021). In a systematic review that examined international police and social work and social service collaborations CIT was not only the most often identified collaboration for mental health crisis; it was also the most identified collaboration found among the 83 collaborations found in the review (Patterson & Swan, 2019).

Research evidence demonstrates that CIT is effective for achieving certain outcomes although not effective for others. As mentioned in Chapter 8, CrimeSolutions is a clearinghouse maintained by the National Institute of Justice (NIJ). The clearinghouse offers information that summarizes the quality of evidence that exists for criminal justice programs or practices. A rating classification scheme reflects the strength of the data or evidence and based on the evidence classifies a program or practice as "Effective, Promising, or No Effects" (National Institute of Justice, Office of Justice Programs, 2020a). As of October 2018, CITs were identified as a practice with numerous additional goals of CIT identified in CrimeSolutions. These goals include reducing police officer injuries and use of force during a mental health crisis response, and reducing arrests among individuals experiencing a mental health crisis. CrimeSolutions assigned CIT a rating of "No Effects" for reducing arrests among individuals experiencing a mental health crisis or use of police officer force when responding to mental health crises (National Institute of Justice, Office of Justice Programs, 2020b).

Skeem and Bibeau (2008) examined police reports over a two-year period in which a CIT response was provided. Approximately 45% of the calls for service included a response to suicide, and 25% included threatening behaviors. Documentation contained in the police reports supported the diversion benefits of CIT given that 74% of the interventions were hospitalization, whereas only 4% involved arrests. Relatedly, Watson and Wood (2017) found that over a three-year period use of the CIT model resulted in more hospitalizations than arrests. De-escalation and other interventions were also provided at the scene, which did not involve hospitalization or arrest.

Willis, Comartin, Victor, Kern, and Kubiak (2021) investigated the use of CIT implemented in a sheriff's office located in a Midwestern state. The objective of the study was to examine the effects of utilizing CIT for individuals with multiple law enforcement contacts who experienced SMI and co-occurring disorders. Interestingly, Willis et al. found that although individuals had numerous law enforcement contacts these contacts actually increased following the implementation of the CIT. They suggested that individuals and their support systems became aware of CIT services and perhaps utilized these services when needed resulting in increased use of CIT.

Co-response teams

A co-response team refers to the use of a team comprised of a police officer and a mental health practitioner or clinician to provide an emergency response for individuals experiencing a mental health crisis. Koziarski, O'Connor, and Frederick (2021) suggested that the use of CIT and co-response teams in Canada has been understudied. Similar to the research conducted by Deane, Steadman, Borum, Veysey, & Morrissey (1999) their study sought to identify the characteristics of CITs and co-response teams in Canada as well as the number of programs that have been implemented. In 2017 and 2018, they surveyed 23 Canadian law enforcement agencies and found 17 (76%) had implemented a CIT or a co-response team. Among these two types of interventions five distinct models were identified: (1) 9 (53%) law enforcement agencies utilized a team comprised of a police officer and a mental health practitioner, (2) 2 (12%) agencies utilized a crisis intervention team that was on call to respond to emergencies, (3) 2 (12%) agencies utilized both a team comprised of a police officer and a mental health practitioner, and the CIT model, (4) 1 (6%) agency utilized both CIT and a co-response team, and (5) 3 agencies (17%) utilized specialty-trained police officers in a co-response team that connected individuals with services or responded to individuals already known to police.

It is not unusual for communities to implement several collaboration models simultaneously to respond to mental health crises. In Denver, CO, both a collaboration formed between a social worker and a paramedic, excluding law enforcement, and a co-responder model comprised of a police officer and a mental health practitioner are utilized (Enos, 2020).

Although co-responder models are an effective mental health crisis response when used in hot spot locations (White & Weisburd, 2018), insufficient data demonstrate that co-responder models are an evidence-based practice (Morabito, Savage, Sneider, & Wallace, 2018). However, among 1,127 calls for service that involved a co-responder model the two most commonly provided interventions were resolving the crisis with the individual remaining at the scene and using EMS to transport the individuals to receive emergency services. The least common interventions included police officers providing transportation to receive emergency services and making an arrest. The two most frequently occurring types of calls involved a mental health crisis experienced by a child and suicide. The least frequent calls involved substance use and offending behaviors (Morabito et al., 2018).

A recommended mental health crisis response

SAMHSA (2020b) provided national guidelines for responding to individuals experiencing a behavioral health or mental health crisis. The guidelines are intended to enhance the crisis response, reduce the costs associated with incarceration and hospitalization, and decrease law enforcement contacts and involvement among individuals experiencing a mental health crisis.

One of the key elements identified in the guidelines is the recommendation to provide a mental health response without law enforcement assistance because including law enforcement has the potential to be ineffective. This can occur due to the presence of armed and uniformed police officers and police vehicles which could exacerbate a crisis situation.

While identifying these concerns about a law enforcement presence SAMHSA (2020b) also recognizes that law enforcement may be necessary at the scene of a mental health crisis for safety reasons. The guidelines identify both minimum expectations and best practices approaches for providing a mental health crisis response. Overall these guidelines include: (1) establishing a regional call center that employs mental health practitioners who answer hotline calls and also use technology to assist individuals experiencing a mental health crisis; (2) implementing a mobile crisis team comprised of a mental health practitioner and a peer which does not include law enforcement unless necessary and the goals of which are to immediately connect individuals with treatment and divert them from criminal justice system involvement; and (3) create crisis receiving and stabilization facilities such as drop-off centers.

Steadman, Deane, Borum, and Morrissey (2000) described the use of a drop-off center as a component of a law enforcement response to mental health crises. To use the drop-off center police officers transport individuals in crisis to the center with pre-arranged assurance that an intake interview will occur and the individual will be admitted. In this way, individuals received timely treatment and police officers were soon available to respond to other police calls for service. Police officers reported this approach was effective.

Clearly, implementing the most appropriate response for individuals experiencing mental health crises does not involve a single approach. Multiple approaches have been developed and implemented both nationally and internationally. Community stakeholders should be included in the decision-making process when considering which model(s) is best suited for a community.

POLICE Model application

The POLICE Model requires data collection and analysis to evaluate a law enforcement collaboration. Determining the most appropriate collaboration outcomes to use to evaluate whether the goals of the collaboration have been achieved is essential. As highlighted in this chapter relevant outcomes for a law enforcement collaboration response to mental health crises include those out-comes that are relevant for law enforcement such as increased knowledge and skills among police officers and outcomes that are relevant for individuals expe-riencing a mental health crisis such as receiving a referral, diversion from jail, and use of psychiatric emergency department services and hospitalization (Compton, Bahoram, Watson, & Oliva, 2008).

It is perhaps easier to measure outcomes that are relevant for police officers, such as the amount of time officers spend responding to a mental health cri-sis than it is to measure outcomes relevant for individuals and their families who receive the law enforcement crisis response and services (Morabito et al., 2018).

Chapter summary

This chapter provided a brief historical overview of the care individuals living with mental illness experienced in the United States. These individuals were incarcerated in jails and prisons during the colonial period before the crea-tion of psychiatric hospitals and their subsequent hospitalization. The present period in the care of individuals living with mental illness is characterized by decriminalization. The practice of decriminalization requires significant coop-eration from law enforcement and other components of the criminal justice system. Prior to decriminalization a practice known as the criminalization of mental illness occurred. During both practices individuals live within the community.

Mental illness can be a contributing factor to homelessness, unemployment, offending behavior including nuisance violations, as well as experiencing a mental health crisis. These situations result in law enforcement contact. Decriminalization posits that individuals are in need of mental health treatment, not incarceration. This chapter also reviewed the two major approaches, CIT and co-responder models, that are used by law enforcement to address mental health crises. Additionally, some of the limitations involved in a law enforcement mental health crisis response were also considered.

Questions for discussion

1. Given the role of law enforcement in responding to mental health crises what are your thoughts about the amount of training time allotted to mental health?
2. Does your local law enforcement agency maintain a specialized unit of police officers or a law enforcement collaboration with mental health practi-tioners or social workers to respond to mental health crises?
3. Compare and contrast the effectiveness of CIT and co-responder models based on research studies you have searched, located, and retrieved.

Activities for further learning

1. Develop a curriculum for mental health training to be delivered to police officers and recruits. Then locate an online sample posted by a law enforcement agency. How does your proposal compare to the sample that you located?
2. Develop a proposal for all states to enact mental health and de-escalation training standards for recruits and veteran police officers. What type of content should be included in your proposal?
3. Does your community provide specialized inpatient and community-based treatment to individuals living with co-occurring disorders? What are the eligibility requirements to receive treatment?

References

Compton, M. T., Bahoram, M., Watson, A. C., & Oliva, J. R. (2008). A comprehensive review of extant research on crisis intervention team (CIT) programs. *The Journal of the American Academy of Psychiatry and the Law, 36*(1), 47–55.

Deane, M. W., Steadman, H. J., Borum, R., Veysey, B. M., & Morrissey, J. P. (1999). Emerging partnerships between mental health and law enforcement. *Psychiatric Services, 50*(1), 99–101.

Dupont, R., & Cochran, S. (2000). Police response to mental health emergencies – Barriers to change. *Journal of the American Academy of Psychiatry and the Law, 28,* 338–344.

Finn, P. (1989). Coordinating services for the mentally ill misdemeanor offender. *Social Service Review, 63*(1), 127–141.

Enos, G. (2020). Crisis response in Denver progresses, with many other communities watching. *Mental Health Weekly, 30*(37), 1–6.

Fyfe, J. J. (2000). Policing the emotionally disturbed. *Journal of the American Academy of Psychiatry and the Law, 28,* 345–347.

Hollander, Y., Lee, S. J., Tahtalian, S., Young, D., & Kulkarni, J. (2012). Challenges relating to the interface between crisis mental health clinicians and police when engaging with people with a mental illness. *Psychiatry, Psychology and Law, 19*(3), 402–411.

Koziarski, J., O'Connor, C., & Frederick, T. (2021). Policing mental health: The composition and perceived challenges of co-response teams and crisis intervention teams in the Canadian context. *Police Practice and Research, 22*(1), 977–995.

Kisely, S., Campbell, L. A., Peddle, S., Hare, S., Pyche, M., Spicer, D., & Moore, B. (2010). A controlled before-and-after evaluation of a mobile crisis partnership between mental health and police services in Nova Scotia. *The Canadian Journal of Psychiatry, 55*(10), 662–668.

Lee, L. H., & Cain, D. S. (2020). Mental health policy for justice-involved persons: Exploring history, perspectives, and models in the United States. *Best Practices in Mental Health, 16*(2), 55–68.

Minkoff, K., & Cline, C. A. (2005). Developing welcoming systems for individuals with co-occurring disorders: The role of the comprehensive continuous integrated system of care model. *Journal of Dual Diagnosis, 1*(1), 65–89.

Mental Health First Aid (n.d.). *Mental health first aid or CIT: What should law enforcement do?* Retrieved from https://www.mentalhealthfirstaid.org/cs/wp-content/uploads/2016/01/FINAL-MHFA-CIT-White-Paper-Annoucement.pdf

Morabito, M. S., Savage, J., Sneider, L., & Wallace, K. (2018). Police response to people with mental illnesses in a major US city: The Boston experience with the co-responder model. *Victims & Offenders*, *13*(8), 1093–1105.

National Institute of Justice, Office of Justice Programs (2020a). *About CrimeSolutions*. Retrieved from CrimeSolutions, https://crimesolutions.ojp.gov/about

National Institute of Justice, Office of Justice Programs (2020b). *Crisis intervention teams (CITs)*. Retrieved from CrimeSolutions, https://crimesolutions.ojp.gov/ratedpractices/81

National Institute of Mental Health (NIMH) (2021). *Mental illness*. Retrieved from https://www.nimh.nih.gov/health/statistics/mental-illness.shtml

Patterson, G. T., & Swan, P. G. (2019). Police social work and social service collaboration strategies one hundred years after Vollmer: A systematic review. *Policing: An International Journal*, *42*(5), 863–886.

Plotkin, M., & Peckerman, T. (2017). *The variability in law enforcement state standards: A 42-state survey on mental health and crisis de-escalation training*. New York: The Council of State Governments.

Skeem, J., & Bibeau, L. (2008). How does violence potential relate to crisis intervention team responses to emergencies?. *Psychiatric Services*, *59*(2), 201–204.

Steadman, H. J., Deane, M. W., Borum, R., & Morrissey, J. P. (2000). Comparing outcomes of major models of police responses to mental health emergencies. *Psychiatric Services*, *51*(5), 645–649.

Substance Abuse and Mental Health Services Administration (SAMHSA) (2020a). *Co-occurring disorders and other health conditions*. Retrieved from https://www.samhsa.gov/medication-assisted-treatment/medications-counseling-related-conditions/co-occurring-disorders

Substance Abuse and Mental Health Services Administration (SAMHSA) (2020b). *National guidelines for behavioral health crisis care best practice toolkit executive summary*. Retrieved from https://www.samhsa.gov/sites/default/files/national-guidelines-for-behavioral-health-crisis-services-executive-summary-02242020.pdf

Sweeney, A., & Gorner, J. (2020). *Chicago considers changes to emergency mental-health response as recent police cases highlight the issue*. Retrieved from https://www.chicagotribune.com/news/criminal-justice/ct-chicago-police-mental-health-response-20201116-wjit5ahx2zh3xoglmopteywedm-story.html

Watson, A. C., & Wood, J. D. (2017). Everyday police work during mental health encounters: A study of call resolutions in Chicago and their implications for diversion. *Behavioral Sciences & the Law*, *35*, 442–455.

White, C., & Weisburd, D. (2018). A co-responder model for policing mental health problems at crime hot spots: Findings from a pilot project. *Policing: A Journal of Policy & Practice*, *12*(2), 194–209.

Willis, T., Comartin, E., Victor, G., Kern, L., & Kubiak, S. (2021). Individuals with mental illness who have multiple encounters with law enforcement. *Journal of Offender Rehabilitation*, *60*(2), 1–18.

University of Memphis (n.d.a). *The CIT program: Background*. Retrieved from http://cit.memphis.edu/overview.php?page=1#:~:text=The%20CIT%20Program%3A%20Background%20In%201987%20police%20officers,the%20young%20man%20died%20of%20multiple%20gunshot%20wounds

University of Memphis (n.d.b). *About CIT*. Retrieved from http://cit.memphis.edu/overview.php?page=2

U.S. Government Accountability Office (GAO) (2018). *Federal law enforcement: DHS and DOJ are working to enhance responses to incidents involving individuals with mental illness*. Retrieved from https://www.gao.gov/products/gao-18-229

11

JUVENILES

Chapter overview

This chapter reviews the role of law enforcement with juveniles. The chapter briefly describes the juvenile justice system as a criminal justice system separate from the adult criminal justice system and explains why the juvenile justice system emerged. These topics are presented through the lens of law enforcement and do not include the other components of the juvenile justice system such as courts and corrections. The role of law enforcement with juveniles is characterized by diversion, rehabilitation, and treatment as opposed to punishment and retribution. Depending on the nature of the offense police officers use more discretion with juveniles, which involves the participation of caretakers and diversion interventions rather than formally processing juveniles in the juvenile justice system.

The chapter also examines the differences between a status offense and juvenile delinquency, defines the age ranges for status offenders and juvenile delinquents, and provides examples of specialized law enforcement programs for juveniles and collaborations. Although an age range that defines a juvenile is articulated in federal legislation, the age ranges that define a juvenile delinquent and a status offender are not uniform among states.

Introduction

Juveniles experience some of the same social problems as adults such as domestic violence, homelessness, alcohol and substance abuse, criminal victimization, sexual assault, and mental illness, to mention but a few. Regarding mental illness, 49.5% of juveniles between the ages of 13 and 18 are living with AMI, and

DOI: 10.4324/9781003132257-11

among these juveniles 22.2% experience severe impairment in their functioning (NIMH, 2021).

Juveniles also experience social problems that are unique to their age groups such as bullying, peer pressure, challenges in teen dating, and parent–child conflict. Like adults experiencing these social problems can contribute to trauma, behavioral, psychological, and physiological reactions. Other reactions include anxiety and depression. Consequently, among juveniles law enforcement contacts may be a result of these experiences.

Further, some juvenile contacts with law enforcement involve juvenile delinquency in which a crime has been committed or status offenses that are only considered offending behavior because of the juvenile's age. The age range for these classifications varies among states. Finally, juveniles may have contacts with law enforcement associated with the "school-to-prison pipeline" and zero-tolerance or other school disciplinary policies. Indeed, each of the issues can result in contact with law enforcement. Addressing these social problems and issues requires specialized law enforcement knowledge and skills. Because police officers have contact with juveniles and their caregivers it is essential that officers understand the policies and procedures that exist for juveniles within their jurisdiction. Law enforcement contacts with youth focus on utilizing police officer discretion, diversion, and rehabilitation including processing juveniles informally rather than formally through the juvenile justice system.

Defining a juvenile

The federal age range used to define a juvenile has been identified by the U.S. Department of Justice. While the definition does not identify the types of criminal offenses which need to be committed by juveniles in order to define a juvenile delinquent the definition does imply that the crime or offense must be similar to that committed by an adult. Consider the following definition:

> A 'juvenile' is a person who has not attained his eighteenth birthday, and 'juvenile delinquency' is the violation of a law of the United States committed by a person prior to his eighteenth birthday which would have been a crime if committed by an adult. A person over eighteen but under twenty-one years of age is also accorded juvenile treatment if the act of juvenile delinquency occurred prior to his eighteenth birthday.
>
> *Department of Justice (2020)*

Understanding the legal age of a juvenile is essential for law enforcement because of the policies and procedures involved in law enforcement contacts with juveniles. The age range has important consequences for juveniles having law enforcement contacts. These contacts with juveniles also require that police officers possess the knowledge and skills to intervene based on the criminal offense and the age of the offender.

Juvenile delinquency

The Department of Justice's (2020) definition of a juvenile delinquent identifies a juvenile delinquent as a juvenile who commits a crime prior to the juvenile's 18th birthday and this definition is established in federal legislation. However, according to the Office of Juvenile Justice and Delinquency Prevention (OJJDP) (2019) the age range used to identify a juvenile delinquent varies among states. OJJDP provides a summary of the age ranges that identify juvenile delinquency among the 50 states in addition to Washington, DC, as of 2018. Among 33 states the lower age range considered a juvenile delinquent is not specified, although one state, North Carolina, identifies age 6 as the lowest age considered a juvenile delinquent. Age 17 is the upper age range to be considered a juvenile delinquent.

Law enforcement agencies in the United States often immediately provide public information about an offender who has been arrested. This information is released well before a trial begins. Images of the arrest are also publicized in the media. This is not the case for juvenile offenders. Because of their age the identity of a juvenile offender is withheld from the media.

Siegel and Senna (1991) report that the treatment of juveniles in the criminal justice system has its origins in the concept of *parens patriae* ("the state is the father," p. 12), established based on English common law, which suggests juvenile delinquency does not imply a criminal law violation and as such juveniles are not criminals. Juvenile offenses are more associated with civil laws which support the well-being of society. Further, some juvenile behaviors are considered status offenses, although these are not criminal law violations. During the 1960s legislation was enacted among states to distinguish between a status offender and a juvenile delinquent to eliminate the classification of the juvenile as a juvenile delinquent.

Status offenses

The *Michigan Guide to Compliance with Laws Governing the Placement of Juveniles in Secure Facilities* (n.d.) provides the definition of a status offense and examples of status offense behaviors:

> A status offender is a juvenile who has been charged with or adjudicated for conduct that would not be a crime if committed by an adult. Examples of status offenses are truancy, curfew violations, incorrigibility, and running away. In addition, underage alcohol offenses are considered to be status offenses for federal compliance purposes, even though state or local law may consider them delinquent offenses.

The Juvenile Justice, Geography, Policy, Practice & Statistics (JJGPS) (n.d.) provided a similar list of status offenses which included: running away, truancy, tobacco and alcohol use, curfew violations, and disobeying parents and school officials. Lastly, in addition to identifying the behaviors listed above Siegel and Senna (1991) identified additional behaviors not included in the above listings. They identified: sexual misconduct, use of profanity, having delinquent friends, and engaging in immoral behaviors.

Similar to the differential age ranges that exist among states to define a juvenile delinquent different age ranges exist that identify a status offender. For status offenses 46 states identify the lower age range as not specified, whereas 49 states including Washington, DC, identify 17 as the upper age range. Only Massachusetts and North Carolina identify age 6 as the lowest age range to be considered a status offense, and only South Carolina identifies age 16 as the upper age range to be considered a status offense. All other states including Washington, DC, identify the upper age range as age 17 (OJJDP, 2019).

Status offenders have law enforcement contacts for many reasons, although perhaps a primary source for law enforcement contacts involves caregivers who are worried and frustrated about a juvenile's behaviors. As the following case example illustrates the parents of a 15-year-old were worried about behaviors associated with status offenses. These behaviors include not following the rules at home established by the parents, violating established curfew times, socializing with peers that did not have parental approval, and truancy.

Case Example

Status Offense Behaviors

The parents of a 15-year-old male telephoned 911, stating that their son was not following the rules at home, staying out late at night beyond a set curfew time, hanging out with the wrong crowd, and skipping school often. The parents informed the operator that they have tried counseling and other interventions and that it does not appear to be effective. They are requesting that police remove him from the home and he is stating that he plans to leave the home.

After conducting an assessment and determining that this is an appropriate family situation for referral to a police social worker the officer made the referral by contacting the police social worker who arrived on the scene to meet with the parents and juvenile.

The police social worker provided crisis intervention, emotional support, and mediation. As the police social worker explored options to resolve the crisis situation the parents remained committed to having their son removed from their home because they felt the situation was beyond their ability to manage, and their son remained determined to leave the home after the police officer and police social worker left.

The police social worker discussed with the family the option of a voluntary, non-secure out-of-home placement in an emergency youth shelter. Additional services provided by the shelter such as developing a plan for the son's return to the home and ongoing counseling were also discussed. Both the parents and their son agreed this would resolve the crisis.

> *Subsequently the police social worker contacted the shelter by telephone. The shelter intake worker spoke with both of the parents and their son. The parents provided verbal consent by telephone, agreeing to have their son placed in the shelter. The son also agreed to the emergency placement and consented to allow the police social worker to transport him to the shelter. Upon packing a few personal items the police social worker transported him in an unmarked police vehicle to the youth shelter and facilitated the intake process upon arrival. The parents were informed that the shelter would provide follow-up the following day.*

In this case example the situation required that the police social worker was knowledgeable about the admission criteria of the voluntary emergency youth shelter. The emergency placement was voluntary and the juvenile was not mandated to be admitted. Therefore, it is imperative that the juvenile and his parents were informed so that they could make an informed decision and provide informed consent.

Persons in need of supervision

A Persons in Need of Supervision (PINS) case is intended for juveniles whose behaviors are status offenses. These juveniles are regarded as in need of supervision or treatment to change their behaviors. A parent or guardian, school official, or an official employed in a city or county agency involved with the juvenile are all eligible to file for a PINS. Before a PINS case is opened the juvenile and parent or guardian must meet with a probation officer to explore options for addressing the behaviors, namely family counseling (New York State Unified Court System, n.d.a). However, in another community within the same state a collaboration established between the New York City Administration for Children's Services (ACS) and the probation department utilizes social workers, not probation officers, to provide referrals and other services to juveniles and their families such as substance abuse treatment and family counseling. The juvenile and parent or guardian meet with a social worker instead of a probation officer to explore these options (New York Stated Unified Court System. (n.d.b).

The procedures for obtaining a PINS vary based on jurisdiction and not all jurisdictions offer PINS. In jurisdictions that offer PINS police officers provide referrals to families, encouraging them to seek a PINS. Whether or not a jurisdiction offers PINS police officers have contacts with juveniles that involve status offense behaviors.

The school-to-prison pipeline

Behaviors associated with the school-to-prison pipeline may result in juveniles receiving either a juvenile delinquent or status offender classification. This situation occurs because certain behaviors and offenses that happen on school grounds are subject to zero tolerance and other strict disciplinary policies. Because truancy is a status offense school officials can initiate the process to classify a juvenile as a status offender. As we saw, in some jurisdictions school officials can initiate a PINS case for truancy and other status offense behaviors.

Numerous law enforcement collaborations have been implemented to address the school-to-prison pipeline. For example, the Philadelphia Police School Diversion Program is a partnership formed between the Philadelphia Police Department, the School District of Philadelphia, Philadelphia's Department of Human Services, and youth service agencies. The goals of the program are to avoid arrests in schools, avoid the use of suspension or detention, and divert youth to receive services from youth services agencies. Any student aged 10 or older who has committed a misdemeanor offense on school property and does not have a prior record is eligible to participate in the program (Goldstein et al., 2019).

The role of law enforcement with juveniles

The role of law enforcement with juveniles is much different than the law enforcement role with adults, particularly adult offenders. Law enforcement contacts with juveniles occur as a result of juvenile delinquency, status offenses, and social problems similar to those experienced by adults. During these law enforcement contacts emphasis is placed on diversion, informal juvenile justice system processing, rehabilitation, and treatment. Police officers also use discretion during the contacts.

Wiley and Esbensen (2016) found juveniles who were stopped and questioned by police officers or arrested were involved in more delinquent behaviors than juveniles who did not have law enforcement contacts. Importantly, the authors note that law enforcement diversion interventions follow a juvenile's contact with law enforcement. This creates a dilemma for police officers that requires further inquiry because law enforcement must respond to juvenile delinquency and status offense behaviors. The authors further note that juvenile law enforcement contacts must be positive and not label juveniles.

Law enforcement specialty programs for juveniles

Numerous specialty programs have been implemented within law enforcement agencies with a focus on police and juvenile interactions. In general, the goal of these programs is to improve law enforcement and juvenile relations and provide positive prosocial activities for juveniles. Although not intended to be an exhaustive review of juvenile programs operated by law enforcement agencies, the following programs are illustrative of perhaps the most well-known law enforcement juvenile programs. These specialty law enforcement programs are national in scope.

Youth officers

Generally, youth officers are specialty trained patrol officers assigned to a law enforcement unit. Their purpose is to provide law enforcement and service functions to juveniles and their caregivers.

School resource officers

School resource officers (SROs) may also be specialty-trained patrol officers. Instead of being assigned to a law enforcement unit these officers' primary assignments are schools. Rhodes (2019) identified the law enforcement functions SROs performed in four Midwestern states. In high schools and schools located in urban areas SROs performed order maintenance and law enforcement functions, whereas SROs involved in community policing strategies performed the service law enforcement function in addition to mentoring and teaching students.

The use of sworn law enforcement officers in schools has become increasingly controversial due to the excessive use of force by officers that has been captured on video and the enforcement of school zero-tolerance policies and other school disciplinary policies that contribute to the school-to-prison pipeline. Although some efforts have been made to increase the use of police officers in schools, including approaches that consider arming teachers due to safety concerns, other approaches call for the removal of police officers from schools. In 2020 during the 116th Congress 2nd Session a Bill titled the *Counseling Not Criminalization in Schools Act* was introduced in the House of Representatives. In order to receive funding under this Bill schools must end contractual agreements with law enforcement agencies and remove police officers from school property. If enacted into law the Bill will provide funding opportunities for schools to hire social workers, nurses, psychologists, and other professionals to provide evidence-based and trauma-informed services (GovTrack.us., 2021).

Police athletic league

An early model of the Police Athletic League (PAL) was formed in New York City in 1914 when the police commissioner created playground areas for children. During this period the Junior Police was also developed for boys. Around 1932 in response to rising juvenile crime the Junior PAL was created. Throughout its evolution PAL has focused on youth development. In the 1940s and 1950s social workers were hired to provide interventions to youth. Presently PAL operates after-school and summer youth programs focused on education and life skills (Police Athletic League, Inc., 2021).

Junior police cadets

The South Bend Police Department, located in South Bend, IN, operates a junior cadet program for youth and young adults aged 14 to 20 years old who are interested in law enforcement. Cadets receive law enforcement training in topics such as writing crime reports, crime investigations, and the use of firearms. Interested applicants must meet the program requirements and submit an application (South Bend Police Department, 2021).

Junior police academy

The Mobile Police Department, located in Mobile, AL, operates a junior police academy for youth between 9 and 12 years old. The purpose of the junior police academy is to provide interaction between police officers and youth and provide team building and field trip activities for youths interested in law enforcement. The application process involves submitting an application, essay, enrollment fee, and achieving a C grade average to be accepted into the one-week academy (City of Mobile Police Department, 2021).

The role of social work with juveniles

The social work profession has a significant history of advocacy on behalf of juveniles as well as participating in criminal justice reforms on behalf of juveniles by recognizing the need for juveniles to be treated differently than adults in the criminal justice system. The first juvenile court in the United States was created in Chicago, IL, resulting from the passage of *An Act to Regulate the Treatment and Control of Dependent, Neglected, and Delinquent* Children (Abbott, as cited in Alexander, 2007). The social work profession was instrumental in establishing this first juvenile court (Fox, as cited in Alexander, 2007). Today, as a result of these efforts a juvenile court has been formed in all 50 states (Ellis & Sowers, 2001). This separate court system is known as a juvenile court in some states and family court in other states.

Social workers are employed in numerous agencies that provide services to youth and their families. Social workers provide services to juveniles in settings such as schools, courts, juvenile probation departments, family counseling and mental health centers, emergency shelters, and youth detention centers.

The following case example demonstrates how a police social worker can provide assistance to both a law enforcement agency and a family experiencing a crisis. In this case example the reasons for the 911 call placed by a 7-year-old was vague. A police officer was dispatched to provide a response and investigate the situation. The example shows the dilemma police officers experience in terms of responding or not responding to situations when a child has telephoned the police. Although a call such as this placed to 911 can occur among youth of any age this example shows that younger youth may also contact law enforcement when experiencing parent–child conflict.

Case Example

Providing a Police Social Work in Response to a Juvenile Police Call

A 7-year-old boy called 911 and informed the operator that he was having problems with his mother. He stated that his mother was discriminating against him and that he would like for a police officer to come to the home and assist him. When questioned by the 911 operator he stated that no violence or abuse had occurred but insisted that he needed a police officer. Other than providing this information he was vague about why he was requesting a police officer. His single mother did not know he had telephoned 911 until a police officer arrived. She had contacted police in the past when her boyfriend became argumentative.

Upon arrival and speaking with the juvenile and his mother the police officer first assessed whether the call involved child abuse or neglect. The officer assessed this was not child maltreatment and ascertained that the youth was angry with his mother because she would not allow him to visit his friend and play at her house. He thought his mother was being unfair and that this was a matter for the police. After completing an assessment and obtaining information about the situation the police officer contacted the police social worker with a request to provide assistance to the family.

The police social worker arrived at the home shortly following the request from the officer. Mediation was provided during which the youth and his mother both discussed their concerns about this situation. The mother stated that she will plan to speak with her son's friend's family to ease her worries about him visiting their home and the son agreed to this plan.

Police and social work collaboration with juveniles

Social workers can provide beneficial services when police officers employ diversion strategies so that youth avoid further juvenile justice system involvement, thereby creating opportunities for social work practice, and when caregivers are arrested social workers can provide services to youth to ensure the well-being of youth (Cantwell, 2013). In some countries it is mandatory that a social worker attend an investigation interview that is conducted by a police officer. The social workers attend the investigative interview together with the caregiver or without the caregiver's attendance (Cantwell, 2013; Pierpoint, 2001). The presence of a social worker can introduce a social work perspective into the law enforcement investigative interview process in numerous ways and provide emotional support for youth.

A police crisis worker reported assisting a law enforcement agency with approximately 20% of parent–child conflicts due to a parent placing limitations on the youth's use of a cellphone or video games. Once parents set limits on the use of these electronics conflict escalated to the point where many times youth became violent toward their parents. In these situations parents subsequently called the police. The police crisis worker describes providing support to the parents, family therapy, and referrals to parenting classes (Schoenberg, 2018).

In an early study of law enforcement collaborations implemented with partners from national organizations that provide youth services, Chaiken (1998) identified some of these agencies, which included the Boys and Girls Club of America, Boy Scouts of America, Girls Incorporated, Girl Scouts of the USA, the National Association of Police Athletic Leagues, the National 4-H Council including USDA 4-H and Youth Development Service, and the YMCA of the USA. Chaiken found that among these diverse youth collaborations when law enforcement partnered with previously established programs such partnerships facilitated the progress of implementing collaborations. More than 100 years ago Vollmer (1919) advocated for law enforcement collaboration with the campfire girls, boy scouts and clubs, and junior police organizations.

As previously mentioned juveniles experience some of the same social problems as adults. Law enforcement collaborations have been implemented to address some of these social problems. For instance, Van Hasselt et al. (2006) described a substance abuse prevention and treatment program for youth consisting of a collaboration between law enforcement and mental health practitioners. Youth were eligible to receive program interventions only upon receiving a referral to the program from law enforcement. Upon examining the program outcomes Van Hasselt et al. observed a decrease in substance use, law enforcement contacts, and school truancy among youth that participated in the program. These youth also had improved academic performance.

POLICE Model application

As Chaiken (1998) found, utilizing previously established youth service programs can provide a useful foundation for forming a collaboration with law enforcement focused on youth services. These collaborations can provide services to youth focused on diverting youth from further juvenile justice system involvement, addressing issues associated with the school-to-prison pipeline, or providing interventions to ameliorate the social problems that juveniles experience.

During the planning phase, prior to beginning the organizing phase, a useful task to accomplish is to locate and retrieve information about community-based youth services agencies. These agencies can be categorized based on the types of services provided. Agencies not included in the initial planning phase can also be approached and invited to participate in considering a collaboration with law enforcement collaboration during the organizing phase. The subsequent tasks will then be guided by determining the most appropriate agencies in support of forming a collaboration and the feasibility of including these agencies.

Chapter summary

This chapter suggested that some of the same social problems experienced by adults are also experienced by juveniles. In addition, juveniles are involved in offending behaviors referred to as juvenile delinquency, as well as behaviors that are offenses due to their age referred to as status offenses. Status offenses are considered offenses only due to a juvenile's age and would not be considered an offense for an adult. These social problems and offenses are likely to be the focus of juvenile contacts with law enforcement. While a federal definition identifying a juvenile was reviewed no uniform age range exists among states to identify a status offender or a juvenile delinquent.

This chapter also briefly reviewed the historical handling of juveniles within the criminal justice system. In Chapter 1, we examined the four components of the criminal justice system. In this chapter we discussed two criminal justice systems that exist, the adult criminal justice system and the juvenile justice system. The juvenile justice system is characterized by the same four criminal justice system components of legislation, law enforcement, courts, and corrections although these four componnents focus on juveniles. As a result of how juveniles were handled in the adult criminal justice system the juvenile justice system emerged. Because of their status, and depending upon the type of offense, juvenile contacts with law enforcement involve the use of a police officer's discretion and diversion interventions. Law enforcement as a component of both the adult criminal justice and the juvenile justice system employs police officers with specialized training, knowledge, and skills to address the issues that juveniles experience. This requires that these officers have an understanding of community resources, legislative policies, and the ability to have positive interactions with juveniles as well as their caregivers. A case example illustrating the approach taken by a police social worker providing crisis intervention for a juvenile and family members was presented.

Questions for discussion

1. What age range is considered a juvenile in your state?
2. Does your state have procedures for persons-in-need-of-supervision and status offenses?
3. Does your local law enforcement agency employ youth officers? Does the local law enforcement agency place police officers in schools? If so, what are your thoughts about the presence of police officers in schools?

Activities for further learning

1. Locate national and local statistics that identify the number of juveniles categorized as status offenders and juvenile delinquents.

2. Prepare a list of emergency services for juveniles in your community such as hotlines, emergency shelters, and community-based counseling and recreational centers. Is a lower and upper age limit identified for these services?
3. Prepare a list of specialty programs for juveniles organized and operated by your local law enforcement agency. Is a lower and upper age limit identified for these programs?

References

Alexander, R., Jr. (2007). Juvenile delinquency and social work practice. In C. A. McNeece & A. R. Roberts (Eds.), *Policy and practice in the justice system* (pp. 181–197). Chicago: Nelson Hall.

Cantwell, N. (2013). *The role of social work in juvenile justice*. Retrieved from http://www.socialserviceworkforce.org/system/files/resource/files/The%20Role%20of%20Social%20Work%20in%20Juvenile%20Justice.pdf

Chaiken, M. R. (1998). *Kids, cops, and communities*. Washington, D.C.: U.S. Department of Justice, Office of Justice Programs, National Institute of Justice.

City of Mobile Police Department (2021). *Junior police academy: Mobile police department*. Retrieved from https://www.mobilepd.org/juniorpoliceacademy/

Department of Justice (2020). *"Juvenile" defined*. Retrieved from https://www.justice.gov/archives/jm/criminal-resource-manual-38-juvenile-defined

Ellis, R. A., & Sowers, K. M. (2001). *Juvenile justice practice: A cross-disciplinary approach to intervention*. Belmont, CA: Wadsworth, Brooks/Cole.

Goldstein, N. E., Cole, L. M., Houck, M., Haney-Caron, E., Holliday, S. B., Kreimer, R., & Bethel, K. (2019). Dismantling the school-to-prison pipeline: The Philadelphia police school diversion program. *Children and Youth Services Review, 101*, 61–69.

GovTrack.us. (2021). *S. 4360 – 116th Congress: Counseling not criminalization in schools act*. Retrieved from https://www.govtrack.us/congress/bills/116/s4360

Juvenile Justice, Geography, Policy, Practice & Statistics (JJGPS) (n.d.). *Status offense issues*. Retrieved from http://www.jjgps.org/status-offense-issues

Michigan Guide to Compliance with Laws Governing the Placement of Juveniles in Secure Facilities (n.d.). Retrieved from https://michigancommitteeonjuvenilejustice.com/site-files/files/Documents/DHS-BJJJuvenileJusticeBookletWebVersion_292401_7.pdf

National Institute of Mental Health (NIMH) (2021). *Mental illness*. Retrieved from https://www.nimh.nih.gov/health/statistics/mental-illness.shtml

New York State Unified Court System (n.d.a). *Persons in need of supervision*. Retrieved from http://ww2.nycourts.gov/courts/7jd/courts/family/case_types/persons_in_need_of_supervision.shtml#:~:text=A%20person%20in%20need%20of%20supervision%20%28PINS%29%20is,drug%20abuse%205%20And%20requires%20supervision%20or%20treatment

New York Stated Unified Court System (n.d.b). *Family assessment program*. Retrieved from https://ww2.nycourts.gov/COURTS/nyc/family/familyassessmentprogram.shtml

Office of Juvenile Justice and Delinquency Prevention (2019). *OJJDP statistical briefing book*. Retrieved from https://www.ojjdp.gov/ojstatbb/structure_process/qa04102.asp?qaDate=2018

Police Athletic League, Inc. (2021). *History*. Retrieved from https://www.palnyc.org/history

Pierpoint, H. (2001). The performance of volunteer appropriate adults: A survey of call outs. *The Howard Journal of Criminal Justice*, *40*(3), 255–271.

Rhodes, T. (2019). School resource officer perceptions and correlates of work roles. *Policing: A Journal of Policy and Practice*, *13*(4), 498–516.

Schoenberg, N. (2018, December 23). Some parents call police over teens' cellphone use. *Chicago Tribune*, Section 6, 5.

Siegel, L. J., & Senna, J. J. (1991). *Juvenile delinquency: Theory, practice and law* (4th ed.). St. Paul, MN: West Publishing Company.

South Bend Police Department (2021). *Junior cadets*. Retrieved from https://police.southbendin.gov/get-involved/junior-cadets

Van Hasselt, V. B., Killam, G., Schlessinger, K. M., DiCicco, T. M., Anzalone Jr, W. F., Leslie, T. L., … & Massey, L. L. (2006). The adolescent drug abuse prevention and treatment (ADAPT) program: A mental health-law enforcement collaboration. *Journal of Child & Adolescent Substance Abuse*, *15*(2), 87–104.

Vollmer, A. (April, 1919). *Writings, the policeman as social worker*. BANC MSS C-B 403, The Bancroft Library, University of California, Berkeley.

Wiley, S. A., & Esbensen, F. A. (2016). The effect of police contact: Does official intervention result in deviance amplification?. *Crime & Delinquency*, *62*(3), 283–307.

12

INTERNATIONAL POLICE AND SOCIAL WORK AND POLICE AND SOCIAL SERVICE COLLABORATION

Chapter overview

The practice of police social work and social work and social service collaborations implemented with law enforcement agencies are not unique to the United States. The use of social workers, social service workers, and other practitioners as collaborators in law enforcement partnerships is international in scope. Although by no means complete this chapter provides examples of international police and social work and social service collaborations, as well as a discussion about the practice of police social work in India.

The collaboration examples were identified in database searches and articles published in English were retrieved. The examples provided in this chapter were guided, in part, based on the approach from a systematic review conducted by Patterson and Swan (2019). Due to the search strategy employed and using only databases for conducting searches numerous collaborations are likely to not be included in this presentation. While this chapter does not endeavor to provide a comprehensive review of international law enforcement collaborations it does provide a brief summary among select collaborations of the types of social problems addressed.

Introduction

Throughout this book, the focus has been the practice of police social work, which occurs when police social workers are employed in law enforcement agencies. This unique type of social work practice has been primarily presented in this book applicable to the United States. Moreover, throughout this book, police social work has been distinguished from police and social work collaboration and police and social service collaboration.

DOI: 10.4324/9781003132257-12

However, discussions about police social work, police and social work, and police and social service collaborations are not limited to the United States. Such collaborations are international in scope, with numerous countries having implemented some form of police and social work or social service collaboration. Law enforcement agencies have identified the need for these collaborations and scholars have disseminated information about their characteristics.

These international collaborations are diverse in scope and the types of social problems addressed range from assisting migrant children to providing interventions to address radicalization and extremism. Although this presentation does not discuss all of the varied groups of professionals involved in these collaborations the professional groups range from child protection workers to health care workers. The collaborations presented in this chapter are summarized in sufficient detail primarily to identify the type of social problems addressed and are not intended to summarize an exhaustive listing of collaborations. Further, the purpose of this chapter is not to identify all of the professionals involved in the collaboration nor the collaboration components (see Patterson & Swan, 2019).

As law enforcement agencies, social workers, social service workers, and other professionals consider establishing joint collaboration it is essential to recognize the wide variation in the existing types of collaborations and social problems that are addressed.

The publication titled *Co-operation between social services and police: The first international ICRA workshop for international practitioners* (International Crime Research Association and International Association for Comparative Studies in Policing Crime Control and Social Order, 1990) reports on the first International Crime Research Association (ICRA) workshop held at the School of Social Work in Esbjerg, Denmark, from January 29 to February 2, 1990. The goals of the workshop were to increase police and social work collaboration and "to promote and contribute to comparative international research in this field" (p. 4). Seven countries were invited to have participants attend the workshop – Denmark, France, Germany, the Netherlands, Norway, Sweden, and the U.K. – although participants from France could not attend. Participants included law enforcement personnel and social workers who provided presentations on the topic of police and social work collaboration in their countries. The presentation provided in this chapter describing international police and social work collaborations shows that each of these countries, except France and Norway, were found in a database search to maintain a police and social work or police and social service collaboration.

Police social work in India

Police social work practice in which police social workers are employed in law enforcement is rare in India (Shetye, 2019; Sinha, 2012). Nevertheless, police and social work collaborations have been implemented in India to assist female victims of crime (Sinha) and intervene in instances of human trafficking and child labor exploitation (Shetye).

Although a need exists to expand the practice of police social work India these efforts are hindered by the government's position to exclude police social workers from employment in law enforcement agencies and the lack of social work educational opportunities to prepare students for this specialized area of social work practice (Sinha, 2017).

Criminal Justice Social Work

The term Criminal Justice Social Work (CJSW) does not concern police social work practice or social work collaboration with law enforcement agencies. Nonetheless, the historical development of CJSW, together with skills and tasks performed by social workers, has implications for police social work practice.

After the Social Work 1968 Act was enacted in Scotland the Scottish Probation Service was eliminated. As a result, probationers under community supervision were mandated to report to social workers instead of probation officers. The established goals for social work practice with offenders included social justice and rehabilitation (McNeill, 2005). These goals are achieved through social work community supervision, as opposed to probation supervision, in which social workers emphasize public safety, reducing re-offending and incarceration, and the reintegration of offenders into society based on best practice approaches (McNeill, Batchelor, Burnett, & Knox, 2005).

The creation of CJSW underscores how the social work profession can be established in criminal justice settings that are typically viewed by social workers as inconsistent with social justice. In addition, CJSW underscores how tasks and interventions that are not associated with social work practice can be performed by social workers to improve client outcomes. Certainly performing the tasks of probation officers may not be appealing to social workers and may make some feel uncomfortable assuming this role. It is a role characterized by social control, court sanctions and mandates, authoritarian settings, and oftentimes elements of coercion. Among the most distressing tasks may be the mandate for a social worker to violate a probationer for not appearing for an appointment or some other behavior that constitutes a violation. As a consequence of a violation an individual under probation supervision could receive sanctions that include incarceration.

Maybee (2000) acknowledged that social workers employed in the CJSW services also share these concerns. Social workers are uncomfortable with probationers reporting requirements to keep appointments and the need to enforce these requirements that may also be attached to sanctions. However, in order for social work interventions to be effective Maybee also articulates the need for social workers to develop best practice approaches to address these concerns.

Assuming tasks formerly performed by probation officers illustrates how the social work profession can engage in ethical social work practice while at the same addressing issues associated social control, court sanctions and mandates, authoritarian settings, and coercion. These are issues facing social workers employed in criminal justice settings including law enforcement agencies. Much can be learned from CJSW.

Examples of international police and social work and police and social service collaborations

As the preceding discussion about police work in India, CJSW in Scotland, and the ICRA workshop have indicated the social work profession has an established history of international involvement with law enforcement and the criminal justice system. Specifically, police and social work collaboration has an extensive history of planning, implementation, and development among various countries. Indeed, a great deal of planning is needed to bring law enforcement and social work together to provide collaborative interventions. While the goals are the same to resolve community social problems, there are numerous challenges that can arise when police and social workers collaborate. These challenges were examined in Chapter 4.

As mentioned police and social work and police and social service collaborations are international in scope. In a comprehensive systematic review that initially examined 3,065 titles before including 81 studies in the systematic review results, Patterson and Swan (2019) investigated the extent of police and social work and police and social service collaborations. The studies were located through database searches and only studies published in English were included. The systematic review included numerous international collaborations. Among the 81 studies, 83 collaborations were described. In addition, among these collaborations 52.2% were implemented in the United States, whereas 47.8% of the total collaborations included in the systematic review were implemented outside of the United States.

Nearly half of the collaborations were implemented outside of the United States, although a very small number of collaborations were found among the different countries. Outside of the United States, the U.K. was found to have implemented the most collaborations, followed by Australia, Canada, Israel, Sweden, and the Netherlands. One police social work or police and social service collaboration was found in each of 11 countries: Germany, Singapore, Cambodia, Hong Kong, Romania, Grenada, Denmark, Taiwan, Austria, Switzerland, and Portugal (Patterson & Swan, 2019).

Because the following description of these collaborations was retrieved from database searches of published literature there is no assurance that these collaborations still exist and some may have ended. The following brief descriptions show the range of possibilities and types of social problems and populations that have been the focus of such collaborations. These international collaborations do not identify the practice of police social work in law enforcement agencies but rather identify police and social work and police and social service collaboration. Among some collaborations other professionals in addition to social work and social service workers are involved.

Domestic violence

Numerous collaborations provide services to women of children and families who are victims of domestic violence. Cooper, Anaf, and Bowden (2008) described police and social work collaboration implemented in Australia to address domestic violence against women perpetrated by gang and organized crime members. Stanley and Humphreys (2014) reported several collaborations implemented to conduct risk assessments and provide services to children and families that experienced domestic violence in several countries. These include the Victorian Risk Assessment Framework, which includes assessments conducted by social workers in Australia, the Multi-Agency Risk Assessment Conferences implemented in England and Wales, and the Multi-Agency Safeguarding Hubs established in England. Collaborations established to provide services to children living in families experiencing domestic violence in Australia have also been described (Humphreys, Healey, Kirkwood, & Nicholson, 2018).

Buchbinder and Eisikovits (2008) examined the characteristics of police and social work collaboration in response to domestic violence in Israel. Jeremiah, Quinn, and Alexis (2018) provided information about the implementation of the United Nations Partnership for Peace (PfP) domestic violence diversion program in Grenada that included courts, police, and social service agencies. Finally, Diemer, Ross, Humphreys, and Healey (2017) described police officers providing referrals to social service providers and collaborating with domestic violence specialists in Australia to address incidents of domestic violence.

Elder abuse and adult protection

Collaborations have also been implemented to address the social problem of elder abuse and to provide adult protection services. Cambridge and Parkes (2006) explained joint collaboration in the UK in adult protection investigations, particularly when a crime has occurred. Additionally, Beaulieu, Côté, and Diaz (2017) identified the Integrated Police Response for Abused Seniors (IPRAS) collaboration to address elder abuse in Canada.

Community policing

Parkinson (1980) described community policing program collaborations formed in Canada between police and social workers employed in numerous social service agencies to which police officers made referrals.

Substance abuse

Copoeru, Moldovan, Agheorghiesei, Ciuhodaru, Seghedin, and Iorga (2013) explained the police and social work and health care provider collaboration to address substance abuse in Romania. Law enforcement collaborations have been implemented in numerous countries to address substance use, as explained by

Waal, Clausen, Gjersing, and Gossop (2014), who identified law enforcement, social work, social services, and health care collaboration to address substance use in public spaces in Austria, Germany, the Netherlands, Portugal, and Switzerland.

Drivers under the influence of drugs and alcohol

Forsman, Hrelja, Henriksson, and Wiklund (2011) identified a collaboration formed between police and social service providers to deliver interventions to drivers under the influence of drugs and alcohol in Sweden.

Mental health

As discussed in Chapter 10 law enforcement officers are first responders to individuals experiencing a mental health crisis or who have other mental health needs. Consequently, the law enforcement service function can be enhanced through collaboration with mental health providers.

Among the international collaborations identified is the Cornwall Criminal Justice Liaison and Diversion Service (CJLDS) implemented in the U.K. as a pilot project collaboration. The focus of the Cornwall CJLDS was to provide interventions to individuals experiencing mental health concerns that did not involve a mental crisis nor require a law enforcement or criminal justice response. Police officers referred individuals to psychiatric nurses (Earl, Cocksedge, Rheeder, Morgan, & Palmer, 2015). Also in the U.K., James (2000) reported a collaboration established in a police station. The purpose of collaboration was to divert individuals with mental health needs away from law enforcement and further criminal justice system involvement and into mental health treatment. Heywood and Vandenabeele (2012) described the development of a police collaboration with mental health providers in a hospital in the U.K. to address criminal offenses committed among hospitalized patients.

Finally, Amirthalingam (2013) described diversion programs comprised of police officers and social workers implemented in Singapore. The programs provide referrals to social services and interventions for low-level offenders who are adults, juveniles, and individuals living with mental illness. Diversion collaborations between police and psychiatric nurses have also been implemented in England and Wales (Kane et al., 2018).

Homelessness

Huey (2008) summarized the Remote Reporting program aimed at assisting individuals in the UK who are homeless with reporting criminal victimization to law enforcement. Social service workers assisted individuals with reporting victimization to police.

Juveniles

Chapter 11 examined the role of law enforcement with juveniles. Several international collaborations have been implemented that attend to this role. McCarthy (2013) reported a collaboration in the U.K. comprised of female police officers, social workers, and community-based agencies. The purpose of the collaborations is to divert juveniles from becoming involved in delinquent behaviors. Pierpoint (2001) described the issues that arise when social workers function as an "appropriate adult" (p. 255) in England and Wales. This function requires that social workers are present during interviews in which law enforcement interviews juveniles to obtain evidence pertaining to a crime in which the juvenile may be a suspect.

Chun, Chui, Chan, and Cheng (2010) identified the Police Attachment to NGOs Program for police training implemented in Hong Kong to prepare police officers to intervene with at-risk youth. Also in attendance during the training were social workers and at-risk youth. The training provided opportunities for police and social work collaborations.

Immigrants

Vanhanen and Heikkilä (2017) explained the Immigrants, Police and Social Work (IPS) project implemented in Finland, the Netherlands, Sweden, Spain, and the U.K. The purpose of the IPS is to assist immigrants with societal integration.

Child maltreatment

Masson (2006) suggested that more collaboration is needed between police and social workers when they utilize interventions to remove maltreated children from their homes in emergency situations in the U.K. Social workers and law enforcement officers in the U.K. jointly interview children who are victims of sexual exploitation (Ahern, Sadler, Lamb, & Gariglietti, 2017). Also in the U.K., Voss, Rushforth, and Powell (2018) described a collaboration established between police, social workers, and medical staff to address child sexual abuse.

Davidov, Sigad, Lev-Wiesel, and Eisikovits (2017) examined the issues that arise during collaboration between police, social workers, psychologists, medical providers, and educators in response to child maltreatment in Israel. Whyte (1997) summarized The Children's Project as having the purpose of addressing child maltreatment. The project was developed based on youth service projects implemented in Scotland. The project involves collaboration between police, social workers, educators, and health care providers.

Sex trafficking

Burkhalter (2012) described a police and social work collaboration established in Cambodia involving social workers from the International Justice Mission to address sex trafficking of young and adult women.

Crime prevention

Clancey, Lee, and Crofts (2012) reported a collaboration developed in Australia to address crime prevention strategies that ranged from domestic violence to diversion for at-risk youth. The interventions were provided by community safety officers with backgrounds in social work, psychology, and social sciences, among other disciplines.

Victims of crime

Identifying collaborations to provide interventions to victims of crime in the United States, Wilson and Segrave (2011) also identified such collaborations in the U.K., Australia, and Canada. These collaborations are comprised of police and victim assistance providers, although some victim services are provided only by specialty-trained police officers. Ekman and Seng (2009) identified a victim assistance unit implemented in a law enforcement agency in Canada to assist victims of crime. Victim assistance providers staff the unit and collaborate with law enforcement. Tien, Wu, Lin, and Wang (2017) described police and social work and medical staff collaboration to assist victims of sexual assault in Taiwan.

Migrant children

Westwood (2012) identified a police and social work collaboration in the U.K. that provides interventions to immigrant children.

Missing persons

Clark (2012) interviewed siblings of missing persons to better understand police collaboration in response to missing person investigations in Australia. Clark concluded that more police and social work collaboration, including other professionals, is needed to enhance the law enforcement response provided to families of missing persons.

Radicalization and extremism

Sestoft, Hansen, and Christensen (2017) describe police and social service and psychiatry (PSP) collaboration implemented in Denmark with the aim of providing services to individuals at risk for radicalization and extremist views. The

PSP added this additional service to already existing services for individuals at risk of other social problems such as suicide, substance abuse, and mental illness. This innovative collaboration exemplifies how currently established collaborations can be adapted to add additional services to address contemporary social problems.

Lessons learned

These examples of established police and social work and social service collaborations illustrate the wide range of collaborations that can be implemented to address contemporary social problems. Many countries are presently experiencing radicalism and extremism, and lawmakers and other stakeholders are seeking approaches to address this problem. This is not a social problem experienced solely in Denmark. Likewise, drivers under the influence of drugs and alcohol are not a social problem only in Sweden. In many countries these drivers have come to the attention of lawmakers and other stakeholders advocating that this social problem be addressed. What is notable about this social problem is the approach to addressing it, and other social problems presented in this chapter, through police and social work and social service collaboration.

The lessons learned from the international police and social work and social service collaborations presented in this chapter have implications for the development and implementation of such collaborations globally. A review and more in-depth examination of these collaborations could be informative for law enforcement agencies, social workers, and other professionals considering implementing a partnership to address community social problems.

POLICE Model application

Through providing a brief presentation summarizing published studies describing international police and social work and social service collaborations this chapter has explored the numerous possibilities for such collaborations. The POLICE Model, with its focus on planning, organizing, listening, implementation, collecting data, and evaluation methods, also has applications for international collaborations. For instance, the presentation of these collaborations has shown the wide range of collaboration possibilities that can be considered during the planning phase. In general, the published studies primarily describe collaboration aims and goals, and as such few outcome studies are available that demonstrate the effectiveness of the collaboration models. Because inadequate available data demonstrate the effectiveness of these collaborations special attention will need to be given to collecting data and evaluation methods during the initial planning phase.

Some international collaborations have been studied using qualitative methods and data. This approach can be invaluable for assessing collaborators' perceptions toward the collaboration because these perceptions can have many uses for enhancing the collaboration. For example, if collaborators perceive that the collaboration is not operating as intended these data can be used to modify aspects of the collaboration.

Chapter summary

As this chapter has shown, international law enforcement collaborations have been implemented in response to a wide range of social problems. These social problems are not unique to the countries where the collaborations were implemented, and, therefore, law enforcement agencies and interested stakeholders in other countries can benefit from examining the types of social problems that are the focus of interventions and the partners involved in the collaboration.

Police social work practice, in which police social workers are employees of law enforcement agencies, was not found among the collaborations. Instead, collaboration partners involved social workers, social service workers, and other professionals. This outcome supports an argument that more police and social work collaborations have been implemented than the employment of police social workers in law enforcement agencies. These internationally implemented collaborations address some of the same social problems discussed earlier in this book in addition to breaking new ground by expanding the possibilities for implementing police and social work and social service collaborations.

Questions for discussion

1. Why is the implementation of police and social work and police and social service collaboration international in scope?
2. Why do you believe that so many different types of international police and social work and police and social services collaborations exist that focus on different social problems?
3. Given the international scope of police and social work and police and social services collaboration do you believe that an international organization should be established to provide guidance, training, and technical assistance? Why or why not? What should be the purpose and goals of such an organization?

Activities for further learning

1. This chapter did not endeavor to provide an exhaustive list of international police and social work and police and social service collaborations. Locate and retrieve an article or report describing an international police and social work or police and social service collaboration. After reading the article or report were you able to identify the components of the collaboration? Was sufficient information provided to determine the effectiveness of the collaboration?

2. After locating an international police and social work or police and social service collaboration, locate information about the social work profession in that country. Compare and contrast information that you find with information about social work practice in the United States.

3. Create a list of international police and social work or police and social service collaborations that you have located that were not included in this chapter.

References

Ahern, E. C., Sadler, L. A., Lamb, M. E., & Gariglietti, G. M. (2017). Practitioner perspectives on child sexual exploitation: Rapport building with young people. *Journal of Child Sexual Abuse, 26*(1), 78–91.

Amirthalingam, K. (2013). Criminal justice and diversionary programmes in Singapore. *Criminal Law Forum, 24*(4), 527–559.

Beaulieu, M., Côté, M., & Diaz, L. (2017). Police and partners: New ways of working together in Montréal. *The Journal of Adult Protection, 19*(6), 406–417.

Buchbinder, E., & Eisikovits, Z. (2008). Collaborative discourse: The case of police and social work relationships in intimate violence intervention in Israel. *Journal of Social Service Research, 34*(4), 1–13.

Burkhalter, H. (2012). Sex trafficking, law enforcement and perpetrator accountability. *Anti-Trafficking Review, 1*(1), 122–123.

Cambridge, P., & Parkes, T. (2006). The management and practice of joint adult protection investigations between health and social services: Issues arising from a training intervention. *Social Work Education, 25*(8), 824–837.

Chun, R. P., Chui, Y. H., Chan, Y. C., & Cheng, H. C. (2010). Police work with youth-at-risk: What can social work contribute?. *The Hong Kong Journal of Social Work, 44*(01), 31–48.

Clancey, G., Lee, M., & Crofts, T. (2012). "We're not Batman" – roles and expectations of local government community safety officers in New South Wales. *Crime Prevention and Community Safety, 14*(4), 235–257.

Clark, J. (2012). "You are going to drop the ball on this …": Using siblings' stories to inform better interprofessional practice when someone goes missing. *Police Practice and Research, 13*(1), 31–43.

Cooper, L., Anaf, J., & Bowden, M. (2008). Can social workers and police be partners when dealing with bikie-gang related domestic violence and sexual assault?. *European Journal of Social Work, 11*(3), 295–311.

Copoeru, I., Moldovan, S., Agheorghiesei, D. T., Ciuhodaru, T., Seghedin, E., & Iorga, M. (2013). The inter-agency cooperation in healthcare and social services for substance misuse and addiction in Romania: A case study. *Revista de Asistenta Sociala, 12*(2), 125–133.

Davidov, J., Sigad, L. I., Lev-Wiesel, R., & Eisikovits, Z. (2017). Cross-disciplinary craftsmanship: The case of child abuse work. *Qualitative Social Work, 16*(5), 717–733.

Diemer, K., Ross, S., Humphreys, C., & Healey, L. (2017). A "double edged sword": Discretion and compulsion in policing domestic violence. *Police Practice and Research, 18*(4), 339–351.

Earl, F., Cocksedge, K., Rheeder, B., Morgan, J., & Palmer, J. (2015). Neighbourhood outreach: A novel approach to Liaison and Diversion. *The Journal of Forensic Psychiatry & Psychology, 26*(5), 573–585.

Ekman, M. S., & Seng, M. J. (2009). On-scene victim assistance units within law enforcement agencies. *Policing: An International Journal of Police Strategies & Management, 32*(40, 719–738.

Forsman, Å., Hrelja, R., Henriksson, P., & Wiklund, M. (2011). Cooperation between police and social treatment services offering treatment to drink and drug drivers – experience in Sweden. *Traffic Injury Prevention, 12*(1), 9–17.

Heywood, D., & Vandenabeele, P. (2012). Setting up a police liaison service in a medium secure hospital. *Mental Health Practice, 16*(2), 24–26.

Huey, L. (2008). "When it comes to violence in my place, I am the police!" Exploring the policing functions of service providers in Edinburgh's Cowgate and Grassmarket. *Policing & Society, 18*(3), 207–224.

Humphreys, C., Healey, L., Kirkwood, D., & Nicholson, D. (2018). Children living with domestic violence: A differential response through multi-agency collaboration. *Australian Social Work, 71*(2), 162–174.

International Crime Research Association and International Association for Comparative Studies in Policing Crime Control and Social Order (1990). *Co-operation between social services and police: The first international ICRA workshop for international practitioners.* Esbjerg, DK: National Commissioner of the Danish Police.

James, D. (2000). Police station diversion schemes: Role and efficacy in central London. *The Journal of Forensic Psychiatry, 11*(3), 532–555.

Jeremiah, R. D., Quinn, C. R., & Alexis, J. M. (2018). Lessons learned: Evaluating the program fidelity of UNWomen Partnership for Peace domestic violence diversion program in the Eastern Caribbean. *Evaluation and Program Planning, 69,* 61–67.

Kane, E., Evans, E., Mitsch, J., Jilani, T., Quinlan, P., Cattell, J., & Khalifa, N. (2018). Police interactions and interventions with suspects flagged as experiencing mental health problems. *Criminal Behaviour and Mental Health, 28*(5), 424–432.

Masson, J. (2006). Emergency powers for child protection. *Journal of Children's Services, 1*(2), 31–40.

Maybee, J. (2000). The challenge ahead for criminal justice social work in Scotland. *Probation Journal, 47*(3), 193–199.

McCarthy, D. J. (2013). Gendering "soft" policing: Multi-agency working, female cops, and the fluidities of police culture/s. *Policing and Society, 23*(2), 261–278.

McNeill, F. (2005). *Offender management in Scotland: The first hundred years.* Retrieved from https://strathprints.strath.ac.uk/38317/1/Offender_management.pdf

McNeill, F., Batchelor, S., Burnett, R., & Knox, J. (2005). *21st century social work: Reducing re-offending-key practice skills.* Edinburgh, UK: Scottish Executive.

Parkinson, G. C. (1980). Cooperation between police and social workers: Hidden issues. *Social Work, 25*(1), 12–18.

Patterson, G. T., & Swan, P. G. (2019). Police social work and social service collaboration strategies one hundred years after Vollmer: A systematic review. *Policing: An International Journal, 42*(5), 863–886.

Pierpoint, H. (2001). The performance of volunteer appropriate adults: A survey of call outs. *The Howard Journal of Criminal Justice, 40*(3), 255–271.

Sestoft, D., Hansen, S. M., & Christensen, A. B. (2017). The police, social services, and psychiatry (PSP) cooperation as a platform for dealing with concerns of radicalization. *International Review of Psychiatry, 29*(4), 350–354.

Shetye, S. (2019). Experiences of working as a social worker with the Delhi police on human trafficking cases: Issues and challenges. *International Journal of Criminal Justice Sciences, 14*(1), 56–66.

Sinha, R. (2012). Social work in police stations: Challenges for front line practice in India. *Practice*, *24*(2), 91–104.

Sinha, R. (2017). Police social work: Active engagement with law enforcement. In M. D. Chong & A. P. Francis (Eds.), *Demystifying criminal justice social work in India* (pp. 85–98). Thousand Oaks, CA: SAGE Publications.

Stanley, N., & Humphreys, C. (2014). Multi-agency risk assessment and management for children and families experiencing domestic violence. *Children and Youth Services Review*, *47*, 78–85.

Tien, L. C., Wu, Y. L., Lin, T. W., & Wang, S. S. C. (2017). Different perceptions of interprofessional collaboration and factors influencing the one-stop service for sexual assault victims in Taiwan. *Journal of Interprofessional Care*, *31*(1), 98–104.

Vanhanen, S., & Heikkilä, E. (2017). Multi-professional work practices in the field of immigrant Integration – examples of collaboration between the police and social work. *Migration Letters*, *14*(2), 273–284.

Voss, L., Rushforth, H., & Powell, C. (2018). Multiagency response to childhood sexual abuse: A case study that explores the role of a specialist centre. *Child Abuse Review*, *27*(3), 209–222.

Waal, H., Clausen, T., Gjersing, L., & Gossop, M. (2014). Open drug scenes: Responses of five European cities. *BMC Public Health*, *14*(1), 1–12.

Westwood, J. L. (2012). Constructing risk and avoiding need: Findings from interviews with social workers and police officers involved in safeguarding work with migrant children. *Child Abuse Review*, *21*(5), 349–361.

Whyte, B. (1997). Crossing boundaries: An exercise in partnership provision. *The British Journal of Social Work*, *27*(5), 679–704.

Wilson, D., & Segrave, M. (2011). Police-based victim services: Australian and international models. *Policing: An International Journal of Police Strategies & Management*, *34*(3), 479–496.

13

THE FUTURE OF POLICE SOCIAL WORK

Chapter overview

This chapter offers recommendations for the future of professional police social work practice. These recommendations are informed by the topics discussed throughout this book. For example, in Chapter 8 law enforcement use of the ITRAC was established. The ITRAC assessed levels of risk among domestic violence incidents for law enforcement agencies. It was also established in Chapter 8 that some law enforcement agencies require that police officers administer and score standardized risk assessment instruments during police calls for service to assess levels of risk for future violence among domestic violence incidents. In the present chapter it is recommended that police social workers administer and score these standardized risk assessment instruments at the scene of a domestic violence call for service. Social workers have expertise administering and scoring standardized risk assessment instruments and can utilize these skills at the scene of a domestic violence incident.

Reflexive scrutiny provides another example and is introduced in this chapter as an approach for police social workers and the social work profession to attend to the critical issues that arise in police social work practice that were discussed in Chapter 4. Such scrutiny can also inform the social work profession about the appropriateness of police social work as a specialty area of social work practice and police and social work collaboration.

The recommendations offered in this chapter are further informed by the use of technology, criminal justice reforms, emerging social problems, and fiscal constraints. The future of police social work is also likely to involve increasing involvement of the social work profession among professional social workers who do not identify as police social workers and are employed in community-based social service agencies rather than law enforcement agencies. Further, the

DOI: 10.4324/9781003132257-13

influence of contemporary movements such as Black Lives Matter, Defund the Police, and community efforts to identify and implement new and innovative methods for responding to 911 emergencies have implications for police social work practice. Lawmakers have begun to enact legislation that addresses some of these concerns and contain provisions to reform law enforcement policies and operations. Finally, this chapter identifies the types of knowledge, skills, and training that police social workers will require to assume these future practice areas.

Introduction

Numerous factors will influence the future of professional police social work practice. These factors include the contemporary movements and societal apprehensions concerning the use of police officers to respond to medical, mental health, and other emergencies, in addition to responding to social problems. Additional concerns arise related to how complaints made against police officers are handled and transforming law enforcement agencies to become responsive to community needs.

The service law enforcement function is likely to continue to include social problems such as parent–child conflict, domestic violence, and neighbor disputes, among others, in the future. Poverty, unemployment and underemployment, and lack of health care or a primary care physician are also contributing factors in police calls for service. Victims of violent crime, and some non-violent crimes, and worries about criminal activity will continue to require a law enforcement response.

Because law enforcement and other first responders, such as emergency medical technicians and paramedics, operate 24 hours, seven days a week throughout the year with mobile services responding within a short amount of time to the location where services have been requested this will further contribute to these agencies providing emergency services.

Taken together, each of these factors necessitates specialized skills and interventions such as referrals to behavioral health providers or community-based social service agencies. Some intervention needs will be more immediate and will be provided through crisis intervention.

In Chapter 3, a recent review of communities that have either implemented or are considering the implementation of unarmed mobile crisis teams was reported. Montoya (2020) described the Los Angeles City Council's proposal to utilize social workers to respond to non-violent police calls for service, a plan in Eugene, Oregon, to utilize crisis intervention workers to respond to some calls for police services, and a proposal in Sacramento, California, to support a civilian emergency response to emergency calls for service instead of law enforcement. In Albuquerque, New Mexico, the mayor is considering utilizing social workers and other professionals to respond to emergency calls for service to assist homeless individuals and those experiencing mental health crises. These professionals would respond instead of dispatching law enforcement, firefighters, and paramedics.

As these examples show many communities are considering expanding opportunities for social workers to respond to emergency situations and provide emergency services. Although these opportunities do not describe the employment of police social workers in law enforcement agencies, it is highly likely that social workers involved in these innovative proposals will collaborate with law enforcement. Further, safety issues may arise when social workers provide an emergency response directly from a 911 dispatcher that requires law enforcement assistance.

Consequently, the lessons learned from police social work practice will remain relevant for the social work profession. Indeed, police and social work collaborations are rapidly increasing, with some collaborations limiting the role of law enforcement and including other partners. For example, in New York City a pilot collaboration includes one social worker partnering with two emergency medical technicians (EMTs). The team will respond to mental health crises without law enforcement and is presently in the early phases of planning (Peltz, 2021). Innovative collaborations such as these are creating additional opportunities for the future of the social work profession. Assuming these opportunities will require training, skills, and technical assistance.

The Breonna Taylor family settlement, in addition to a financial settlement, includes police reforms involving social work. The Louisville Metro Police located in Louisville, Kentucky, were executing a no-knock warrant during a drug investigation when they broke the door and entered Breonna Taylor's apartment. Taylor's boyfriend thought a break-in was occurring and, legally owning a gun, fired shots at whom he thought were intruders. A police officer sustained injuries from the gunfire, after which police officers returned gunshots shooting and killing Breonna Taylor. Approximately six months after her death, Taylor's family received a $12 million settlement. Among other provisions of the settlement include a commitment from Louisville, Kentucky, to employ social workers to provide assistance during particular calls for police service (Morales, Joseph, & Carrega, 2020).

Reflexive scrutiny

Garrett (2004) proposed that the social work profession engages in "reflexive scrutiny" (p. 92) activities to examine the issues associated with police and social work collaboration suggesting that when collaboration occurs "troubling facets of policing were apt to be ignored" (p. 92).

Garrett proposed these activities are necessary as a result of increasing police social work practice, police and social work collaboration, and its expansion to address additional social problems. Further, because priority has been given to developing effective collaborations characterized by positive interdisciplinary relationships between police officers and social workers the difficulties that arise require more attention. To assume these activities Garrett further proposed that both social work educational programs and professional social work training include more content regarding law enforcement and called for creating a unique social work degree that places emphasis on interdisciplinary collaboration given that so much of social work practice is interdisciplinary in scope. In this way, the social work profession can emphasize and address the problematic issues that arise in interdisciplinary collaborations through the development of knowledge and skills.

The topics presented in Chapter 1 can provide a starting point for the social work profession to begin the process of reflexive scrutiny, particularly the topics that identify the mission of law enforcement agencies, the three law enforcement functions, law enforcement tasks, and the organizational structure of law enforcement agencies. The service law enforcement function, which is the focus of Chapter 2, underscores the fact that the majority of law enforcement tasks involve providing a service response similar to social services. Furthermore, Chapter 4 introduced numerous critical issues that arise in police social work practice and police and social work collaboration. These issues can provide an additional starting point for reflexive scrutiny activities.

Reflexive scrutiny activities should also include an examination of ethical issues. The NASW Code of Ethics (2021) identifies the ethical responsibilities for social workers when involved in interdisciplinary collaboration. These responsibilities include applying social work knowledge, values, and skills to make a contribution to the collaboration decisions and following appropriate protocols to resolve ethical issues that arise in interdisciplinary collaboration activity.

Building capacity for the social work profession to respond to 911 emergencies

As discussed earlier in this chapter and as Garrett (2004) reported, police social work practice and police and social collaboration are expanding to include a response to more social problems. So too are collaborations formed between social work and other professionals, excluding law enforcement, to address emergency situations.

Individuals experience crisis situations due to numerous situations well-known to the social work profession. These situations include poverty, homelessness, and lack of resources such as transportation, inadequate health care, and underemployment or unemployment, among others.

Numerous underserved communities also lack emergency services. Further, some individuals are unaware or unable to access essential services, further exacerbating the need to provide emergency services. As a consequence individuals may utilize a variety of emergency services such as the 911 operator, law enforcement, and emergency medical services.

Presently the social work profession is experiencing a defining moment due to concerns about the safety and social justice issues that arise, particularly when people of color seek emergency services from 911 calls or during contacts with law enforcement. Combined, the expansion of the social work profession in providing emergency services and safety and social justice concerns have contributed to the profession exploring innovative interventions for emergency situations that come to the attention of the 911 operator.

Patterson and Swan (2019) conducted a systematic review following the Campbell Collaboration recommendations for systematic reviews. The purpose of the review was to identify in the published literature the types of police social work, police and social work, and police and social service collaborations that were found. Additionally, collaboration components and tasks, partners, social problems addressed and the populations receiving services, types of services provided, and the geographic location of the collaboration were also identified.

The search strategy and inclusion criteria were defined prior to the search of 11 databases. Among these databases 3,065 titles were found. After a two-member research team screened the titles, eliminated duplicates, and reviewed relevant full-text studies, 81 studies were included in the systematic review. Among the 81 studies, 83 collaborations were found. CIT was found most often (6.0%). The remaining collaborations either were only found one time among the studies (63.6%) or were not branded with a name. These studies did not provide the necessary data to assess collaboration effectiveness. The results of the systematic review found the following 15 categories of social problems:

- Domestic violence (20.2%)
- Mental illness (13.1%)
- Crime (10.7%)
- Juvenile delinquency (8.3%)
- Substance abuse (7.1%)
- Child maltreatment (7.1%)
- Sexual assault (6.0%)
- Child sexual assault (6.0%)
- Community social problems (6.0%)
- Missing persons (4.8%)
- Social problems affecting children (2.4%)
- Terrorism (2.4%)
- Victims of crime (2.4%)
- Medical needs (2.4%)
- Human trafficking (1.2%)

Interdisciplinary collaboration is an important component of police and social work partnerships. However, social workers involved in such partnerships also collaborate with other professionals when providing emergency services. In addition to law enforcement, Patterson and Swan (2019) identified the following 11 groups of professionals:

- Social workers (19.9%)
- Mental health practitioners (13.0%)

- Medical providers (13.0%)
- Child protection workers (7.5%)
- Social service workers (5.5%)
- Advocates (4.8%)
- Prosecutors (4.1%)
- Educators (3.4%)
- Volunteers (2.1%)
- Probation officers (1.4%)
- Attorneys (0.7%)

The results of the systematic review have implications for the social work profession to build capacity to respond to 911 emergencies by means of (1) application of the professional value of social justice when providing information, services, and resources, particularly in emergency crisis situations; (2) strengthening social work academic and continuing education to include the knowledge and skills to perform emergency crisis interventions, interdisciplinary collaboration with 911 operators, law enforcement, emergency medical services, and health care providers; key skills include providing crisis intervention, short-term and brief counseling, police case status information, follow-up with clients and service providers, referrals, and using technology; and (3) expanding agency-based practice to implement new and innovative organizational models of collaboration that can be used to respond to emergencies which are flexible based on community need. These collaborations may not necessarily require replication of brand-named collaboration.

Lastly, opportunities for social work educational programs are also likely to increase and shape the future of police social work practice. To provide one example, these educational programs can assist law enforcement agencies by developing a Community Resource Manual (CRM) that contains useful information for police officers to provide referrals categorized by the most frequent types of calls for service and calls for service that are less frequent. Because social work educational programs utilize an extensive network of agencies that provide field education opportunities for student interns it should be feasible to develop a CRM. The CRM should also include brief information such as contact telephone numbers and a contact person where feasible, agency location, and hours of operation. This information can be placed in alphabetical order or categorized in the CRM by the type of social problem or need.

Trauma-informed law enforcement agencies

Trauma-informed social work practice has been identified as advanced practice in which social workers are knowledgeable about trauma outcomes experienced by professionals (including social workers) as well as the outcomes experienced among different populations. Social workers should have the knowledge and skills to intervene when individuals are experiencing trauma including assisting agencies with becoming trauma-informed agencies (Council on Social Work Education, 2012).

The Substance Abuse and Mental Health Services Administration (2014) defines a trauma-informed agency and also identifies trauma-informed programs as follows: "A program, organization, or system that is trauma-informed realizes the widespread impact of trauma and understands potential paths for recovery; recognizes the signs and symptoms of trauma in clients, families, staff, and others involved with the system; and responds by fully integrating knowledge about trauma into policies, procedures, and practices, and seeks to actively resist re-traumatization" (p. 9).

Based on this definition an entire law enforcement agency may not be transformed into a trauma-informed agency, although programs or units within law enforcement agencies can become trauma-informed programs. A police social worker applying knowledge and skills in trauma-informed practice can be useful in this regard.

The following examples demonstrate how trauma-informed practices can be integrated into law enforcement agencies. The first example shows integration within an academic institution. The University at Buffalo School of Social Work formed a collaboration with the University Police (UP) focused on providing education and training to UP police officers. The goal is for officers to utilize trauma-informed skills in their work to reduce traumatic police encounters on campus (Gambini, 2020). The second example shows the integration of a program within a law enforcement agency. The Greensboro Child Response Initiative (CRI) is an example of a trauma-informed collaboration implemented between police and mental health practitioners. CRI is housed in the Greensboro Police Department and provides services to children affected by violence to reduce negative mental health and trauma outcomes (Graves, Ward, Crotts, & Pitts, 2019). As this example illustrates law enforcement agencies can implement trauma-informed practices in specific programs within the agency. This is particularly relevant for programs and units that primarily provide the service law enforcement function.

Numerous resources are available to assist law enforcement agencies and police social workers with implementing trauma-informed practices. The International Association of Chiefs of Police and Yale Child Study Center (2017) published a toolkit with the purpose of improving the law enforcement response for children who have been exposed to violence and are experiencing trauma outcomes. The publication includes a law enforcement organizational assessment instrument as well as an instrument that can be useful for developing law enforcement agency interventions for children. Importantly, the toolkit provides the knowledge necessary for police officers to recognize trauma outcomes among children and the methods necessary for developing collaborations with mental health practitioners having expertise in providing interventions to children experiencing trauma.

The Substance Abuse and Mental Health Services Administration (2020) GAINS Center provides training for police officers, CIT trainers, and other criminal justice professionals focused on reducing traumatic criminal justice encounters and providing trauma-informed interventions. In addition to these groups train-the-trainer sessions are also offered to behavioral health practitioners, including social workers, to become trained to provide trauma-informed community-based criminal justice training.

Risk assessment for domestic violence

Assessing future risk for domestic violence utilizing standardized risk assessment instruments creates opportunities for police social workers and police and social work collaboration. Graduate social work educational programs typically include research courses that teach students about the importance of reliability and validity when administering standardized instruments including scoring procedures. Professional social workers also administer a wide range of standardized instruments to assess risk for child maltreatment, substance abuse, depression, and suicide, among numerous other presenting problems for which individuals seek assistance.

Just as the ITRAC agency provides risk assessment results for future domestic violence for law enforcement agencies police social workers, and other professional social workers, can administer, score and interpret the scores for a law enforcement agency at the scene of the domestic violence call for service. In this way police social workers and police officers do not rely on professional judgment, which could be inaccurate. While the ITRAC only examined police reports to conduct risk assessments administering risk assessment instruments at the scene is more immediate and has the potential to free police officers from conducting risk assessments, thereby allowing officers more time to perform other law enforcement tasks. Furthermore, police social workers can use a trauma-informed approach when conducting risk assessments for domestic violence.

Social justice

Social work students, as well as social workers new to the profession, may be surprised to learn that the ethical practice of social justice includes the professional value of social justice in which services are provided. Images of dismantling an unjust institution or opposing an injustice may appear when the concept of social justice is mentioned. Recall that the primary function performed by law enforcement is the service function.

This value of social justice is identified in the NASW Code of Ethics (2021) and involves providing information, services, and resources. Consequently, the basic provision of information and services and connecting individuals and families with resources during a crisis situation are consistent with ethical social work practice and the value of social justice.

Moreover, because law enforcement agencies are associated with social control, authoritarianism, and a paramilitary agency structure that responds to emergency crisis situations the practice of police social work and police and social collaboration may perhaps be viewed as inconsistent with social justice. The provision of service is consistent with social justice. Police social workers and social work collaboration partners also engage in social change activities and possess information about oppression and diversity when adhering to the value of social justice.

The influence of contemporary social justice movements

The Civil Rights movement had a profound influence on American policing. Contemporary social justice movements such as Defund the Police and Black Lives Matter also have an influence on contemporary policing. Ray (2020) suggested that the concept of Defund the Police does not imply abolishing law enforcement agencies. Instead, the concept refers to reallocating funding from a law enforcement agency budget and reallocating funds to support social service agencies addressing substance abuse and mental health, for example. The aim is to reallocate tax funds used to support law enforcement to social service agencies. This approach is intended to enhance well-being among community residents and reduce crime and violent law enforcement encounters. Ray identified numerous municipalities that are exploring the reallocation of large amounts of tax funds. For instance, Los Angeles is considering reallocating $100 million, Prince George's County is considering allocating $20 million, and Baltimore is considering reallocating $22 million from the law enforcement budget.

The reallocation of funds and increase in the budgets of social service agencies will create opportunities for social workers, social service workers, and behavioral health providers. Given that communities will continue to require emergency and non-emergency assistance with social problems enhancing the budgets of social service agencies appears appropriate. Moreover, law enforcement agencies may welcome responding to fewer social problems.

The Black Lives Matter movement has been described as the largest movement in U.S. history based on the number of individuals participating in Black Lives Matter protests (Buchanan, Bui, & Patel, 2020). These protests, among other concerns, resulted from concerns about police violence in communities of color, demands for police reforms, and an end to police violence.

Irrespective of the policing reforms that are implemented to reduce violent law enforcement encounters and police misconduct communities will also continue to rely on a law enforcement response that involves the service law enforcement function given the numerous types of social problems that come to the attention of law enforcement. This cannot be a neglected area of law enforcement.

Civilian Complaint Review Boards

The purpose of a Civilian Complaint Review Board (CCRB) or Citizens Police Review Board (CPRB) is to investigate civilian complaints filed against police officers for misconduct. In general, law enforcement agencies often resist oversight from CCRBs, particularly when these boards request to make disciplinary decisions for the police officers involved in complaints. Often given reasons include a lack of civilian understanding of the challenges inherent in law enforcement. Although some CCRBs are independent of law enforcement agency oversight law enforcement officials are not members of the board and do not contribute to decisions; therefore law enforcement officials may challenge the CCRBs findings, thereby limiting the implementation of any CCRB findings (Prenzler & Ronken, 2001).

Among the six international models used to investigate complaints filed against police officers for misconduct, Goldsmith (1988) reported that five of the models are comprised of civilians. These models range from the employment of civilians in a law enforcement agency to investigate complaints with senior law enforcement officials determining discipline to the use of external CCRBs.

Case Example

What Is the Expected Response to Intimate Partner Violence

Prepared By Emma Lucas–Darby and Elizabeth C. Pittinger

She needed assistance and dialed 911. She gave her address, there was commotion, the call disconnected. Two officers were dispatched. They encountered a man at a window indicating everything was okay but refused to answer questions. A perimeter check of the exterior yielded nothing suspicious. They left. Approximately 24 hours later, the caller did not answer calls and did not pick up her son as expected. Her family contacted the police for a welfare check. Police forced entry into the residence and found the caller beneath her decorated Christmas tree, deceased from a gunshot wound to the head and neck. Across town her estranged boyfriend was holding SWAT at bay, confessed to killing the caller, then killed himself.

Was this situation handled appropriately? The dispatcher stated a female had called and initially was calm, but some commotion followed, and the line disconnected. This sketchy information presented unknown trouble warranting a heightened response by the officers. The on-scene facts and the dispatch information presented the likelihood of a domestic situation. The officers failed to identify and determine if the man at the window was authorized to be there. They failed to observe the well-being of the caller despite the knowledge that the caller was female. They missed the nuances of the holiday and associated stress that can motivate a despondent person to do terrible things. Could procedural triage by a social worker or crisis intervention team have influenced the response to this call?

Curiosity regarding the man at the window and his reluctance to answer questions should have piqued the officers' suspicions and initiated further investigation. The fact that no disturbance was observed from outside the dwelling was not determinative of interior conditions. Discomfort with the inability to observe and speak to the female caller should have led to persistence until contact was made. The suicide note of the assailant suggests that the deficient police response possibly resulted in the caller's death.

This case illustrates the need for support personnel including skilled social workers whose focus is on the problem and risk assessment of circumstances leading to a 911 call for help. This victim did everything she was counseled to do to protect herself. Was this deficient response the result of the officers' casual disregard of the circumstances, complacency, ignorance, and/or bias? Was it a systemic failure or lack of expertise? Would consultation with a social worker throughout the response have influenced police tactics and thoroughness? Circumstances surrounding this case ignited a vigorous public campaign by women's organizations and victim advocates. City Council responded by codifying protective assessment standards. Still, as public safety priorities are reorganized, the response to domestic calls must be reinforced with holistic incident management.

Many questions emerged from this incident regarding protocols for police responses to these types of calls (DeAngelo, 2013). Questioned were the responsibilities of the officers to solicit supervisory assistance, the responsibilities of the shift supervisors to monitor calls for service, and the disposition of those calls by responding officers. The local CPRB also was concerned about the officers' inaction regarding assessment of the presenting risk to the caller. The CPRB identified recommendations that were adopted by the local police department including:

1. *The police should develop a specific protocol for responding to calls dispatched as "unknown trouble," which includes specific instructions for officers to gather pertinent information including whether or not the caller or witness is on scene. When on-scene the officer must observe the caller in person and require a report from dispatch on callback efforts.*
2. *Responding police officers should continue to ask if there are weapons involved in a call and if there is any indication that the call is domestic related. Call takers/dispatchers should ask if the call is a domestic call; a simple yes/no answer is all that is needed.*
3. *Implement intensive training in domestic violence for police officers, call takers, and dispatchers conducted by professional experts rather than other officers or generic trainers.*

These recommendations are aligned with action steps identified by women's and activist groups (Civil Rights Advocacy, 2013).

Could social workers embedded in police departments provide timely guidance for handling cases of this nature? Victims of domestic violence are likely to call the police when subjected to abuse and domestic discord. With training that increases awareness of the many dynamics affecting a domestic violence case, responders have greater awareness of required actions that should be considered when on a call (Lindsey, 2020;

Ward-Lasher, Messing, & Hart, 2017). Optimally, a crisis intervention team or social worker would be involved immediately and would assist police officers on disturbance calls and provide direct focus on risk management (Corcoran, Stephenson, Perryman, & Allen, 2001).

Social work has an essential role in cases involving intimate partner violence. More police departments have implemented protocols and intervention strategies which include social workers and crisis intervention teams. These approaches are especially promising for calls involving intimate partner violence and domestic disturbance calls. Even after training, police officers may not have appropriate knowledge about intimate partner violence or risks factors for homicide (Ward-Lasher, Messing & Hart, 2017). The inclusion of a social worker allows for direct focus on risk assessment and the caller, thereby allowing officers to focus on the offender and situational safety. Involving social workers from 911 call reception through response may enhance the quality and reliability of risk assessment as the situation evolves and ultimately lead to safer incident management and prompt compassionate support for the victim.

This case example illustrates how social work training and expertise providing interventions that address a specific social problem such as domestic violence can be used to provide constructive recommendations to a law enforcement agency. These recommendations were provided following a law enforcement response in which mistakes were made. The example further highlights the benefits of conducting risk assessment and ensuring the safety of a victim of domestic violence. While civilian participation in the CCRB does not require a social work degree and CCRB members can hold other degrees as well as being employed in other occupations, social work expertise is clearly beneficial. Notably, this case example did not include recommendations intended for disciplinary actions for the police officers involved in the response.

As Table 13.1 shows, when civilians are members of CCRBs having the responsibility to conduct an investigation independent of the law enforcement agency and given power to issue subpoenas during the course of the investigation, three categories of complaints made against police officers are investigated. Either the board investigates all complaints, only certain types of complaints, or no officer complaints are investigated.

Table 13.1 also shows that in 2016 among communities with a population of 250,000 or more residents the majority of CCRBs (31.9%) do not have the authority to investigate any complaints made against police officers. This is also the case in communities with a population of 9,999 residents or less (6.9%). Among all law enforcement agencies the majority of CCRBs (6.8%) do not investigate complaints. However, as the table also shows CCRBs do investigate either all police officer complaints or only specific types of complaints, and 16.6% of police officers are employed in agencies that maintain a CCRB authorized to investigate all complaints made against officers (Brooks, Davis, & Hyland, 2020).

TABLE 13.1 Percent of local police departments with a civilian-complaint review board, by size of population served, 2016

Population served	Total (%)	All complaints	Certain complaints	No complaints
250,000 or more	51.1	14.9	3.2	31.9
50,000–249,999	15.0	1.2	0.9	12.8
10,000–49,999	8.2	1.3	2.5	4.1
9,999 or less	11.5	3.0	1.8	6.9
All departments	11.3	2.6	1.9	6.8
All officers	35.4	16.6	4.0	14.1

Reprinted with permission. Brooks, C., Davis, E., & Hyland, S. (2020). *Local police departments: Policies and procedures, 2016.* NCJ 254826. Washington, D.C.: U.S. Department of Justice, Office of Justice Programs, Bureau of Justice Statistics.

Social work advocacy activity focused on establishing and maintaining a CCRB having the authority to conduct investigations of all complaints made against police officers is a worthwhile endeavor. Such oversight of law enforcement can address the issues of "police policing themselves."

Emerging social problems

Although scams, identify theft, and cybercrimes are not new problems the increased use of technology has perhaps contributed to an increase in the numbers of individuals victimized by these crimes. Victims will require a wide variety of social and other services including law enforcement assistance to claim and recover losses.

Agency-based social work practice and police collaboration

An approach to establishing a collaboration with a law enforcement agency is to develop the partnership between a law enforcement and a community-based social service agency. This approach can be more appealing than forming a collaboration that would require funding, office space, hiring, and training partners. Nevertheless, one obstacle involving the use of a community-based social service agency is reassigning existing staff, even on a limited basis, to the newly formed collaboration. Obtaining buy-in from collaboration partners also needs to be addressed.

Public health and public safety

The future of police social work is likely to see an increased need to attend to public health and public safety needs. The Covid-19 pandemic and accompanying mental health and physical health issues, and opioid use, among health concerns, will require knowledge about health matters. Criminal justice reforms such as the release of low-level and non-violent offenders and no cash bail legislation will require knowledge about public safety concerns.

POLICE Model application

As innovative areas for police social work and professional social work practice emerge participating in practice-informed research and research-informed practice is particularly relevant. Police social work practice should be informed by research findings that identify effective crisis and emergency interventions. The delivery of effective interventions not only benefits community residents who experience improved outcomes but also demonstrates to law enforcement agencies or other agencies that maintaining collaboration is an effective method for achieving the intended outcomes.

Moreover, because some possibilities for the future of police social work practices will involve innovative collaborations and interventions the POLICE Model can be useful for conducting practice-informed research. Keep in mind that although the collaboration partners involved in the steps contained in the POLICE Model may not be police officers the steps of the model will continue to be applicable.

As social work educational programs and the social work profession develop interdisciplinary collaborations that build capacity for the profession to respond to 911 emergencies these collaborations should include information about efficacy and disseminate this information for replication among communities. Costs analysis would also be beneficial. Such endeavors would provide critical information for stakeholders considering implementation in their community.

Chapter summary

Although by no means exhaustive this concluding chapter provided several recommendations for future directions regarding the practice of professional police social work. It was important to repeat one last time in this final chapter that the term police social work refers to the employment of a professional social worker in a law enforcement agency with the purpose of assisting police officers with the service law enforcement function. Also as mentioned elsewhere in this book, not all social workers who collaborate with law enforcement professionally identify as a police social worker, and not all police collaboration partners are social workers. Consequently, some recommendations for the future of police social work practice presented in this chapter were discussed considering opportunities for social workers who are employed in community-based social service agencies. Some recommendations also have implications for professionals who are not social workers. These professionals, such as social service workers, are employed in social service agencies that collaborate with law enforcement. However, as discussed earlier in this book the social work profession has played a central role in establishing collaboration with law enforcement.

This concluding chapter also recommended numerous specific tasks for social work educators and the social work profession such as building professional capacity for social work to respond to 311 or 911 emergencies. It was recommended that this could be achieved by enhancing social work educational and continuing education opportunities to emphasize content necessary for police social work collaboration and skills for responding to emergencies. This includes expanding the capacity of the profession to provide information, services, and resources in emergency crisis situations consistent with the professional value of social justice. Exploring options for responding to 311 or 911 emergencies will also create opportunities for social workers employed in social service agencies.

Additional recommendations for the future of police social work practice include assisting law enforcement agencies with transforming into trauma-informed law enforcement agencies or developing trauma-informed programs, assisting law enforcement agencies with conducting risk assessments during domestic violence calls for service, assuming a leadership role that critically examines police social work as a specialty area of social work practice through reflexive scrutiny activities, and continuing to address emerging public safety issues that arise a result of criminal justice reforms as well as emerging public health issues.

Indeed, as society becomes increasingly apprehensive about the use of armed and uniformed police officers to respond to social problems involving individuals experiencing a crisis, in addition to expressing concerns about the safety of the public during a law enforcement response, innovative proposals will continue to be developed. Moreover, these apprehensions will likely be accompanied by questions as to whether other specialty-trained professionals are better prepared than law enforcement to respond to these situations. These issues will necessitate that the social work profession continues its rich historical tradition of reimagining new and innovative ways to assist communities in crisis, which has included employment in law enforcement agencies.

Questions for discussion

1. Can you identify additional contemporary social problems that could be the focus of police social work and police and social work collaboration?
2. What type of critical issues that present challenges in law enforcement and the social work profession should be addressed by police social workers in the future?
3. Do you believe that the practice of police social work and police and social work collaborations should increase or decrease in the future? Why? Include a discussion of the benefits and challenges of police social work practice and police and social work collaborations in your response.

Activities for further learning

1. Locate information about the law enforcement response to a public health emergency. Consider the way in which the social work profession could assist law enforcement with the public health emergency.

2. Prepare a proposal to transform a law enforcement agency into a trauma-informed law enforcement agency. Be sure to include the role of law enforcement agencies and the social work profession in your proposal.
3. Prepare a proposal for the social work profession to respond to 911 emergencies. Be sure to include the values of the social work profession in your proposal as well as the role of other stakeholders such as 911 operators, law enforcement, and emergency medical technicians.

References

Brooks, C., Davis, E., & Hyland, S. (2020). *Local police departments: Policies and procedures, 2016.* NCJ 254826. Washington, D.C.: U.S. Department of Justice, Office of Justice Programs, Bureau of Justice Statistics.

Buchanan, L., Bui, Q., & Patel, J. K. (2020). *Black lives matter may be the largest movement in U.S. history.* Retrieved from https://www.nytimes.com/interactive/2020/07/03/us/george-floyd-protests-crowd-size.html

Civil Rights Advocacy (2013, May 8). *Update on Pittsburgh's domestic violence policies.* Retrieved from https://civilrightsadvocacy.net/category/people/kasandra-wade/

Corcoran, J., Stephenson, M., Perryman, D., & Allen, S. (2001). Perceptions and utilization of a police-social work crisis intervention approach for domestic violence. *The Journal of Contemporary Human Services, 84*(4), 394–395.

Council on Social Work Education (2012). *Advanced social work practice in trauma.* Alexandria, VA: Council on Social Work Education.

DeAngelo, G. (2013). *Fatal disconnect: Lessons in community police policy development from the response to the murder of Ka'Sandra Wade – A case study.* Unpublished Master of Public Health, University of Pittsburgh, Graduate School of Public Health. Retrieved from http://d-scholarship.pitt.edu/20067/1/DeAngelo_HPM_Essa_2013_12.pdf

Gambini, B. (2020). *Police training focuses on trauma-informed practices.* Retrieved from http://www.buffalo.edu/ubnow/stories/2020/09/trauma-informed-policing.html

Goldsmith, A. J. (1988). New directions in police complaints procedures: Some conceptual and comparative departures. *Police Studies: The International Review of Police Development, 11*(2), 60–71.

Graves, K. N., Ward, M., Crotts, D. K., & Pitts, W. (2019). The Greensboro child response initiative: A trauma-informed, mental health-law enforcement model for children exposed to violence. *Journal of Aggression, Maltreatment & Trauma, 28*(5), 526–544.

International Association of Chiefs of Police and Yale Child Study Center (2017). *Enhancing police responses to children exposed to violence: A toolkit for law enforcement.* Washington, D.C.: Office Juvenile Justice and Delinquency Prevention, Office of Justice Programs, U.S. Department of Justice.

Lindsey, V. (2020). Deconstructing/constructing working alliance between police and social workers. *Social Work Advocates,* 8–9.

Montoya, K. (2020). *L.A. council wants social workers, not LAPD officers, to respond to non-violent police calls – KTLA.* Retrieved from https://ktla.com/news/local-news/l-a-council-wants-social-workers-not-lapd-officers-to-respond-to-non-violent-police-calls/

Morales, M., Joseph, E., & Carrega, C. (2020). *Louisville agrees to pay Breonna Taylor's family $12 million and enact police reforms in historic settlement.* Retrieved from https://www.cnn.com/2020/09/15/us/breonna-taylor-louisville-settlement/index.html

Patterson, G. T., & Swan, P. G. (2019). Police social work and social service collaboration strategies one hundred years after Vollmer: A systematic review. *Policing: An International Journal, 42*(5), 863–886.

Peltz, J. (2021). *NYC to test no-police mental health crisis response in Harlem.* Retrieved from https://www.nbcnewyork.com/news/local/nyc-to-test-no-police-mental-health-crisis-response-in-harlem/2903212/

Prenzler, T., & Ronken, C. (2001). Models of police oversight: A critique. *Policing and Society: An International Journal, 11*(2), 151–180.

Ray, R. (2020). *What does 'defund the police' mean and does it have merit?* Retrieved from https://www.brookings.edu/blog/fixgov/2020/06/19/what-does-defund-the-police-mean-and-does-it-have-merit/

Substance Abuse and Mental Health Services Administration (2014) *SAMHSA's concept of trauma and guidance for a trauma-informed approach.* HHS Publication No. (SMA) 14-4884. Rockville, MD: Substance Abuse and Mental Health Services Administration.

Substance Abuse and Mental Health Services Administration (2020). *Trauma training for criminal justice professionals.* Retrieved from https://www.samhsa.gov/gains-center/trauma-training-criminal-justice-professionals

Ward-Lasher, A., Messing, J. T., & Hart, B. (2017). Policing intimate partner violence: Attitudes toward risk assessment and collaboration with social workers. *Social Work, 62*(3), 211–218.

INDEX

Made in the USA
Monee, IL
12 September 2022

13853172R00138